BEING HUMAN IN
GOD'S
WORLD

BEING HUMAN IN GOD'S WORLD

D.F.M. STRAUSS

PAIDEIA
PRESS

PAIDEIA
PRESS

www.paideiapress.ca

Being Human in God's World, D.F.M. Strauss

This English edition is a publication of Paideia Press (3248 Twenty First St., Jordan Station, Ontario, Canada L0R 1S0). Copyright © 2020 by Paideia Press.

All rights reserved. Except for brief quotations in critical publications or reviews, no part of this book may be reproduced in any manner without prior written permission from Paideia Press at the address above.

Scripture quotations, unless otherwise indicated, are taken from The Holy Bible, New International Version® NIV®

Copyright © 1973 1978 1984 2011 by Biblica, Inc. TM

Used by permission. All rights reserved worldwide.

ISBN 978-088815-261-9

Cataloguing-in-Publication data:

Printed in the United States of America

Preface

From time immemorial human beings were perplexed by the mighty complexity of the world we live in. Although a sense of wonder and awe accompanied the human consciousness almost throughout the gradual development of understanding ourselves and reality, the adventurous fascination of being human increasingly ventured to grasp rationally the nature and meaning of reality – including the mystery of the human being.

Since the rise of the various special sciences this concern more than often became a victim of an overestimation of the capabilities of rational concept formation. Eventually it turned out that this rationalistic legacy is not itself founded in reason, but (as Karl Popper realized) in a *faith* in reason. Ultimately we here discern the fact that both philosophy and the special sciences are rooted in a direction-giving life- and world-view. Similarly, the special sciences are, both in terms of their history and in terms of the basic questions operative in them, dependent upon all-embracing philosophical perspectives – a main concern throughout this book.

It is remarkable that amidst the wide range of questions and problems confronting understanding the world, the mystery of *being human* itself constantly demands scrutiny and reflection – the reason why Chapter 2 treats the uniqueness of humankind in more detail.

Only against this background can we proceed by engaging ourselves in an analysis of the remarkable *interrelatedness* of things, events and properties within the rich structural diversity evinced by created reality. Due to the fact that our analysis constantly stumbles upon issues which play a dominant role in the history of philosophy and the special sciences, those readers interested in diverse special sciences may frequently encounter unexpected relevant perspectives. The growing cultural climate of *disintegration* and *fragmentation* particularly emphasized by what is currently known as *postmodernism* made it necessary to give it special attention in the last chapter, where the *pre*-modern roots of *post*-modernity are elucidated!

D.F.M. Strauss
February 13, 1999

Contents

Chapter 1: Life View and Philosophy
- 1.1 Introduction — 13
- 1.2 Life View and Scholarship (Science) — 15
  - 1.2.1 The Will of God — 16
  - 1.2.2 Life view divergence – the example from the Old Testament interest-ban — 20
- 1.3 The heart of the gospel — 25
  - 1.3.1 The directional dilemma of science — 27
  - 1.3.2 Unity and Diversity — 29
  - 1.3.3 The discussion about church and society in South Africa — 32
  - 1.3.4 Key questions for an institute-centrism and nature-grace dualism — 34
  - 1.3.5 Identity and Ideology — 37

Chapter 2: The mystery of Human Existence
- 2.1. The Human Being: Fascinating and Unique — 41
- 2.2 Does humankind really descend from animal ancestors? — 44
  - 2.2.1 Cornerstones of neo-Darwinism — 45
  - 2.2.2 Mutation extended across all borders — 46
  - 2.2.3 Adaption and biochemical "hope"? — 47
  - 2.2.4 What do the fossils say? — 48
  - 2.2.5 Is humankind really unique? — 50
  - 2.2.6 Some remarkable characteristics of the human being — 51

		2.2.7	Why animals cannot speak	52
		2.2.8	Can animals think and form concepts?	53
		2.2.9	Tools and the unique nature of being human	55
		2.2.10	Human and animal experience of reality	56
		2.2.11	The lack of specialization in a human being's physical equipment	57
		2.2.12	The unique biotic developmental character of human beings	59
	2.3	Provisional overview		60
	2.4	The recurrent question: what does it mean to be human?		61
	2.5	The temporal 'Gestalt' of being human		67
	2.6	The value of a comprehensive philosophical view		69

Chapter 3: Creation – Unity and Diversity

	3.1	Our experience of reality		77
		3.1.1	Some problems in the history of philosophy	78
			3.1.1.1 'Everything is number'	79
			3.1.1.2 Persistence as opposed to changeability	80
		3.1.2 Plato's theory of ideas		83
	3.2	Entities and their properties		84
		3.2.1	The process of dying	85
			3.2.1.1 The bodily integrity of a person – a public legal interest	85
			3.2.1.2 The dignity of being human	87
			3.2.1.3 Euthanasia	87
			3.2.1.4 The sensitive and biotic facets of the process of dying	88
			3.2.1.5 One 'moment of death'?	89
			3.2.1.6 'Dead' but artificially 'alive'?!	90
		3.2.2	Establishing relations among diverse things	91
		3.2.3	Dichotomous pairs in language	92
		3.2.4	The multi-faceted uniqueness of things	93

3.3.	The diversity of aspects in our experience of reality	94
	3.3.1 Characteristics of a modal aspect	95
	3.3.2 The unique nature of number and space	97
	3.3.2.1 Arithmetizing mathematics	97
	3.3.2.2 A stumbling block	97
	3.3.2.3 The whole-parts relation	98
	3.3.3 Perpetual motion	100
	3.3.4 Constancy and change	101
	3.3.4.1 The core of Einstein's theory of relativity	103
	3.3.4.2 An alternative formulation of the first law of thermodynamics	104
	3.3.4.3 The theory of relativity and relativism	105
	3.3.5 What is … ?	106
	3.3.5.1 The impasse of historicism	107
	3.3.5.2 The meaning of faith	109
	3.3.6 Provisional reflection	111
	3.3.7 What are principles?	111
	3.3.7.1 Principle and application	112
	3.3.7.2 Are principles valid for all time?	113
	3.3.7.3 The historical distance between positive expressions of principles	115
	3.3.7.4 Central appeal and contemporary expressions	116
	3.3.8 Problems with the "new mathematics": Is a line a set of points? (the spatial subject-object relation)	120
3.4	Conclusion	122

Chapter 4: Creational Reality – Kingdoms and Societal Forms of Life

| 4.1 | From aspects to things | 127 |
| 4.2 | Natural things | 130 |

		4.2.1	Material things	130
		4.2.2	Living things	134
			4.2.2.1 Mechanistic reduction of the identity of living things	136
		4.2.3	An alternative structural theoretical approach	138
		4.2.4	The animal kingdom	141
	4.3	Interaction in human society		143
		4.3.1	The correlation between collective and communal relationships on the one hand and coordinational relationships on the other hand	145
		4.3.2	The nature of an undifferentiated society	146
		4.3.3	The structure of a some societal life forms	149
			4.3.3.1 The state	149
			4.3.3.2 The nature of the state as public legal institution –	152
	4.4	Marriage – divorce or living together?		154
	4.5	Church and Kingdom		158
		4.5.1	Continuity and discontinuity	158
		4.5.2	The Kingdom of God	160
	4.6	Societal forms – the "internal" and "external" coherence among aspects		163

Chapter 5: The University

	5.1	The emergence of the university		169
	5.2	The uniqueness of scientific thought		171
		5.2.1	The uniqueness of the university	174
		5.2.2	Structural typicality and university aims	178
	5.3	The structure of education		179
	5.4	A few closing philosophical distinctions and insights		185
		5.4.1	Analogy and Metaphor	185
		5.4.2	Concept and idea / analogy and metaphor	186
		5.4.3	Nominalism	190
		5.4.4	The development of Humanistic thought	191

5.5		The problematic status of postmodernism	192
	5.5.1	The transition from universality to change and individuality	197
	5.5.2	Unresolved problems: the emergence of language as new horizon	198
	5.5.3	The "old face" of "postmodernity": Conclusion	201
Literature			203
Index			217

Chapter 1
Life View and Philosophy

1.1 Introduction

ALTHOUGH OUR SCHOOL SYSTEM and school syllabi only refer to philosophy here and there, philosophy is actually the mother-science from which all other sciences originated – including the subjects given at school.

Normally, the matriculated scholar is only vaguely aware of thinkers from Greek philosophy – figures like Socrates, Plato and Aristotle. Some may be only aware of an anecdote about some philosopher – for instance the story about Socrates who had to drink the poison goblet because he would mislead the youth.[1]

The way in which philosophy has remained the foundation and basis on which the different areas of science (also known as special-sciences or academic disciplines) have continually developed, will scarcely enjoy attention in school teaching. Yet, we can only truly obtain a complete perspective on school subjects like mathematics, physics, biology, history, geography, languages etc. when we view these different subject areas from a philosophical perspective. On the one hand it provides a historical illumination and on the other hand, through such a philosophical angle, we become capable of unmasking the directing and determining ground problems of every subject area. Additionally, we

---

1. When he was given the opportunity to escape, he did not want to – to show that he was the best citizen of the Athenian democracy. He also wanted to indicate how evil the Athenian democracy had become – so bad that they didn't even have place for their **best** citizen!

develop a sense of the melting pot of spiritual tendencies which were not only functioning on the scientific scene in a particular cultural time, but also what coloured and leavened the society of a particular time. Philosophy as the scientific study of reality in its totality therefore undergirds whatever goes on in any particular discipline.

By illustration, we will give a short lay-out of the influence of modern pessimistic nihilism which had such a striking impact on Europe and SA after the Second World War – through the so-called existential philosophy – especially on the literature and art of the nineteen sixties. In church teaching, this philosophical tendency led to an incredible accentuation of the uniqueness and "authentic" situation of the individual – who is *personally* and *concretely* within the "moment" addressed by God. What happens in society with its big organizational structures is not really important – only personal salvation counts.[2] The reaction to this could not be avoided – resulting in a philosophical tendency which rebelled against this abstraction of the societal realities in which people stood.

The problems in different societies led increasingly to philosophers asking the question whether there wasn't also much evil locked in these societal structures, with their powerful organizational grasp on so many facets of modern life. The most well-known result of this approach is connected to a philosophical tendency which was linked to the thought of Karl Marx in coalition with sociology – the so-called (neo-Marxist) *Frankfurter school*. From this angle especially, we received radical and very negative societal criticism – only the destruction and shattering of the existing structures (the so-called status quo) offers hope for a new future where freedom and games, pleasure and eroticism would be the daily routine of humankind. This can only be achieved – so argue these neo-Marxists thinkers – through a *continued revolutionary process*.[3] The effect of this philosophy also became tangible in SA. The nineteen seventies represent *engagement* for us – a theme which was even dealt with in a meeting of the SA Academy of Arts and

---

2   This view also became closely linked with the pietistic view which narrows our Christian life calling to a personal religious experience.

3   Cf. the influence which this thought direction had on the student uprising in the late sixties.

Scinces. And it would surely not be excessive also to see a connection between neo-Marxist societal criticism and the burning involvement of the different societal life forms (i.a. even the church) in the difficult political questions of SA in the nineteen eighties. In 1985 and 1986 it became increasingly clear that neo-Marxist perceptions gave direction to various white and black groupings. In passing we may remark that the ideology of a 'people'/'nation'/'volk' that was dominant during the entire *Apartheid*-era, actually shows the influence of the romantic reaction to the 18th century (the so-called Enlightenment period) – a reaction in which philosophers moved beyond the *abstract individual* and started to emphasize the *people* in a cultural-ethnic sense.

However, this journey only touches a fraction of the reach and horizon of philosophy. It can be said that philosophy is aimed at the interconnectedness of everything in created reality – it gives us a complete picture, a total view on creation with its rich diversity of facets, structures and facts. As of old creation was also depicted by the term cosmos – and from the Greek lingual heritage we also name the study of anything with the help of the suffix *-logy* (= *-skill* or *knowledge*). Subsequently, we can designate the encompassing field of philosophy with the term *cosmology*.[4]

What is presented here is a guide for students who are confronted with philosophy for the first time. The intention is to provide a specific systematic perspective on created reality – coupled with a consideration of important problems from the history of philosophy which we are still addressing, and we want to show each student of philosophy that philosophical distinctions are not only meaningful and relevant for all disciplines, but can also open up illuminating perspectives for some of the most everyday situations and events.

1.2 Life View and Scholarship (Science)

Especially when referring to nature, we can easily refer to the *order for* nature or the *orderliness of* nature. Equally familiar are the expressions law and orderliness. However obvious these expressions may be, it is simply so that some tendencies in the house of science are not satis-

---

4 The term ontology is sometimes also used – it is derived from that which exists – that which ὄν.

fied with them. The key question is **how** we see the origin of this order/law and orderliness/lawfulness. Modern biological literature in the grip of the neo-Darwinian theory of evolution do not want to know anything about any *order-diversity*. A prominent neo-Darwinist thinker, George Gaylard Simpson, states his conviction clearly: "Organisms are not types and they do not have types" (1968:8-9). This approach also flourishes in the philosophical thought climate of the West, which departed from the biblical creational faith especially from the time of the Renaissance (15th century A.D.).

This remark highlights something important: *all* forms of science – philosophy as cosmological-totality science and all other academic disciplines – in the final instance, rest on specific life view choices. To form a better image of the way in which life view convictions function, we begin by pausing for a moment at the question: how do we know the will of the Lord?

1.2.1 The Will of God

Christianity has wrestled with this central question in the Christian life and world view for the past two thousand years. How should I shape my life? Naturally a Christian would say: according to the will of God! But what is the will of the Lord in concrete situations of daily life?

The answer seems simple if we just ask: what does the Bible say? [5]It is virtually standard practice within the Christian tradition that this question shows that the Bible really contains the guidelines/principles/directions for life and that the answer to the question: what does the Bible say? can only be found if attention is given to specific (con-)*texts*. Is the reformation not correct in its valuation of the Bible as the *norm* for faith life? Of course the subsequent penetrating question which can be posed against this is whether or not the Bible gives *decisive answers* for *every facet* of complicated modern life? Does the Bible really say anything concrete about the *nuclear energy* which is hidden in the atom and the catastrophic misuse humankind can make of it? Does the Bible say anything about *Apartheid*? Does the Bible say anything

---

5 Normally theologians will also point at the guidance of the Holy Spirit in the life of a Christian. In what follows the implicit assumption is that this guidance can never contradict God's *Law-Word* for creation.

about *human rights*? What about problems like *inflation, technocracy* or the power of modern *organization* and *communication*? Which texts are to be highlighted to find decisive answers about these and many other contemporary problems?

To put it another way: is it fair to come to the conclusion that if no appropriate texts about a specific issue are found in the Bible, that then the Bible has *no* authority over that issue or terrain of life? At this point something important becomes clear: *if* the authority of the Bible were dependent on the fact there are directly applicable texts for every possible situation and every possible facet of life, *then* it would obviously imply that the Bible simply does not hold authority over the complete life of a person because it cannot be denied that there are many issues about which we find no direct texts in the Bible. This impasse shows us that we could possibly be the victims of a false (and unbiblical!) expectation of what precisely the Bible is and what it offers us.

It is the problem we posed in the beginning that makes it possible for us to expose the critical problem in this false expectation of what the Bible actually is.

Let us approach the matter from a completely practical angle: could we say that the heavenly bodies answer to the will of God in their movement? Is it part of the will of God that pregnancy in humans normally lasts nine months? Do logically correct arguments answer to the will of God? Could we say that God expects us to be thrifty; to be alert; to act with style; to be upright? to be honest? to be fair? etc.?

In the old Testament wisdom literature, this insight is placed within the context of the wisdom of God which is shed over creation. The Law which God set for all His creatures is his actual will for creaturely existence – in the reformational philosophical tradition it is also said that creation is grounded in the sovereign creational will of God (cf. the poetic worship of Rev. 4:11 "because You created everything; through Your will everything came into being and was created").

On the grounds of the biblical faith about creation we accept that God has established his law for being a creature (cf. *inter alia* Ps. 148 and 119).

Every creature displays its being subjected to God's law by acting in terms of the law – i.e. by functioning in an *orderly* fashion, i.e., *lawfully*. The commands which God established for human life do not naturally possess a natural law character, but a normative nature, i.e. they approach humankind in the form of principles (rules/requirements of ought to be). That is why we know of both lawful and unlawful actions (norm-conformative and anti-normative deeds) as a result of the fall.

Even in the Old Testament we find remarkable contexts where it seems evident that the orderliness of the creatures serves as a connecting point through which to understand the will of God for being a creature (i.e. God's creational law).

In Isaiah 28:26ff. we learn that God gave humankind the knowledge to do things as they should be done; black cumin and cumin are removed with a stick; grain is ground for bread; a.s.f. Things should be handled in *this* or *that* way according to their God-given nature. Thanks to the *orderliness* of these things we find the path to the *order* which God established *for* things. Through this orderliness, God teaches us how we should deal with his creatures – taking into consideration his will for their existence.

The most striking thing here is that there is no specific Bible verse which tells us more about the nature and handling of cumin and grain – this knowledge is made possible by the fact that God in his providential faithfulness maintains his Law-Word for creation. Human life implicitly or explicitly rests on a *trust* in God's providential maintenance of his will for *being a creature*.

If we were to ask: how can we find knowledge about the law for the atom? the answer is clear, considering the above light the Bible has shed on it: not by investigating some or other text in the Old and/or New Testament, but by investigating the *orderliness* of concretely existing atoms in their functioning. This investigation flows from the ultimate heart commitment and acceptance of the biblical perspective of God as the Law-giver! In the *atom-ness* of every individual atom the particular atom exhibits in a universal way that it is subject to the (universal) God-established *law for* being-an-atom.

Some years ago, during a visitor's lecture at the theology Faculty of

University of the Free State, prof. Gordon Spykman[6] used the following striking example:

> If we possess the task of finding God's Law-Word for the development of a child, it won't help looking for specific Bible verses. What must be done is to study the orderliness of children-in-development, because it is solely through this method that we can find insight into the law God established for child-development.

The highly acclaimed Western technological advances are only possible thanks to the provident faithfulness with which God upholds his law for creaturely existence. Every tool reflects the given reality that the orderliness of God's creatures brought humankind's technical fantasy on the path of God's law for these creatures which, with the help of this specific tool, can be controlled. This is directly connected to the human God-given cultural task, viz. to fill the earth, to subject and control it.

A question which could clearly crop up here is: isn't the sinfulness of humankind a serious obstacle in this regard. How do I find God's will for my thoughts if I am confronted with an *illogical* formation of concepts or configurations.[7]

The remarkable part here is that the identification of an *il*-logical argument is only possible in that an appeal (even if only implicitly) is made to the logical norms established by God for thinking. Actually, only if we use logical norms as the measurement for judgement can we say that a specific argumentation is illogical. Sinful disobedience never escapes the God-established principles to which it remains subject – at most it can parasitize on it in disobedience! The Scriptural Word refers us to God's Law-Word, i.e. his Creator's will which determines and delimits the existence of all creatures, under which the human existence in all its life activities and life forms falls. Whoever realizes from this Scripturally-founded perspective that God refers us to his Law-Word through the orderliness of his creatures, does not have to be embar-

---

6   At that stage professor in *Biblical Studies* at Calvin College (Grand Rapids) in the USA.

7   Compare the well-known example of an illogical concept: "square circle", from the British mathematician and philosopher, Bertrand Russell.

rassed when having to defend the principal task of practicing science at a university.

For the practice of science, this Scripturally-founded perspective on the *law for* and *lawfulness within* creation (*order for* and *orderliness of* creation) is of conclusive importance – both because it also calls us to an honouring of the order-diversity within creation which cannot be negated without human thought running into serious (theoretical) antinomies.[8]

Naturally, the Christian life and world view is not the only spiritual power active in the history of Western civilization. In opposition to it – and often parasitically – we find many other life views.

Let us demonstrate some of the implications of what we have argued by using historical data, particularly looking at the problem of *interest*.

1.2.2 Life view divergence – the example from the Old Testament interest-ban

Within the context of Israel's life as the Old Testament covenant people, there was a ban on charging interest to a fellow Israelite – interest was allowed to be charged to strangers (foreigners) (cf. Deut. 23:20). Charging interest to a fellow Israelite was a transgression of the commandment "you may not steal" (Deut. 5:19). Despite the fact that the Old Testament constitution – which was prefiguratively referential – was finalized and fulfilled with the coming (crucifixion and resurrection) of Christ, the Roman Catholic church tradition wrongfully clung to this interest ban throughout the Middle Ages. Those who do business in the market place (buying and selling) are busy with an inferior sphere of economic gain – a less holy practice upon which someone who moves on the elevated level of morality and spirituality must look down. Only the spiritual-moral life of humankind could be part of the saving grace in Christ, according to this Roman vision – a grace sphere which embraces the church institute (as supernatural grace-institution) and which is entirely elevated above the less holy "natural (worldly)

---

8   We will not go into the fact that the Bible offers many expressions of obedience which also makes an appeal to the God-established Law-Word for human beings.

life" of humans – where everyday actions (like labour and economic business) take place.⁹ This life view division of life rests on the central Roman ground motive of nature and grace (supernature).

The meaning of Christ's work of salvation is reduced to the supernatural grace sphere to which Christianity is delimited (for Rome, church = Christianity). The practical effect of this ground motive division of life was expressed in many divisions which we now know only too well: sacred (holy) versus profane (worldly/earthly): calling versus career; church (-institute) versus world (non-church life forms like the state, business and university); theology versus philosophy; spiritual versus temporal; sacred versus everyday; eternal life versus temporal life; soul versus body; faith versus reason; and so forth.

It is particularly notable that virtually all reformers of the 16th century were in favour of the continuation of the interest ban – with one exception: Calvin! He was the only reformer that realized that there was nothing in God's creation that was inferior or which was created sinful. God the Father, who in his omnipotence, created a good creation – a creation which, through the Word, carries God's power (Heb. 1:3) and a creation which tells of God's honour and proclaims the work of his hands (Ps. 19:2). Humankind is created as the crown of creation and (as fellow worker with God) the human being is crowned with honour and glory by God. (Ps. 8:6, cf. also Heb. 2:6-8). Through the effects of sin, everything which God created is drawn into service of the idol which mastered the human heart and to which the human person gave himself/herself in self-deceiving piety. The result of sin is that every good creational talent is misused through the sin in the heart of a person – through disobedience and apostasy. No sinful misuse of the creational talent ever abolishes the God-obeying and correct use of it. However much humankind is guilty of economic malpractice and

---

9   In a medieval legend we learn of a person who found demons in every nook and cranny in a monastery, but surprisingly only one demon was found on a tower in the marketplace. When the person mentioned being surprised, a cleric responded with the following explanation: There is a greater need for demons in a monastery because many are needed to seduce the monks. At the marketplace however, one is more than sufficient, because everyone there is already a devil! This legend shows clearly how negatively the medieval tradition devaluated the mercantile estate. (Cf. Goudzwaard, 1960:137).

waste, or hate and enmity towards fellow human beings, humankind remains called to be thrifty in the economic use of things in creation (incl. the precious and irreplaceable resources on earth), or to act in a loving and respectful way towards fellow human beings.

Precisely because Calvin took the encompassing nature of the good creation[10] seriously, he could answer to the impact on the entire creation. Sin did not just affect one specific terrain of human life, but led humankind, in its heart, and therefore in all expressions of life and societal life forms, to *apostasy*. Therefore the sinful heart of human beings brings disobedience to God's creational will on every terrain of creation.

Let us take a closer look at this fundamental statement for a moment. Through sin humankind is brought to disobedience to the creational requirements of God for *logical thinking* (as seen in sophistry and contradiction), for *cultural formation* (history teems with revolutionary and reactionary tendencies – and obedient *reformation* is seldom encountered), for *social dealings* and *activities* (indecency, thoughtlessness and rudeness so often dominates our social activities), for *love relationships* in their various expressions (discord, quarreling, hate, jealousy and tension in spheres where we are called to marital love, family love, love for our country etc.), and even for *religious* (faith) *life* (on the one hand sin leads to the service of idols and on the other hand Christians experience how sin undermines the vitality of their faith, smother sacrificiality, undercut their willingness for the formation of correct faith distinctions and often leads to loveless lack of warmth for their fellow human beings). Only when the implications of the impact of sin in the life of humankind is fully realized, is there room for understanding the impact of the creation-wide salvation in the life of the reborn Christian. Only then can one, with Calvin, realize that there is not a single terrain of creation which is not part of the encompassing (total) and freeing meaning of Christ's work of salvation. Thanks to Christ's gracious redemption, the reborn person (even as saved sinner) can once

---

10 Bohatec emphasizes that Calvin considers all estates equal. All estates are equal in God's sight, the relationship of the merchants to God is not mediated by the clerical "spiritual estate", because, for Calvin, the way to God's grace was no longer blocked by the salvific mediation of the church institute.

again come to obedience to God on every terrain in creation in service to the Great King of creation, who rules over everything – and also over the total life of those redeemed.

Precisely through salvation, the reborn, the new elect race of God, answer, in obedience to the requirements of God for being a child of the Kingdom, for being a citizen of God's Kingdom, on all life's terrains. Everything humans perform, whether they eat or drink or do anything, (cf. 1 Cor. 10:31 and Col. 3:17) is therefore *kingdom work* which should happen in obedience to God's will. Therefore, it was completely biblically true for Calvin to *restore* the nature of *economic labour* to its original place – according to Calvin, every career is a calling, a God-given task which can be carried out well or badly. Compared to Luther, Zwingli and other reformers, Calvin did pioneering work through the removal of the interest ban and the honourable reinstitution of the economic terrain of creation, which was of conclusive importance for the economic development of the West during the past four centuries. The economic flourishing of the Protestant countries of the past – think of the "golden age" which the Netherlands experienced in the 17th century – is a direct result of the fact that Christians fulfilled their economic calling in a renewed and responsible fashion – no longer viewing this terrain as inferior and as belonging to the lower natural/worldly life of humankind.

Of course the modern rejection of God, which places the (idolized) human person central, viz. *humanism*, warps this healthy economic development and makes it subject to the sinful urge of humankind, to the selfish and greedy materialism of our age. The fathers of modern capitalism proclaimed unabashedly that economic salvation and prosperity for all people could only occur when everyone is allowed to pursue his or her own interest in an unrestricted and optimal way.

At the beginning of this century, Max Weber achieved fame[11] with a writing in which he distinguishes the *puritan work ethic* and *sober lifestyle* as one of the causes of modern *capitalism*, understanding it as a consequence of the characteristic world-view of the reformation (protestantism). The puritan work ethic of the English worker was

---

11 Die protestantische Ethik und der Geist des Kapitalismus – originally published in a social sciences journal in 1904 and 1905.

described strikingly with the expression: *worldly asceticism* (*innerweltliche Askese*) – from which it is apparent that he still signifies the nature of the Christian in Roman Catholic terms. Additionally, since then various authoritative studies have appeared in which it is proved that the fundamental ideas of Calvin can hardly be seen as the point of departure for the humanistic accent on *self-interest* and *greed* which is at the root of Western *capitalistic materialism*.[12]

The exploitation and excesses to which this humanistic selfishness led, degraded the worker during the Industrial Revolution (at the end of the 18th and beginning of the 19th centuries) to such a degree of vulnerability that it gave rise to the *socialistic reaction* of Marx's communistic life view. In our day and age every Christian is impressed by the life importance and danger of the ideological powers of our age – the capitalistic materialism on the one hand and the socialistic materialism on the other.

Those who realize that the original nature of capitalism, as preached by the well-known American economist Milton Freeman, the Austrian Nobel prizewinner Von Hayek and the South African economist prof. Jan Lombard, historically gave rise to the modern trade union movement, the labour parties and communism, would be much less disposed to the unqualified acceptance of the capitalistic free-market system.

With the help of this historically-coloured factual explanation of the development of the problem surrounding the Old Testamental interest ban, we have seen not only the basic elements of the Roman and modern humanistic life and world views, because at the same time attention could be paid to the essential characteristics of the Christian life and world view. To sketch this more clearly, we pause at another ground pillar of our Christian life and world view.

---

12 In mitigation it must be said that Weber himself warns against a too simplistic approach which claims "that the spirit of capitalism ... could only have arisen as a result of certain effects of the Reformation, or even that capitalism as an economic system is a creation of the Reformation" (1970:91). On the same page he adds: "In itself, the fact that certain important forms of capitalistic business organization are known to be considerably older than the reformation is a sufficient refutation of such a claim."

1.3 The heart of the gospel

When we confront the continuing Roman influence on society with the requirements of the Christian life and world view, the question arises whether the Bible recognizes a division of life into a lower worldly sphere and an elevated sphere of grace. The natural life of humankind outside the church is subordinated to the elevated spiritual sphere of grace to which the church as an institution belongs. The central message of the Bible, after all, is the *kingdom* (basileia) of God (his lordship over everything – cf. Ps. 103:22 and especially the four gospels where the term *basileia* appears about 100 times). *At first*, the kingdom of God refers to the full stretch of God's lordship in Christ over sinless creation. *After the fall*, it refers to God's rule over the believer and unbeliever, and *from Christ's crucifixion* and *resurrection*, it refers on the one side to the *coming kingdom* of God and on the other side to the lordship of God in the reborn hearts of the saved. Where people reborn in Christ live in accordance with God's will – whether they are eating or drinking or doing anything – *there the kingdom has already come*.

Creation embraces both the creatures which God created as well as the God ordained order for creature-ness – the creational Law-Word of God to which the Bible refers as the genuine and reliable Scriptural Word. We have seen briefly that not only natural laws belong to the creational order (cf. Ps. 148), because the ordinances and commands of God (his Law-Word) which normatively guide every facet and societal life form have been given as the creational will of God – it contains God's kingdom-will for *being human* – as it is summarized in the constitutional basic law of the kingdom: the requirement of service of love to God and one's neighbour with all one's heart. The differentiated variety of commands spring from this root-law which God established for the different facets of human comings and goings.[13]

The opposition (antithesis) of sin and salvation (evil and good)

---

13 Note that this variety of commands cannot be deduced from the encompassing meaning of the love commandment – it only offers a differentiated specification of it. When the commandment for neighbourly love requires that one must love one's neighbour as oneself, it does not imply that you must love your neighbour's wife in the same way as your own wife! The specification of God's Law-Word for the different facets of a person's life can simply not be deduced from the central love commandment.

shows the direction distinction within the good order of God's creation: for or against Christ on all life terrains. Sin gives (as we have already seen) an idolatrous direction to the possibilities of creation – think only of *illogical* thoughts, *wasteful* activities, *unjust* actions, the formation of *unbelief*, etc. On the other side salvation in Christ frees us from the creationally-wide rule of sin and calls us to turn away from evil and, out of fear of the Lord in all terrains of life, to live in obedience to his will (cf. Job 28:28; Eccl. 6:16 and Rom. 12:21). Christians and non-Christians do not live in *two different worlds* (terrains) but in *one and the same creation* (*-al order*) of God. Christians and non-Christians are not separated by the creation in which they (communally) live, but by the *opposed directional choices* out of which they live. Christians and non-Christians do the same kinds of things – but they do them *differently*, i.e., from their different *directional orientations*: both think, love, buy and socialize, but within these shared dimensions of creation they life out their respective life orientations springing from different directional choices.

We strip the biblical meaning of creation, fall and redemption of its power if we identify the *directional distinction* between sin and salvation (evil and good) with certain parts of God's creation – which is good in a structural sense. It leads unavoidably to an *unbiblical dualism* which identifies sin with a specific "area" (terrain) of creation (eg. the non-church life forms like the state, business, nation, school and university as the "world" which as Christian faith collectivity forms the opposite of the "natural sinful world"). In radical contrast to each dualistic view, the Bible teaches unambiguously that on every terrain of creation we must turn away from evil by obeying God's will. In other words: salvation does not mean moving away from *any terrain* of life, but precisely the *moving towards* every terrain – in order then to turn away from evil by proclaiming God's kingdom. Therefore, we could say that where all non-Biblical ground motives do not distinguish between the unity and goodness of creation and consistently ignore the directional antithesis between *good* and *evil*, the biblical ground motive is the only one opening up a non-dialectical view on the relation between *structure* and *direction*.

1.3.1 The directional dilemma of science

Al Wolters points out that the development of Western philosophy was consistently a victim of what he calls the "metaphysical soteriology", i.e., a philosophical theory of salvation. Besides the task of analyzing and making appropriate differentiations about the diversity in creation, popular philosophy every now and then saw philosophical thoughts as a way to holiness, to a virtuous life (Plato), as a lifestyle which led to good (Plotinus), to come to rational self-perfection (Descartes), to change reality through philosophical thought activities (in a heaven on earth, the worker's paradise – Marx) etc. The role which the many philosophical tendencies fulfill is to localize the source of evil somewhere in reality and to lead humankind to a domain of safety, integrity and even salvation.

> **Remark:** At this point we come across the many root-symbols which signify these supposed created places of rest for humankind's restless heart. Think of the drawing power of such "shelters" as happiness, prosperity, wealth, success, freedom, and so forth. My colleague, dr. Johan Visagie, talks with justification of "pastoral shelters" – i.e. places from which humankind in its deepest insecurity and lack of rest can apparently come to rest. One thinks of the great Dutch historian, Huizinga, who asks in his work *Geschonden wereld* whether art could not bring about renewal in the sunken Western culture. The late D F Malherbe recognized this as an overestimation of the aesthetic aspect of reality, "Art cannot be a lasting city for the restless heart of a person. Art can give passing satisfaction, momentary joyous experiences, but art itself is caught in turmoil, by nature referring us to Him who is the Origin of all things" (1947:85). In his *Confessions* (written in 400 AD) Augustine already emphasizes this foundational biblical truth: the human heart knows no peace before it comes to rest in God.

The Bible does not localize evil in a terrain, but in the *apostate direction* of the human heart, while salvation is equally a *directional* matter (seek the Kingdom of God – on every terrain). If we look at philosophy (and the different existing special sciences) from the depth perspective of world-view, the most remarkable fact is that we are constantly confronted by what we could call a surrogate salvific appeal. In other words, we are confronted with a way of liberation, with a call to move away from one terrain of creation to "the kingdom of freedom/virtue/self-perfection/goodness/autonomy" etc. This means that the directional contrast between *good* and *evil* is understood in *structural* terms, i.e., is identified with *specific opposed terrains*. For Greek philosophers, *evil* is found in the *material* world; for the existential philosopher of the 20th century, it is found in societal structures which threaten the *individual freedom* of a person; for the neo-Marxist and the social conflict theorist (cf. Hegel, Simmel and Dahrendorf) it is found in the *authority structure* of societal life forms; for other thinkers in the supposed inevitability of natural causality, and for others in the appearance of freedom which an individual is supposed to possess. This apostate style of practicing science – in philosophy and in special sciences – still indicates the way to good, to the meaning of life and to freedom, according to Wolters – in short, the path to salvation – as the escape from one terrain of creation to another terrain of creation: for example by moving to rationality, to forming, to the collective whole (of the nation, the state or the church), to freedom etc.

Each of these ways to salvation rests on a misvaluation of a well-created part of creation with an inner inevitability, on a depreciation of something in creation (a fundamental characteristic already of the ancient heresy of *gnosticism*), while at the same time coming to the idolization (absolutising) of something in creation – a point of departure of all idolatrous service which brings honour, meant for the Creator, to a creature.

> **Remark:** Wolters concludes correctly: "It is in this feature of traditional philosophy, which I have called the 'metaphysical soteriology' (and which has been blunted but not completely eradicated, in most Christian philosophies) that its religious nature comes most clearly to the fore. In my view, it ought to be a mark of philosophy which seeks to be as radical as the Bible that it renounces this whole enterprise, and simply accepts, as a point of departure, that every creature of God is good, and that sin and salvation are matters of opposing religious direction, not of good and evil sectors of the created order. All aspects of created life and reality are in principle equally good, and all are in principle equally subject to perversion and renewal" (1981:10-11).

1.3.2 Unity and Diversity

Because rebirth – as passport to God's kingdom – touches the root (i.e. the heart) of the existence of the Christian, it cannot be identified with a specific sector (terrain) of human life.

Membership in the church as institute does not encompass all one's life-relationships – one also act (without ceasing to be a member of the church) in other capacities – for example as Christian parent, Christian spouse, Christian lecturer and so forth. If the new root of being a Christian – being reborn in Christ as a branch of the true vine[14] – is identified with a diverging expression of their existence (viz. membership of the church institute) we must – that is if we are *consistent* – with Rome, "churchify" the whole of life rather than "Christian-ize" life.

If salvation (rebirth) isn't just a sector or terrain of life, but includes all the divergent expressions from the heart (the root) which embraces all of life, then this primary root-orientation of the saved (reborn, elect) in Christ, as the new nation of God (reborn humanity in Christ), cannot be identified, as Rome does, with merely *one* of the many creational relations of humankind, viz. the church as an institute. We do not act in marriage, family, state or university as "reborn church members", but as spouses, fathers or lecturers reborn in Christ. Also in the church institute, we can only act as members of the *ecclesia*, the 'body-elect', reborn in Christ.

When the New Testament refers vividly to the joint close connection of the saved in Christ – for example as the bride of Christ, the elect, the body of Christ etc. – we must constantly establish from the context whether it is used simply as an indication of a specific (even though relatively undifferentiated)[15] branch in the lives of the reborn

---

14 Note that rebirth in Christ, although it does claim the heart of the individual person, is not just an individual matter, because the Bible constantly stresses that those who are reborn in Christ belong together to reborn humanity, the new elect race of God, the shoots of the True Vine.

15 An extensive quotation from Paul Schrotenboer (who passed away in July 1998), previously secretary of the Reformed-ecumenical Synod, is applicable. It concerns the differentiation between the church institute and the new nation of God and it illuminates simultaneously the relatively undifferentiated nature of the New Testamental society: "We must distinguish between the people of God, the Body of Christ, the new Nation, the holy people, the pillar and

(for example, when they interact religiously) and when it is a radical (penetrating to the root), central (reaching the centre of one's life) and a total (all inclusive) meaning, indicating the descent to kingdom service on every terrain of life of the new humanity (as royal priesthood, elect people, a holy nation – cf. 1 Pet. 2:5 and 9). This total root meaning is found, for example, in Eph. 1:22 and Col. 1:18, as well as Matt. 16:18. The same applies to opening statements in Paul's epistles where a radical, central and total (i.e. RCT-) meaning of the nation of God (the elect) is proclaimed. Cf. also 1 Pet.1:1ff. where three RCT-indications are found in the first four verses (namely: strangerhood, election, and descent). Unfortunately, in the latest Afrikaans Bible translation in such central contexts the word is translated without qualification with the word "church". In such contexts, confusion could be avoided with a more literal translation, for example with the word "elect". That way the reader can avoid the danger of incorrectly identifying the central relation to Christ with the church as institute (as one life relationship next to and in distinction from others which are similarly rooted in the new humanity).

When, for example, the Bible speaks about the unity in Christ, it shows that being reborn is not a singular relation – the New Testament emphasizes the common relationship of the reborn in Christ – that is where the expressions like the body of Christ etc. come from. Often when these and similar expressions are used in the New Testament, it refers to that one all-governing relationship in Christ. It can only be called *radical* (R), *central* (C) and *total* (T). The appropriate abbreviation

---

ground of the truth and the institutional church today. This is a necessary distinction. However the new Testament did not make this distinction for there was yet no such thing as the *'institutional'* church, as distinct from God's people's activity in labour, commerce, education, and the state. To an extent they were busy as Christians in all their ways if living (more consistently than Christian people are today). *But these differences were not institutionalized.* These 'areas' did not yet exist as distinct societal zones. The lines between church and school were not yet visible. Church and home were also much more closely related, judging from the fact that the people of God were sometimes identified as the church that met in a certain person's house. The people of God was then at a very early stage. Right from the start they were organized, but they did not have a distinct organization for worship, for their cultic activity" (1971:110).

which we have already used above is: RCT.

Every other relation of which a person can be part, is, although rooted in this central RCT-relationship, still **d**ifferentiated (a branch of the root) (D), **p**eripheral (standing on the edge and not in the centre of life) (P) and **p**artial (P). A number of DPP-relations (being a Christian spouse, being a student etc. – contra being a non-Christian spouse, co-religionist, being a student, etc.) stand against the one primary RCT-relation (being a Christian or a non-Christian) of being human. Only if the church institute encompassed my life radically, centrally and totally (as Rome teaches), would it be qualified to be the true RCT-relation in my life. This is scarcely the case, because although I do not stop being a member of the church in other DPP-relations (like fatherhood, state citizenship, ethnicity, etc.), I never act in any of the non-church DPP-relationships in my position as church member – even the preacher must constantly act in other capacities, for instance as spouse, parent, citizen, Afrikaner, purchaser, art appreciator in the theater, language-user in social interaction, etc. Conversely, the same perspective applies: although I do not stop being an Afrikaner, lecturer or spouse when I am politically or ecclesiastically occupied, I still never act on political or church terrain as (i.e. in my capacity of) Afrikaner, lecturer or spouse.

The prevalent theological tradition which misconstrues the gospel of God's kingdom, does not only continue a Roman element (with the two-terrain teaching which flows from it), but also fails to recognize any collective RCT-indication in the Bible (for example, those mentioned in Eph. 1:22 and Col. 1:18).

> Remark: Although prof. Johan Heyns maintains that the kingdom is primary, he incorrectly identifies all other collective RCT-indications with the church *institute*. Fortunately, he does it in an inconsistent way – cf. Strauss, 1980:256-259. This flawed identification caused him serious embarrassment in a Sunday evening TV-debate (June 1987) with dr. Willie Lubbe. He expressed his concern about the origin of the *Afrikaanse* Protestant Church who split from the "body of Christ". Dr. Lubbe immediately reacted by saying that they had not left the *body of Christ*, but only the *Dutch Reformed Church*! Since the reformation the protestant church

denominations have struggled with the question of how the traditional Roman identification of the church institute with the body of Christ can be overcome – but continue to fall into the same traps.

1.3.3 The discussion about church and society in South Africa

During the last few decades we have noticed clear differences on the theological front about the relationship between church and society. On the one side we find those who think that the many "natural differences" between peoples (concerning their race, cultural group, language preference, political affiliation and so forth) are not removed by the "grace" in the church as organization (institution) because there we experience a special ("supernatural") unity in Christ. On the other side, a starting-point is chosen in the primary unity in Christ – also understood in terms of the institutional church (i.e. DPP instead of RCT). It is considered to be *normative* and therefore must serve (as ecclesiastical unity) as an *example of reconciliation* for the "sinful world", which must follow this unity by manifesting reconciliation in civil, economic, ethnic, and racial areas as well.

The nature-grace split of life as well as the accompanying limitation of the meaning of Christ's salvation to the sphere of the church institute (i.e., note that both approaches are church-centred) underlies these extreme positions in the theological discussion. The only difference which exists, based on this fundamental similarity, is found in the question of what the relationship between the two terrains of grace and nature is: the first view starts with nature and ends in grace[16] while the other extreme begins with grace and wants to end with nature!

If we want to measure and confront the biblical implications of the abovementioned explanation of RCT (indeed the ABC of the biblical gospel of the kingdom!) in this theological dilemma, we must stress anew that our central and all-demanding (RCT) unity in Christ on every terrain of God's kingdom coinciding with its creational unique nature (sovereignty in its own sphere) ought to be expressed – without any DPP-relation as substitute for the Christ-provided RCT-unity

---

16 This is faithful to the statement of Thomas Aquinas, the supreme medieval protagonist of Roman Catholic thought (1225-1274), that "grace" does not abolish "nature", but completes it – *gratia naturam non tollit, sed perficit*.

ever being seen, or identified therewith – it would come down to an exchange of root and branch. With this we would be freed from the haunting Roman conception that our central unity in Christ only possessed implications for the church as an institute.[17]

Because our central unity in Christ is not the result of any human activity (it is given by Christ), a serious question mark must be placed over attempts to *organize* this central unity *visibly* on any DPP-terrain. What **can** be organized, is only the *implications* of the Christian calling on a particular life terrain – but even then, the unity brought about on a particular terrain may never be identified with the central unity shared through the power of redemption. How can one make our unity in Christ "visible" on a terrain like marriage or Christian politics? Must we uphold a *macro*-polygamous/-polyandrous marriage?

The church institute possesses the calling to spread the creation wide biblical gospel of the kingdom in a unique ecclesiastic way. If faithfully done, the church will make an essential and invaluable contribution to the reintegration of the life vision of Christian people which was so flagrantly disarmed through the continuing Roman dualistic heritage. Then the church members will realize that the message of the gospel is not the *church institute*, but the *kingdom of God* which still calls forth its correlate – the *citizens* of the kingdom, in the RCT sense of the word. God's kingdom rule in Christ over the lives of the redeemed, includes all terrains of society – also that of the church institute. When the church fulfills its task in this way, its members will be encouraged and enabled to express their Christian calling on terrains like Christian politics, Christian business and economics, Christian scholarship ("science") and art. In the *Report* which was delivered about "Church and Society" at the General Synod of 1986 (Dutch Reformed Church), the status of the believer, the encompassing nature of the Kingdom and the Kingship of Christ on all life terrains were correctly stressed. Unfortunately, there are quite a few "2-terrain ideas": "church" and "world"; the church as example; even explicitly the statement that, against the societal structures which come from creation, the church

---

17 Note: "has implications" does not mean that we can ever organize the central religious unity on any DPP-terrain. On the basis of this radical solidarity, Christians can only organize DPP-units that are different in nature.

is the only societal structure which is a fruit of God's re-creation. This nature-grace deviation also explains why almost throughout there is talk of "making our unity in Christ visible" in such a way that our RCT-unity in Christ is clearly being identified with the DPP-unity of the church (-institute) as faith community.

1.3.4 Key questions for an "institute centered view" and for the dualism between nature and grace

Whenever an instance of identifying the central bond in Christ with the church as an institute is encountered, the pitfall entailed in it ought to be challenged by means of asking two straight-forward questions:

(a) Is sin a terrain of creation? and (b) How do we define the borders of the church?

Re (a):

What does question (a) imply? From what has been said thus far it should be quite clear that there is no single terrain of creation that is sinful *as such*, however much the fall from God comes to expression within every terrain of life. If we want to claim that a specific terrain of life is inherently *sinful*, we must be willing to say which terrain it is. Is it the *economic* terrain, as Rome believed? Or is it perhaps the terrain of *science and scholarship*, like the revolutionary utopian thinkers of the 20th century believed, (such as Herbert Marcuse, Claus Koch, Robert Jungk and others)? If the answer to any similar question is "yes", then it means that we were saved by Christ from that particular sinful terrain, in order to move to the "terrain of salvation" – the latter is then by necessity seen as the sphere of the *church institute* and of *morality*. Salvation then entails that we must *move away* from the "terrain of sin" and *move towards* the "terrain of grace" ("salvation"). When we hear references in church to the "sinful world out there", there is a subtle but unmistakable terrain distinction: *here* is the terrain of grace and salvation and *out there* we find the terrain of the sinful world!

Those who are serious about the biblical distinction between good and evil (cf. Job. 28:28 again), clearly realize that the antithesis between *good* and *evil* is a *directional* opposition within the order of God's *good* creation. If sin comes to expression within every terrain of creation, then it also means that salvation *equally* applies to all terrains of creation.

In other words: neither sin nor salvation as such are *terrains* in creation, because both express a heart orientation in human beings which is radical, central and total (RCT) and which consequently have reverberations across the entire scope of creation. No dualism – but a biblical perspective on *one terrain*, creation (the kingdom of God) with *two directions* – idolatrous or obedient to God.[18]

An answer to question (b) would show us unambiguously whether our thoughts are caught up in the central biblical ground motive of creation, fall and redemption, i.e. if we believe in the distinctiveness of *structure* and *direction*. In principle, there are two possible answers to this question about the *delimitation* of the "church":

(i) we can firstly give a definitive indication which refers to the nature of the church as a life form distinct from other life forms (like the state, business, university, etc.) – then we are delimiting one *societal structure* amongst others;

(ii) secondly, we can define the church in terms of a *directional perspective* – then we indicate the fundamental antithesis of *direction*, present in the structure of creation since the fall, between the *kingdom of God* and the *kingdom of darkness*, or, between those who are part of God's elect and those who are not. This second delimitation regards the RCT-dimension of creation, while the first one focuses on the DPP-dimension.

Even within the reformational tradition, the view exists that we must identify (i) and (ii), in other words that the church as institutional DPP-relationship is nothing less than the RCT-relationship of the new humanity in Christ. The unacceptability of this identification is evident from the following:

(a) It implies irrevocably that the meaning of salvation – which holds

---

18 In the testimony of the Reformed Ecumenical Synod about human rights from the year 1983 we read the following correction to dualist world views: "Dualist world-views always misconstrue the biblical idea of antithesis. The antithesis gets defined, not in terms of a spiritual warfare which is being waged in every sector of life, but along structural lines. It places one set of societal structures off against another – for example, church against state, a mission station against a political party. Christians then end up fighting the wrong battles" (RES, 1983:76).

a radical, central and total directional appeal to all life terrains – is limited to *one* terrain of creation, viz. the terrain of the church as institute.[19]

(b) From this it is obvious that our thinking is in the grip of an unbiblical dualism, because then salvation is identified with a particular terrain of creation, namely the terrain of the church and religion.

(c) The opposite of this implication only underlines the unbiblical dualistic effect of this identification of the *directional* delimitation with the *structural* delimitation, because then it follows without saying that the "terrain of sin" stands opposed to the "terrain of salvation" – we are saved in order to move from the one to the other.

(d) Once at this point, there are a number of options:

(i) a total dualism can be preached – then we meet asceticism and a monastic mentality, an exclusion in the kingdom of the supposedly exclusively redeemed terrain of creation with disgust and avoidance of everything that opposes it as "the sinful world";

(ii) or we meet a milder attitude where the "church" is not considered so estranged from the world but has the calling to act as example of reconciliation (the "area" of God's concern with creation) to shine its light over the different terrains of the "sinful world" sometimes supported by Kuyper's view of the church as "organism";

(iii) finally, this (quasi-platonic "example" idea) can be taken up so seriously that we are considered to be called to express this "unity" not only visibly within the church, but also visibly within every

---

[19] The form in which identification comes to the fore is in the critical question which church institute (even within the protestant tradition there are many different denominations) must actually be seen as "the body of Christ"? There can still be hypocrites in the institutional church. Can that also be the case with the body of Christ? Although the reformation rejected the Roman identification of the body of Christ with the (Roman) church as institute, some of this Roman heritage still lives particularly when we think that the body of Christ is only expressed in the church as institute, without the realization of the fact that being a Christian (Christ-reborn humanity) should have expression in every facet of life – obedient to the RCT-requirement of the kingdom: service of love to God and neighbour with the whole heart in all its expressions of life.

sector of society.

To summarize: Whoever starts with the acceptance that there is no one terrain of creation which is sinful as such, has taken leave of the view that sin and salvation are "terrains" of creation. It involves nothing but the recognition of the distinction of structure and direction as we have shown earlier. Precisely this basis makes it impossible to reconcile the church as life form (institute)[20] with the central directional division which exists between the elect race of God and apostate humanity.

Whoever delimits the church in a central sense by means of a structural limit only identifies a particular terrain of creation which does not as such exhaust the meaning of salvation (except if we run into a false nature-grace dualism).

1.3.5 Identity and Ideology[21]

From the previous explanation, it is not difficult to give a brief indication of the question of *identity* and the nature of an *ideology*.

In South Africa, we are often confronted with the question: am I first an Afrikaner or a South African? What finally determines my identity, my ethnicity or my state citizenship? Most Afrikaners tend to say that they are first Afrikaners and then South Africans whereas English speaking South Africans tend to say that they are first South Africans. In reality, these people possess, simultaneously, a differentiated variety of (DPP) relationships – without the possibility of elevating anyone of these branches to the primary relationship of being human. I have, for example, simultaneously a (DPP) identity as Sotho (i.e. a Sotho identity), a South African identity, a cultic-religious identity (eg. a member of a specific church denomination), a marriage identity, an academic identity (eg. a Kovsie), etc.

When we fall prey to identifying the central religious dimension with any of its branches – we are in the grip of an unbiblical *ideology*.

---

20 That is, as Christian faith consociation distinct from the state as legal consociation, business as economic consociation, the university as academic consociation, etc.

21 Compare in this regard the excellent work by P.G. Schoeman: Ideology, Culture and Education, Bloemfontein: Tekskor, 1998.

That is why any attempt to identify any differentiated (DPP) relationship with our (RCT) relationship in Christ is ideological and therefore idolatrous. An ideology desires to seduce humankind into finding its last life anchor in some or other temporal relationship, i.e. to find a temporary haven ("pastoral home") for the restless heart of a person. When the Afrikaner nation is seen as the *true* Israel, as the nation of God, we meet an *ethnic ideology* which exchanges root and branch. Whoever is encompassed in Christ, shares in a RCT-relation which transcends ethnic differences – in Christ we are no longer Jew and Greek (cf. Gal. 3:28).

The ideology of Fascism puts the state as life form at the centre, while Rome is guilty of a church ideology because it puts the church as institute equal to the body of Christ in its central meaning.[22] The tragic irony is that this Roman view still lives, although modified, in our reformational tradition, (as we have seen above in connection with the theological discussion about church and society), tempered – although not principially overcome – by the differentiation between church as institute and church as organism.

By way of illustration, we observe the double ideologically-loaded content that the principle name Christian-national receives:

A well-known cultural leader, prof. Tjaart van der Walt (theologian and former Rector of the University of Potchefstroom), once explained the issue as follows:

> The symbol of the cross serves for him to explain the differentiation between "vertical" and "horizontal" – "vertical" refers to the relation to God (*Christian*) and "horizontal" the relation to fellow-Afrikaners (*national*).

What is wrong with this explanation? Both the *root* of being a Christian as well as each branch of his or her life, *simultaneously* serve as the crux of *three relations* in which s/he stands: The three "co-ordinates" of the root and each branch of a person's existence indicate the

---

22 Cf. the Roman *Corpus Christianum* idea which comes down practically to the attempt to "churchify" the whole of life instead of "christianizing" it. In the year 1302, Pope Bonifacius VII formulated his famous bull, the conclusion of which states typically in terms of the church ideology: outside the Roman church there is no salvation.

simultaneous involvement in the relation to God, to fellow human beings and to the whole of creation. Therefore humankind's central relation to God is not only *vertical*, because the Bible stresses that the body of Christ, the new nation of God, those who were elect in Christ, are *collectively* ("horizontally") bound together.[23] As a result of the Roman heritage, we tend sometimes to tear apart this mutual involvement of fellow believers who share in a collective calling. When this happens the central relation to God as so-called "vertical"relation is understood to refer to the branch of the church as institute, while the "horizontal" co-ordinate of the central religious dimension refers to the sphere of another DPP-relationship – (*Afrikaner*) ethnicity – which results in a twofold ideological stance where *Christian-national* means that the life of a person is actually exhausted by the church as institute and the Afrikaner nation as a cultural community.[24] This content is doubly ideological because that which is centrally horizontal refers to the nation, and that which is centrally vertical refers to the church institute – both merely branches of our life, which furthermore as branches still have a share in both the "vertical" and "horizontal co-ordinate".

At the end of this first Chapter, it is good to pause for a moment to see what our methodology has been thus far, and what it will be in the following Chapters. Because philosophical distinction is not strange to everyday life experience, it makes it easier to use examples and problems which appeal to daily life. It is equally useful in certain explanations to make use of philosophical insights and distinctions implicitly without explaining them. Later on, when these implicit explanations are used, one can draw from a particular pre-knowledge. This methodology will also be used in the Chapters which follow.

---

23 In other words, the Bible stresses the collective nature of our RCT-relationship in Christ.

24 In other words, the nation receives the central-horizontal co-ordinate and the church institute the central-vertical co-ordinate.

QUESTIONS FOR CHAPTER 1

1. Elucidate the relationship between life and world view and scholarship with reference to the will of God.
2. Discuss the divergence between the Roman Catholic, the Reformational and modern Humanistic world and life views using the example of the Old Testament interest ban.
3. Characterize the heart of the gospel with particular reference to the way in which the kingdom perspective of the Scriptures distinguishes between structure and direction.
4. What are the implications of the structure-direction dilemma for scholarship?
5. Explain the unity within the multiplicity of societal ties humans share by making a distinction between radical, central and total on the one hand and differentiated, peripheral and partial on the other hand.
6. Analyse the two key questions that should be asked to every church centristic perspective and to each two realm doctrine (dualism). Define the nature of identity and ideology.

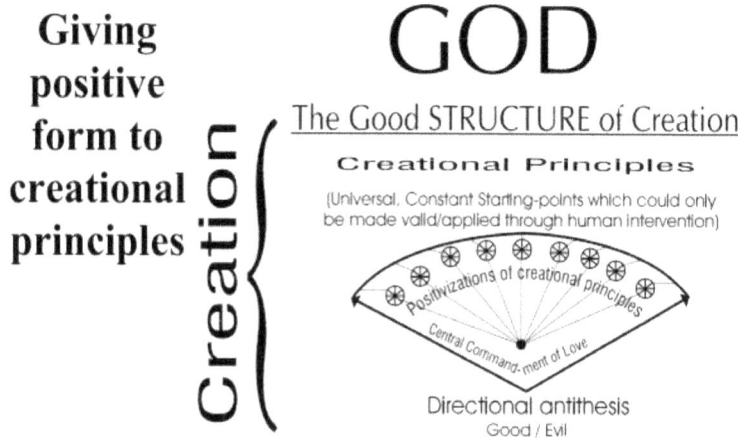

Chapter 2
The mystery of Human Existence

2.1 The Human Being: Fascinating and Unique

AMIDST THE EXPANDING CONTEMPLATION of the universe the central question of the unique nature of humanity returns ever unanswered. This fundamental puzzle exerts such an urgent appeal on scientific reflection that early Greek thinkers already held the opinion that there is no meaning to the attainment of knowledge about all else if humankind does not know itself. As Heraclitus declares: "I investigate myself" (Diels-Krantz, B. Fragment 101).[1] His reflection is situated within the context of an aspiration to discover a cosmic order which is valid for everything (cf. B Fr. 30). What he says about the nature of a human being, furthermore, is formulated with the relation between God and humankind taken into account – with as negative limit the relation between a human being and a beast. Note his simile: "The most beautiful ape is despicable in comparison to the human race. The most wise human being, however, stands to God as an ape ..." (B Fr. 82, 83). Humankind, for Heraclitus, is situated between beast and God – a problem echoing even into the 20th century in the title of a book by an eminent zoologist: *Homo Sapiens, From animal to demigod* (B. Rensch).

Socrates deepens and internalizes the Greek question concerning

---

1 The Nobel prize winner, Walter Gilbert (lecturer in biochemistry at Harvard University), claims that the instruction "know thyself" actually refers to (biological) knowledge of the human "genome"! Cf. Elseviers Weekblad, 5 September 1987: 87ff.

the nature of a human being. He wants to know who he is himself: is he related to the many-headed animal TIPON (the mythological symbol of the *flowing stream of life* without any *set limit* or *form*), or does he share in the more *measured*, simple *divine* nature (the prominence of the *form motive* in Greek thought). The term **know** gains a new significance: it no longer refers to the acceptance of a pre-existent truth, but to *investigation, searching* (cf. Landmann, 1962:67).

In search of the uniqueness of a person, Plato realized that distinctive characteristics would have to be taken into account. To distinguish always implies the identification of differences between two compared entities – requiring some or other basis for comparison. In one of his later periods Plato is of the opinion that a person might be described as a "bipedal living being without feathers". In terms of this basis of comparison little room is left, however, for the distinctive nature of being human. According to an anecdote mentioned by M. Landmann Diogenes plucked a cock as an example of Plato's human being, upon which Plato added to his definition: "with flat toenails".

In the **Phaedo** – the first dialogue in which Plato's famed theory of ideas comes to fruition – one finds an approach constitutive of the traditional Western dualistic view of being human. In this view a person is seen as the union of two entities: a rational soul and a material body. Plato introduced the existence of ideas[2] in an effort to make sense of the possibility to know things. He had learned from Heraclitus that all things accessible to sensory perception are in an ever-fluctuating state. It is therefore impossible to know these things. This conclusion rests on the presupposition that everything is *changeable*. But then what Plato considers to be the essential being of things (their static **eidos**, their αὐτός τό εἶδος), is also constantly changing. However, this Plato could not accept, since things can be known. He wishes to acknowledge that the so-called *essence* of things could not also be subject to continuous change (cf. his youth dialogue: Cratylus 439 c- 440 a).

In **Phaedo** Plato explains that that which is invisible (and constant), can only be thought about rationally, while that which is visible

---

2   According to him these ideas are foundational to the transient sensorily perceivable things as invisible, unchanging essential forms.

(and changeable), can only be observed through the senses. When the soul investigates without the mediation of the body, it is directed at the world of the pure and eternal, immortal and unchanging, constant and equally natured things (79d). The soul exhibits the greatest similarity to the divine, immortal, conceivable, simple indissoluble, constant and 'self-identical', while the body bears the greatest similarity to the human, mortal, multifarious, non-conceivable, dissoluble and never-constant (80b:1-6).

In Plato's greatest dialogue, **Politeia** (The republic) – representing the culmination of the first phase of his theory of ideas – he defends (in preparation of his ideal state with its three classes) a tripartite understanding of the soul (cf. 436ff.). These three parts of the soul[3] continued via the Middle Ages to exert an influence on the traditional understanding of the "abilities" of the soul (even in 20th century Reformed theology): *thought*, *will* and *feeling* – compare also Hitler's estates in Nazi Germany and the *id*, *ego* and *superego* in the depth psychology of Sigmund Freud.

On the other hand it also continued to exert an influence on the classifications of biological systematics. It has been assumed as of old that a person has something which is missing in animals: rational insight (wisdom/sapiens) – thence the typification **Homo sapiens**. Since Darwin, admittedly, this biological classification has been placed within a climate of thought which links humankind in a continuous line of descent to its supposedly animal forebears – a line which has to extend back (via lower animals, plants, pre-organic systems, macro-molecules, atoms and elementary particles) to some supposed primal configuration – at which point an end must be called so as to prevent the continuation of the material-physical "origin" into nothingness. (Such a continuation would exert an influence towards the idea of some sort of creation.)

A remarkable recent phenomenon is that a number of prominent biologists, who apparently are trying to accept a coherent, supposedly continuous line of descent, are at once also increasingly recognizing

---

3   Namely the *logistikon*, *thumoeides* and *epithumétikon*, i.e. thought, fervour and desire.

the qualitative differences which characterize the unique nature of a person. An illustration is the following statement by Simpson (1971:270):

> Man has certain basic diagnostic features which set him off most sharply from any other animal and which have involved other developments not only increasing this sharp distinction but also making it an absolute difference in kind and not only a relative difference of degree.

Despite this growing sensitivity for the unique nature of a person, hardly any scientific discipline today manages to escape the claims of the variants of evolutionism. The obvious shortcoming in this claim is the pretence that the origin of humankind is a matter purely of biological theory.[4] In reality it is fairly obvious that every biological theory is subject to particular philosophical preconceptions. In reflecting for a moment whether humankind really descends from animal forebears we can also set the practice of philosophy in motion by laying some foundation stones for the development of a philosophical view of being human which recognizes the unique nature of a person.

2.2 Does humankind really descend from animal ancestors?

There is sense in distinguishing between "evolution" (gradual development) and "evolutionism" (gradual development across all barriers – from lifeless material things like atoms and molecules, to plants, animals and eventually human beings, the supposed culmination of the evolutionary process). Evolution as gradual, continuous development is by no means a new concept. The Greek philosopher Anaximander already claimed six centuries before Christ that living creatures came into existence in a rising line after one another. This theory was however only elaborated in a modern biological-scientific manner during the 19th century by Jean Lamarck (1744-1829). It was as a reaction to Lamarck's work that the famous Charles Darwin published his "The Origin of Species" in 1859.

Diametrically opposed points of view emerged in biology since the end of the 19th century. The still prominent mechanistic approach presumes that all living entities can be completely understood in terms

---

4   Biology is the science which studies living things from the perspective of the biotic aspect of reality.

of physical, non-living material particles – particularly the interactions of atoms, molecules and macromolecules out of which they consist. Alternatively vitalism ("vita" means *life*) teaches that all living things exist by virtue of the presence of some or other immaterial "life force". The mechanistic approach exalts the physical aspect of created reality as the explanatory principle of origin – and sees everything as transformations of material particles which continuously and completely by chance cause all forms of life, while (neo-)vitalism starts with the *biotical aspect* of reality.[5] Since living things exhibit a remarkable purposiveness and finality, neo-vitalism emphasizes this teleological (purposiveness) feature of living entities and as a consequence it rejects the blind faith in fate of neo-Darwinism.[6]

The multiplicity of opinions in modern biology makes it nonsense to speak of evolutionary theory as if it is a single, uniform body of opinion. Without denial a number of different evolutionary theories exist, while even non-evolutionary opinions are quite common in contemporary biology.

Let us examine some of the pitfalls and problem areas in the conceptual world of the most well-known evolutionary theory – physicalist (mechanistic) neo-Darwinism.

2.2.1 Cornerstones of neo-Darwinism

"Mutation" is the conceptual term for the supposed phenomenon of sudden drastic, and subsequently inheritable, changes in the biotic structure of living things.[7] It has to serve as explanation for the ori-

---

5 Another well-known vitalist thinker is Albert Schweitzer.

6 Other biological points of view, such as organismic biology, emergence evolutionism, panpsychism and holism are not discussed here.

7 The two strings of the nucleonic acid are ordered in a double spiral structure and can double themselves. Every nucleotide (nucleotides are present in the nucleonic acid–DNA: Desoxirhibonuclein acid – and are formed of the link between a sugar with a nitrogen-inclusive base on the one side and a phosphoric acid complement on the other side) attracts its complement out of the nucleotides freely present in the environment, leading to the formation of two new DNA-spirals which are faultless copies of the original. It could happen, as a result of chemical influences, cosmic or Röntgen radiation, that one or more of the nucleotides fall away or are added, changing the genetic information of the DNA-molecule. This "fault" can then again be faultlessly copied.

gin of more developed types. Unfortunately, all known mutations are detrimental. Neo-Darwinists are forced by their position to see these disadvantaged mutants (i.e. those individual living entities that came into being as an effect of mutations) as the *advantaged* living entities with a better chance to survive. In order to temper this far-fetchedness, the aid of *natural selection*, or "accidental purposiveness", is called in. This caused the eminent geneticist Dobzhansky to remark, "mutation alone, uncontrolled by natural selection, could only result in degeneration, decay and extinction" (1967:41).

With "natural selection" Darwin had in mind the continual struggle for survival in which only the fittest survive. As a result, mainstream Darwinist evolutionary theory holds that these two phenomena, mutation and natural selection, always act in coherence. This makes it possible for the disadvantaged organism to emerge as the advantaged. In this manner all transformations and links between different living things can be explained: from the lowest form of plant and animal life [8]to humankind.

It is scientifically clear, however, that no single molecule, however complex its structure, could be alive. The term "molecular biology" is actually an internal contradiction. In his later development even the well-known neo-Darwinist, G.G. Simpson, had to admit, "Since biology is the study of life (it may rather be "living things" – DFMS) and molecules, as such, are not alive, the term 'molecular biology' is self-contradictory" (1969:6).

2.2.2 Mutation extended across all borders

Despite the limitations in Darwinistic evolutionary theory, neo-Darwinists blithely extend the working of mutations across all barriers. In this manner they attempt to gain scientific status for a theory founded on speculation and which cannot be controlled scientifically.

Mutations can bring about changes in individual genes, chromosomes, or even a number of chromosomes (e.g. in the case of polyploide).

8   Grouped together as the protista – a number of living things which are grouped apart as a result of their simple structure (biotic organization) – such as algae, bacteria, fungi, slime, and protozoa.

Extensive and widely-known studies of the fruit fly[9] have contributed considerably to our knowledge of micro-evolution.[10] Practically, this has brought about the current situation in which the breeding (artificial selection) of plants and improved animal breeds has become an everyday occurrence. The previously-mentioned geneticist, T. Dobzhansky, nonetheless observes that all the mutations of the fruit fly still belong to the species **Drosophila** – the same as that to which their ancestors belonged.

The eminent Swiss biologist, Adolf Portmann, questions with reason the neo-Darwinist attempt to take the long and uncontrollable step from microevolution to macro-evolution.[11] He claims that the knowledge we currently possess, based on experiments, is far too little to explain such awesome phenomena as fossils (studied in paleontology). In consequence he finds it unjustified to derive the larger animals from simpler earlier forms (1969: 30).

2.2.3 Adaption and biochemical "hope"?

Explanations of evolution by means of adaption commonly refers to true and controllable instances of adaption. Much is made of the white moth in England which became black in very polluted areas during the industrial revolution, since birds could catch the white moths more easily against the dark background, thereby increasing the chances of survival of the black moths. This does not, however, provide any proof of macro-evolution. After all, the black moths still belong to the same species as the white moths.

New directions in biochemistry have begun to investigate the dimension of possible relationships, with particular attention to the molecular building blocks of organisms.

This investigation concerns the nature of proteins – including he-

---

9   Known as *Drosophila melanogaster* it has a life cycle of ten days, which means that great quantities can be bred with great success.

10 Micro-evolution is development within the nature of a single species – "small scale evolution" – in distinction from macro-evolution which poses development across all typical barriers, and across the barriers of more common systematic units, such as genera, families, orders, classes and phyla.

11 Cf. His discussion of the matter in his work on the problems of life (1967: 113-121).

moglobin, albumin, etc. It also concerns the nature of Enzymes which, built up out of 20 different amino aids, performs a catalytic function in metabolic processes (building up and taking apart processes) of cells (sometimes as many as 100 000 are found in a single cell). Finally, this new direction in biochemistry investigates blood group antigens (which cause the formation of antibodies) etc.

To arrive at intricate "family trees" on the basis of this information is impossible, since this sort of analysis does not provide information on the time factor – essential for any theory of descent.

W. Henke and H. Rothe mention additionally that all efforts until now to draw "family trees" on the basis of biochemical research, have been unsatisfactory, due to the numerous unproven presuppositions regarding evolutionary tempo on a molecular level (1980: 17). They also make this remarkable statement: "It (the drawing up of family trees on the basis of biochemical information – D.S.) indicates furthermore quite prominent deviations from those 'family trees' constructed in terms of morphological measures".

2.2.4 What do the fossils say?

The responsibility for fostering the credibility of the neo-Darwinist evolutionary hypothesis rests largely on paleontology (the study of unearthed fossils).

At its deepest, evolutionary theory attempts to answer the question of the origin of living organisms during a virtually inconceivable past. Its pretense is to satisfactorily explain events in the process of biotic development over a period of some three billion years (three thousand million years). It is obvious that such a pretense cannot be bolstered by means of direct "verification", observation or experimentation. The acceptability of the "family trees" sketched by paleontologists is additionally dependent on such fossils as are found. Already since the publication of Darwin's controversial writings much evolutionistic hope has been placed on the conclusiveness of such finds. Much trusting expectation was spent on the discovery of "missing links". The hope was cherished that paleontology would clear up the mystery of the major moments in the historical descent of plants, animals and human beings.[12]

Into the 1960's most evolutionists still believed that modern human beings descended from the southern apes, with Java and Peking forms as links. The latter had been dated back some 500 000 years. This is now dated back to 1 million years. Subsequent discoveries, however, upset these hypotheses.

Since the beginning of the 1960's, L.S.B. Leakey has made known several fossil finds which belong, according to standard classification, to a separate species within the genus *Homo* – *Homo habilis*. This form, however, was supposed to be two million years old, while being contemporary with humankind's supposed ancestors, the southern apes. In 1972 Richard Leakey found skull fragments (given the registration number 1470) which, though almost three times older than the Peking and Java forms (currently grouped together by Leakey as the Homo erectus), still has a brain volume almost as large, and without the prominent brow of the erectus-forms.[13] Skull 1470 is also currently considered as a Homo habilis type (cf. Henke and Rothe, 1980:95).

In the last couple of decades the history of the emergence of the homonids (human-like) experienced so many alterations as a consequence of new discoveries that it can be assumed that this situation will only become more complex. L.S.B. Leakey (with Napier and Tobi-

---

12 The following gives a summary history of the paleontological appearance of a few relevant plants, animals, and human beings: unicellular algae are the most ancient (3100 million years: *Archaeosphairoides babartonensis*). A few invertebrate animal phyla are known from the pre-Cambrium (such as *Trilobita, Porifera*, and *Coelenterata*). In the *Paleosoicum* different kinds of fish: Agnatha (jawless fish), *Placodermi Chondrichtyes, Actinopterygii, Crossopterygii*, as well as Amphibians and Reptiles; in the *Mesozoicum* Mammals as well as the first primeval bird *Archaeopteryx* (discovered in 1861). Supposed ancestors of human beings are: the Southern apes (*Australopithecines* 5-1 million years), *Homo habilis* (3-2 million years), Java- and Peking-apeman (currently *Homo erectus* – 1 million years), Neanderthal people (about 100000 years) and *Homo sapiens recens* (40000 years).

13 Leakey, R.E.: *Skull 1470, Discovery in Kenya of the earliest suggestion of the genus Homo – nearly three million years old*, National Geographic, Vol.143, no.6, June 1973, p.820. Cf. also pp.822,823,828. Later Kamoya Kimieu, a colleague of Richard Leakey, discovered a well-preserved Homo erectus skeleton on the west side of Lake Turkana in Kenya – it is about 1,6 million years old and is probably that of a young boy of about 12 years old (cf. *Newsweek*, 29 October, 1984, p.39).

as) abandoned e.g. brain volume as a characteristic of the genus Homo. It has become increasingly clear that the features regarding the human build and form (i.e. anatomical and morphological measures) are inadequate to define a human person.

It is interesting to note that the following was written in one of the world's most authoritative pro-evolutionist journals, "Evolution", in 1974. The paleontologist D.B. Kitts wrote that the spatial distribution and succession in time of organisms with which paleontologists work, are founded in the ordering principles of geology, and not in any biological theory. Paleontology therefore provides information inaccessible by means of biological principles alone. For this reason paleontologists cannot substantiate evolution; "We can leave the fossil record free of a theory of evolution. An evolutionist, however, cannot leave the fossil record free of the evolutionary hypothesis" (1974: 466). This is a leading paleontologist saying explicitly that evolution is a provisional (theoretical-hypothetical) presupposition. Kitts also remarks that many biological thinkers become convinced evolutionists on the grounds of a theory already inherently evolutionistic. This is yet another instance of people believing what they want to believe.

With regard to the "missing links", Kitts says: "Evolution requires intermediate forms between species and paleontology does not provide them" (1974:467). With regard to Darwin's hope of a continuous line of descent without gaps, he declares: "Most of the gaps were still there a century later and some paleontologists were no longer willing to explain them away geologically."[14]

On the basis of phenomena and characteristics to which we have direct access we can ask the question of a person's unique nature. Against the background of these preceding considerations, which emphasize the important problem points in the supposed descent of humankind from non-human ancestors, we briefly pay attention to this question.

2.2.5 Is humankind really unique?

As of young, children learn that people and animals differ. An animal

---

14 The so-called 'punctuated equilibria' introduced by S. Gould is nothing but an attempt to come to grips with the overall image of discontinuity presented by the paleontological record.

is an animal and a human is a human. This knowledge, which the child can check with its senses, is challenged for the first time when the child is taught that people are actually *Mammals*. Consequently, conflict and doubt grows in the mind of the child. On the one side is the growing child's reality-conforming experience of life, on the other side the scientific knowledge with which they come into contact.

There are of course many similarities between human beings and animals, particularly between humans and Mammals, the latter being a class of Vertebrates, which is a subphylum of the Chordata. Whenever similarities are indicated, however, it also implies differences. It would, after all, be impossible to notice similarities without differences – things would simply be identical. And where differences exist, we are not dealing with exactly the same thing. To emphasize similarities exclusively and subsequently conclude to identity, is scientifically indefensible.

As of old it has been accepted that a human person possesses something lacking in animals: rational insight or wisdom. Thence the name ascribed to a person in biological classification: *Homo* (the genus) *sapiens* (the species name, which means "wisdom"). Darwinism, however, has linked this wise person with animal ancestors, and prior to them with the lower animals, sub-organic systems (such as viruses), macro-molecules, atoms, and elementary particles all the way back to the supposed primal mass. By choice this was the end of the process, since an extension of the process through the material into nothingness would come to close to the biblical idea of creation. What, however, is meant by the unique nature of humankind?

2.2.6 Some remarkable characteristics of the human being

Some thinkers are of the opinion that language is the particular characteristic which distinguishes humankind from animals. By means of language humanity owns and utilizes a consciousness of the past and the future, a consciousness including the knowledge of the individual person's limited lifespan. It is interesting, understandable and noteworthy that the evolutionist Dobzhansky considers the awareness of death as typifying the distinctive characteristic of human beings. Some thinkers are even of the opinion that the ability to commit suicide typifies the unique nature of being human.

Animal communication does not refer to the past or the future. It refers to the vital here and now. For this reason animal signs have strictly one content for every single sign.

All human utterances can signify a number of things, depending on the context, intention, or even, in the case of written language, the punctuation. Compare this with the famous dance of the bees which always indicates by means of the (i) tempo, (ii) direction and (iii) angle of the figure eight executed, the (i) distance, (ii) location, and (iii) direction of the found source. Human language, on the other hand, presupposes a freedom of choice and the concomitant multiplicity of meaning, requiring interpretation, which in turn requires interpretation from the addressee. It presupposes the responsible free activity of the human being, which requires responsible choices.[15]

2.2.7 Why animals cannot speak

The order of primates, under which humankind is classified evolutionistically, is noticeably poor in nuanced sounds – with the obvious exception of the human being. The sounds of Mammals simply do not compare with, for example, birdsong.

The 'man'-apes (anthropoids, i.e. the orangutan, gorilla, chimpanzee, and gibbon), are as a result of anatomical shortcomings, born incapable of speech. It is interesting to note that the human larynx is positioned in exactly the same way as that of all other Mammals at birth. One reason for this is that the human infant needs a way for milk to flow which is separate from the windpipe. The baby can breath calmly while drinking. Exactly because of this the human infant is incapable of speech, like all Mammals. Only by means of the gradual removal of this division, caused by the downward movement of larynx – freeing the larger pharynx cavity – is the human person enabled to speak. Only human beings possess an intermediate area in between the nasal cavity and the larynx where air and food channels freely cross.[16] As Laitman

---

15 This is why there is a difference in principle between the learning of certain signs by chimpanzees and gorillas and all human language usage – these animals are simply not free to react **responsibly** to norms.

16 When the mobile epiglottis does not handle the "traffic" effectively, we suffo-

observes:

> "This high position permits the epiglottis to pass up behind the soft palate to lock the larynx into the nasopharynx, providing a direct air channel from the nose through the nasopharynx, larynx and trachea to the lungs. ... In essence, two separate pathways are created: a respiratory tract from the nose to the lungs, and a digestive tract from the oral cavity to the esophagus. While this basic mammalian pattern – found with variations from dolphins to apes – enables an individual to breathe and swallow simultaneously, it severely limits the array of sounds an animal can produce. ... While some animals can approximate some human speech sounds, they are anatomically incapable of producing the range of sounds necessary for complete, articulate speech" (1985: 282).

Strictly speaking human beings do not possess any speech organs. No one single human organ is responsible for the production of language sounds on its own. Furthermore, every organ involved in the process of speech, possesses a primary function which would continue undisturbed even if people never spoke. When people talk they take these organs in service, namely the brain, lungs, larynx, palate, teeth, lips, and nasal cavity.

The highly developed and delicate interaction among these anatomically diverse organs in the process of talking and singing, is so amazing that the attempt to explain it evolutionistically must be doomed to everlasting failure.[17]

2.2.8 Can animals think and form concepts?

The German zoologist, Bernard Rensch, who believes that animals can form a-verbal concepts (concepts without words), admits that only a human being can form a concept of causal relationships. Only a human being can make deductions, accompanied by parts of speech such as "in consequence of", "because", "in case", etc. The human equipment to come to logical conclusions is lacking in animals.

The capacity of anthropoids to distinguish between objects giv-

---

cate. Cf. Goerttler, 1972:249 and Portmann, 1973:397-424.

17 Cf. the similar comments by P. Overhage in his work of 1972:250, as well as his work of 1977:109-112.

en in sense perception, and even to associate these with one another (compare the sort of signs taught to gorillas), still do not provide conclusive evidence that these animals can function actively – reason logically – in the logical aspect of reality.[18] This truth can be tested simply by asking whether animals can distinguish between logical and illogical concepts. Use for example the concept of a "square circle".[19] An attempt at Münster to get chimpanzees to copy drawings of squares and triangles lasted six months, and met with no success. How then could a chimpanzee be brought to form the concept of a "square circle", or even to realize that it is illogical?

Portmann typifies the peculiar human freedom of choice as follows: "The narrow limitations of animal interests is opposed to our freedom of choice and direction. Animals can escape the bonds of their urges only to a limited extent, while I myself can, in every moment, in accordance with my entire observance, turn my entire inwardly participative dedication to some or other matter, however insignificant it may appear" (1974: 102). What is truly human is apparent evinced in a person's erect stature, free hand, opposing thumb, and spiritually-characterized facial expression. K. Lorenz says that a human being is a *specialist in non-specialization*.

Gehlen is inclined to see the typically human functions as compensation for a person's lack of instinctive certainty and environmental fixation.[20] The opposite is however the case. The physical, biotic and sensitive-psychic dimensions of human existence stands in service of and is directed towards a person's normative character. A person can think logically, speak, interact socially, and form culture. The freedom

---

18 Cf. e.g. the arguments of R.E. Leakey and R. Lewin, 1978:202ff.

19 Don't think of a boxing ring in this regard – it demonstrates the freedom of *metaphoric* or *figurative* language! This example of an *illogical concept* comes from Immanuel Kant (1724-1804) – see his *Prolegomena zu einer jeden künftigen Metaphysik die als Wissenschaft word auftreten können*, 1783 §52b, p.341 and was also used by Bertrand Russell (1872-1970) who is particularly known for the three volume work: *Principia Mathematica* (3 volumes, 1910-1913) – with A.N. Whitehead. This work aimed to pursue the *logicist* program in logic and the foundation of mathematics, i.e. to reduce all of mathematics to logic.

20 This typification derives, as we shall see below, from the thought of the Swiss biologist, Adolf Portmann.

of decision and the need to reflect rationally (expressed in the great variety evident in the formation of culture) characteristic of human existence, requires a non-specialized and relatively instinct-poor foundation. Portmann speaks in this regard of our "second nature", the transformed formation of a world of culture. From the perspective of the normative-cultural character of our human activities, we should perhaps rather speak of of our "first nature".

2.2.9 Tools and the unique nature of being human

The use of tools was originally seen as a distinction from animals. Since it has been shown that animals do use tools, this criterion has been changed. With reference to Oakley's definition of a human being, Overhage emphasizes our distinguishing ability to make, rather than merely use, tools (1974: 359). Despite the continuing placement of humankind in the animal kingdom, Simpson defines a human being summarily as "the only living animal that uses tools to make tools" (1969:91).

This description, however, typifies the nature of technique, since, differently from other widely divergent cultural products such as money, cars and test tubes (respectively economically, socially and academically qualified), tools are the only artificially made cultural products (their technical formative foundation) made to make something else with (their technical formative qualification).

The importance of technical cultural products (tools) as a distinctive criterion has increased as it became clear that anatomical and morphological criteria come far too short in the evaluation of fossils. There is an increasing dependence on evidence of typically human cultural activity, which has increasingly brought archaeology into the picture. The archaeologist K.J. Narr indicated already in 1959 that "largely descent researchers with a natural scientific bent have sought anew the border between the human being and an animal where the particular spirituality of a person appears in singular indications of cultural activity" (1959:393).

The obvious and distinctive human cultural activities are particularly closely bound to the free formative fantasy of a person which is the foundation of all technical inventions. As Von Königsberg states with reason, a person is a cultural being, "without culture no **Dasein** (concrete existence – D.S.) worthy of being human can be contemplated" (Von Königswald, 1968:150). Mentioning the fact that human tools are conceptualized particularly with a view to future use, he states explicitly that true invention took place already in the earliest phase of the **paleolithicum** (the earlier stone age) (1968:167). The presence of a person's inventive formative fantasy provides the foundation for practically useful archaeological criteria in terms of which typically human tools can be distinguished:

(a) The form of the produced tool may not be suggested or determined by the original raw material (e.g. in distinction from a stick from which irritating leafs and twigs need merely be removed);
(b) the function of the tools may not be suggested (a rock in its natural shape is a strengthening of the fist; a stick an elongation of the arm or fingers), that is, tools may not be merely extended physical organs;
(c) the manner of production may not be suggested, with appeal to the technical moment which implies that tools must be formed by means of (formed or unformed) tools (cf. Narr, 1974: 105 and Narr, 1976:99-101).

The fact that the earliest human tools had multiple purposes and only gained a relative task-specific speciality in due course, indicates that the means-endrelation is inherent to all tools. The typically human use of tools presupposes a person's analytical ability which enables him to distinguish means and ends.

A philosophical analysis of the unique nature of a human being must advance to the question of the particular manner in which one experiences reality.

2.2.10 Human and animal experience of reality

Portmann considers the animal nature to be instinctively assured and environmentally bound (1969:86). Animals experience reality exclusively out of their natural inclination, directed at that which is physically, biotically and psychic-sensitively important to them. Animals experience reality in terms of that which is negotiable and not negotiable, edible and inedible, in terms of same sex and opposite sex, comforting and alarming. J. Von Uexküll illustrated the environmental (Umwelt-) restriction of the animal by means of his oak tree example: "Each Umwelt isolates out of the oak tree a particular part ... In all the various Umwelten of its various inhabitants the same oak plays a widely divergent role, sometimes with particular and then again with none of its parts. The same part can be large or small, the same wood hard and soft, it can serve as a means of shelter or attack" (Von Uexküll, 1970:98, 100). Human experience of the oak tree transcends these natural aspects of reality to which animal experience is restricted. The natural scientist sees the tree as an object of analytical study, the hiker as something with a particular aesthetic attraction, the criminal as a hiding place from the law, the woodworker as material from which to make furniture, and so forth. This human experiential perspective with its rich variety is linked to a person's cultural calling which enables a person to be variably settled in any environment by means of cultural formation.

Since those facets of reality in which a person functions in a typically human way are not instinctively assured or bound, but are directed at a person's normatively qualified, responsible freedom of choice,[21] humankind has a flexibility which makes incredible specialization possible in differentiated civilizations. Even Simpson emphasizes this: "Such specialization, which is nongenetic, requires individual flexibility and could not occur in a mainly instinctive animal" (1969:90).[22]

Such normative specialization, however, requires and presupposes an unspecialized bio-psychic foundation – a further characteristic unique to being human.

2.2.11 The lack of specialization in a human being's physical equipment

In contrast with the instinctively assured and environmentally bound

---

21 We have already referred to this in the brief discussion on opposites such as logical-illogical, historical-unhistorical, social-unsocial, and so forth – opposites which all presuppose universal measures, "ought" demands, and principles.

22 Contrast this with the closed nature of animal existence. As Hart comments, "A worker ant is just that – and all its functions are geared to being a worker ant. A human being, on the other hand, has multiple roles to play and is not exhausted in any of them" (1984:146).

specialized way in which animals are adapted to their natural environment, a person enters this world with unspecialized physical equipment: that person possesses no natural adaption to a particular environment, and is distinctively unspecialized, physically and bio-psychically, in comparison to animals. Human teeth are not adapted to either eating plants or animals. The lack of gaps between the eye teeth and premolars (which is specialized into e.g. fangs in anthropoids) is also an archaic (primitive, in the sense of unspecialized) characteristic of human teeth in comparison with animal teeth. The human hand and foot is equally archaic in comparison with those of the anthropoids (cf. Gehlen, 1971:86 ff.) G. Altner notes that even anthropoid teeth are relatively unspecialized, but cannot deny the general trend of the mentioned data (as emphasized by e.g. Gehlen) (1972:199-202).

> **Comment:** Since Dollo formulated the law of irreversible specialization, existing anthropoids lost their claim to ancestry of humanity, since it is impossible to deduce the unspecialized characteristics from the progressively specialized nature of the anthropoids. This leaves two equally limited possibilities:
>
> (i) construct a hypothetical primal form which could serve as basis andpoint of departure for the specialization of the anthropoids (but then these would be descended from human beings), or
>
> (ii) negate the law of Dollo with reference to e.g. neoteny (rejuvenation phenomena among animals, L. Bolk) and the theory of self-domestication (K. Lorenz).[23]

Gehlen typifies a human being – in comparison to the natural inclination of animals – as a defective creature (1971: 20, 30, 83, 354). He neatly turns around the position that animals have no mind: a human being lacks something, since s/he is so unspecialized! Gehlen returns to the position of J.G.Herder who said in 1770 (the Ursprung der Sprache) the following regarding humankind: "This instinctless, miserable creature, emerging so lonely from the hands of nature, was from the very first moment a free-acting, inventive creature who had to help himself and could not but do so" (quoted by Altner, 1972: 157).

---

23 Cf. resp. Bolk, 1926 en Lorenz, 1973, as well as my more extensive treatment in 1988.

Even though human beings are not entirely without instinct, their natural inclinations do come considerably short in comparison with the abilities of animals. Humankind is earthbound, unable to soar through the air like a bird. A human being is much slower than many wild animals and lacks a naturally protective hairy hide. Human senses are considerably limited in comparison with the acuity of animal senses. Human beings possess no naturally dangerous weapons, especially in comparison with the muscular strength, claws or jaws of carnivores. There are animals which can register supersonic waves, see ultraviolet rays as light, fish which can sense electrical fields and birds which use the magnetic poles of the earth as navigating devices – all senses lacking in a human being.[24]

A human being only appears an unspecialized and defective creature when the natural inclinations of animals are used as the single basis of comparison. As Hans Freyer objects: the human being is first fictitiously portrayed *as* an animal, after which it appears that as such (i.e., as an animal), a human being is highly *incomplete* and even *impossible*!

What picture do we get when we look at the human being and at animals in terms of common factors – as revealed in the biotic functioning of both?

2.2.12 The unique biotic developmental character of human beings

The pioneering work of Portmann on this terrain has not only indicated that human beings cannot be pigeonholed in either of the two developmental types which he identified in the animal kingdom,[25] but that in comparison with the typical animal growth rhythms – which are gradual and continuous – the human growth rhythm has two phases of acceleration.

---

24 Portmann discusses this in one of his works: *Der Mensch ein Mängelwesen?* in Portmann, 1970:200ff.

25 Namely the *Nesthocker* (nest-huggers) and the *Nestflüchter* (nest-leavers). The latter are animals who have a way of movement, stature and proportions at birth similar to their adult form, with open eyelids and hearing channels and little dependency on the parents. *Nesthocker*, on the other hand, are born in helpless dependence, with closed eyes and ears and dependent on care in a prepared nest.

In comparison with the Nestflüchter human beings are born a year too early. Portmann calls this the "social uterus period" which enables the newborn human to gain by means of cultural contact and transference that which the animal instinctively has at birth (1969: cf. Chapters II, III, V, and VI). During the first year of life the human baby develops at double the rate of the anthropoids, after which a slowing down in growth tempo takes place until the ninth year. After this period of childhood there is another period of rapid growth culminating in the fifteenth year (during which puberty stage sexual maturity is reached) – after which the process of growth slows down again until maturity is reached at about twenty or twenty-two years.

Similar to this long period of youth (during which a person must master and internalize the expansive cultural tradition within which that person lives), human beings also possess a similarly long period of adulthood within which to transfer this cultural inheritance of generations effectively and educationally. This biotic developmental dynamics shows that each period of development must be seen as completely interwoven with the characteristic human form of life.

2.3 Provisional overview

Out of the data brought to the fore in the preceding discussion regarding the origin and nature of humankind it has gradually become clear that what is involved is an encompassing philosophical view of humankind transcending the limits of any *specific discipline*. We already mentioned at the beginning that it is impossible to maintain the pretense that what is involved is a mere biological scientific theory. What is involved fundamentally is a philosophical view of reality which continues to reveal a particular underlying life- and worldview and directive foundational motive.

It is consequently not so simple to attempt a reconciliation between the Christian worldview and the idea of unplanned, coincidental evolution across all limits. We are often told that we may as well believe that God merely created by means of evolution. That God created humankind as the crown of creation is however a central element of our biblical faith in creation. All of creation is directed at the human being as the holder of God's cultural mandate on earth – the human being has a cultural calling and task. This meaningful and orderly universal anthropocentricity is excluded in principle by neo-Darwinism in its combination of mutation and natural selection. In this view the idea of a divine plan of creation makes no sense – least of all that humankind should be part of this plan. As neo-Darwinism teaches, being human is merely the result of a meaningless and completely coincidental material-energetic process which did not foresee this development, as Simpson commented on occasion: "He was not planned".

The biblical Christian knows that there is nothing in creation, not even a single facet, in which the human heart can find rest. God alone may receive the honour as the true Creator of all things. He created everything according to its own nature (Genesis 1) with humankind as the crown of creation (Genesis 1:28), crowned with glory and honour (Psalm 8:6). No superficial attempt at reconciliation can bridge the gap between a biblically founded view of science and the many variations of the evolutionary theory. No Christian can abandon his or her heart to the deification of the created, and so attempt to serve two lords at once.

2.4 The recurrent question: What does it mean to be human?

At this central point we are confronted anew by the question: who and what is a person actually? At the beginning of this chapter we referred to the mystery of human existence. The course of our exposition could even have given the impression that science could provide the solution to this riddle. Anyone seriously attempting to ascertain what exactly is known scientifically about humankind today is soon overwhelmed by the sheer magnitude of this knowledge – so much is known that no single individual could hope to be up to date with it all.

Investigations of the microdimensions of human existence has spectacularly expanded the scientific horizon during the past five decades. We only need to think back to the early 1950's when biologists and biochemists unveiled the mysteries of the DNA-molecule. More and more becomes known all the time about the complex duplication mechanics in the cell during reproduction and about the human 'genome'. Biological engineering is developing at an astounding rate – so much so that the inhuman possibilities with regard to the future genetic manipulation of humanity are truly disturbing. These developments probably have as their all-encompassing background the rise of depth psychology during the first half of the 20th century – with such great psychologists as Freud, Adler and Jung in the vanguard. Many previously unexplained phenomena were suddenly wrenched into the centre of scientific interest. The astounding world of the sub- or unconscious was placed on the table and it became possible to discuss scientifically what has become virtually general knowledge today – e.g. pathological schizophrenia (the personality problem of Dr. Jekyll and Mr. Hyde).

It has not been only the natural sciences which advanced considerably in recent decades. Owing to developments in abstract mathematics during the 19th century and at the beginning of the 20th century (such as the famous **Principia Mathematica** of Russell and Whitehead during the years 1910-1913), we are on the one hand for the first time in a position to plumb the depths of logical reasoning – already accessible to Greek thought[26] – in terms of mathematical logic, while on the other hand we have been enabled by means of the micro-electronic developments in our day – developments entirely dependent on insights in the field of mathematical logic – to develop one of humankind's most astounding tools as yet, the computer. By means of the historical and ethnological sciences humankind has also gained a considerably enriched perspective on the previously unknown origins of its cultural heritage, while we know more than ever about the striking stylistic figures which distinguishes 20th century peoples culturally from such truly undifferentiated cultures as still live in bygone historical eras.[27]

We could continue in this vein to bring examples of the advances of modern science to attention – without coming any closer to the

---

26 Euclides, the great Greek mathematician, developed an arithmetical proof stating that there are an infinite number of prime numbers. (Prime numbers are all natural numbers which can be divided only by 1 and themselves). In this proof subtle use is made of means of evidence and conclusion which could only be explicitly accounted for by means of mathematical logic in the 2oth century. (Cf. Gentzen, 1967:14-25).

27 In Africa there are even tribes who haven't yet entered the stone age, still living in cultures with soft objects of daily use.

elusive riddle – who and what is a person himself/herself?

The influential personalistic philosopher and ethicist, Martin Buber, developed a dualistic view of reality in one of his works which places all emphasis on the personal encounter of human beings in love. This personal encounter in love is then placed dialectically against all impersonal relations between human beings and the external world. This work is called "**Ich und Du**" (1923).

According to Buber, reality reveals itself to humankind in two ways, since the "I" stands in two kinds of fundamental relations: the I-Thou relationship and the I-It relationship. For Buber no I-in-itself exists, since the word I always encompasses one of these two relationships. He and She falls within the I-It relationship. The world as we experience it, with the It, He, and She, even with internal experiences or secrets reserved for the initiated, already consists of Its, Objects. Experiences of this world are not reciprocal, and affect only human beings, who experience them. Thus, the world-as-experience belongs with the fundamental term I-It. In contrast to this is the fundamental term I-Thou, which is the basis for the world-of-relationship that knows no inner barriers since only Its are mutually delimited. The I-Thou relationship exists in the presence of encounter, since only in this relationship does the present reveal itself. The objects of the I-It relationship, however, are experienced in the past. The individual Thou becomes It after the experience of encounter, and the individual It can become Thou by stepping into the experience of encounter.

Love is the distinguishing mark of the personal I-Thou relationship. Buber develops his approach in a world-historical and religious context (he was Jewish). Every great culture draws its spark of life continually out of an original experience of encounter, out of an answer to the Thou. When these renewing relational occasions are lost, a culture stultifies and becomes subject to that fate which rests on every human being in the full weight of a dead world mass. Liberation from this situation, to being children of God, according to Buber, comes only out of new experiences of encounter, a fateful answer of human beings to their Thou. Only in this way can a culture renew itself. In the dominant idea of fate, which subjects humankind to social, cultural, psychic, historical and other laws, it is forgotten that no-one can meet fate unless he proceeds from a position of freedom. Notice this internal dialectical tension in Buber's thought: natural law and freedom reciprocally presuppose and threaten each other.

According to Buber, faith in fate surrenders humankind to the overpowering grip of the It-World, whereas a person becomes free in the I-Thou relationship, free also of the grip of a rationally obvious system (Buber's reaction against rationalism)[28] a freedom indicated fundamentally by liberation from faith in unfreedom. The meaning of life is to be found, according to Buber, in the embrace of fate and freedom.

The word love is central in this supposed encounter between person and person. Does it provide insight into the mystery of human existence? Can we truly say that love is the actual core of human existence – or at least that it **should**? Both Classical Greek and Eastern philosophy emphasized the ethical (moral) nature of a person – as can be seen in the typification of an individual as a *rational-moral* creature. Let us look briefly at the possibility of seeing love as the essence of being human.

We are immediately confronted by two problems: (i) it is very difficult to define love and (ii) love reveals itself in many ways.

About four decades ago the famous Dutch philosopher, Herman Dooyeweerd, gave attention to this problem in a lecture given in America. With reference to attempts to typify human beings in terms of love he said:

> "The personalistic and existential views of man attempted to fictionalize the I-Thou relationship as a relationship of love – an inner encounter of human persons. But in the earthly horizon of time even these relationships of love reveal a variety of meaning and typical character". He continues to bring the various relationships of love within which man stands to attention by means of a series of questions: "Does this refer to the love between marriage partners or that between parents and children? Or is it the relationship of love between co-religionists in related Reformed churches which we have in mind? Or maybe the relationship of love

---

28 We shall discuss the nature of rationalism and a few other isms in philosophy and the special sciences later.

among compatriots with a common love for the same fatherland? Or maybe we have the general love of a neighbour in the moral relationships of our temporal life in mind?" (1960:12).

It is clear that Dooyeweerd is paying attention to what we called DPP-relations in Chapter 1. Each of these exemplifies another differentiated human relationship of love – family love, marriage love, patriotism, and so forth. None of these DPP-relationships, however, can be reconciled with the central, radical and total bond of humanity – the RCT-dimension of our existence.[29]

To further complicate matters we use the same word for the RCT-dimension of creation as we do for one of the multitude of DDP-relations in which people engage. The Bible regularly uses the word **love** for a differentiated given which refers to a particular facet, among others, of human existence. As often, the Bible uses **love** in an RCT-sense.

When love is used in a differentiated sense it should not be confused with love in the central sense – as it is expressed, among others in the central commandment of love. This commandment, which demands that we love God and our neighbour with all our heart, belongs to the RCT-dimension of creation and contains, for exactly this reason, an appeal for all the facets of our existence. When we talk about marriage, family or patriotic love, however, we are referring to only a sector of our existence and not the totality thereof. In biblical usage this difference is obviously present. In distinction from those portions of Scripture which pertinently refer to the central sense of the commandment of love (e.g. Matt. 22: 37-40, Deut. 6:5, Lev. 19:18), we find many portions in which love is placed in a row next to other facets of reality. The statements in Gal. 5: 22 and I Tim. 6:11 refer, for example, to the "fruit of the Spirit", and then mentions "love, joy, peace, …" and so forth and mentions that towards which we should be striving:

---

29 In Chapter 1 we saw that a distinction can be drawn between the **one** encompassing and determinative relationship of a person – referred to as RCT (Radical, Central and Total) – and the various differentiated relationships within which people exists and within which they are only engaged in a partial and peripheral way (i.e., DPP-relations).

"faith, endurance and gentleness".[30]

In terms of these distinctions it is clear that the term **love** cannot be used without distinction to indicate the core of human personality. If it is used, however, to reflect the central religious meaning of the commandment of love, we have indeed moved a step closer to the mystery of human existence. Scripture refers to the heart of human existence – which is, according to the poet of Proverbs, the wellspring of life (Proverbs 4:23). It is fundamentally a matter of self-knowledge, knowledge of the heart of human existence.

Can a person attain self-knowledge autonomously? As a result of the fall, which struck at one's heart – which is why Christ requires a reborn heart – humankind has been tempted, in sinful apostasy, to try and find somewhere in creation a pseudo-place of rest – and, as we have already noted, it is only possible to find ultimate rest in God. For this reason Calvin could emphasize that true knowledge of humankind depends upon true knowledge of God. Of course the opposite is also true: fallen humankind designs an anthropology in the light of its idolatry. In modern times human beings have been greatly impressed by the machine-like control of reality – with the result that a mechanical or mechanistic view of humankind necessarily followed. As the second half of the 20th century stands increasingly in the sign of the power of the computer, we find increasingly that human beings are being understood in computer terms: a person as super-computer. David Lyons has recently shown to what extent all of society is being understood in these terms, as is strikingly suggested in the title of his book: "The Silicon Society".

The human self is nothing in itself, that is, it does not exist separately from the three central relationships in which God has placed human beings. First of all human beings stand in relation to God, then in relation to their neighbours, and lastly in relation to the totality of created temporal reality. Each of these three relationships are engaged in both the DPP- and RCT-relationships in which human beings take

---

30 Note, by the way, that the same thing happens with regard to the word *faith*: it is sometimes used in the sense of a total heart commitment to God and sometimes – as in this instance (I Tim. 6:11) – to indicate a virtue which is valued next to and in distinction from others.

part. My relation to God is for instance not an esoteric inner room-experience which can be divorced from my being a citizen, husband, member of an ethnic community or student, since exactly in all these positions do I live out my love of God or idol. Similarly every relationship with a fellow human being – however differentiated and peripheral it may be – continues to appeal to the whole self, the heart of that neighbour. Finally every facet of creation is anchored religiously. We must realize that even the most apparently everyday actions are still directed out of the heart at either God or idol. Paul mentions these sort of activities – like eating and drinking – for good reason when it concerns the honour of God: "So whether you eat or drink or whatever you do, do it all for the glory of God." (I Cor. 10: 31).

It can only be a stumbling block for the centuries-old hubris of Western people – who have, since the time of Greek philosophy, developed a limitless trust in the capacities of *human reason* – to be told that humankind cannot come to true knowledge of the self by means of its own rational insight – only by means of true knowledge of God. True knowledge of God cannot be a human discovery, it can only be received from Christ in the reborn heart. When it comes to this deepest and most central question of life, fallen and sinful humankind cannot give anything. In this regard, as Dooyeweerd has noted, humankind can only piously *listen* and *receive*.

2.5 The temporal 'Gestalt' of being human

In view of the fact that being human does not stand in relation only to the entire temporal reality of creation, but indeed has part also in the various dimensions of creation, we can indicate the multiple similarities between human beings and other created entities. While material things – atoms, molecules, macro-molecules and macro-systems – clearly belong to the kingdom of physically-qualified things, human existence is by no means excluded from this sphere. Our physical existence is, after all, bound to the necessary presence of all the substances out of which we are formed – from the four "organic" elements (hydrogen, oxygen, carbon and nitrogen) to the variety of inorganic substances which are equally necessary for our existence. Of course the entire matter is complicated if we would want to pay attention additionally to the complex macro-molecular bonds present in the human body, even if it only affirms that being human has a part in the physical dimension in the sense that the bodily existence of a human being is founded in this physical-chemical substructure.

This is not the end of the story, since human beings also have distinctive similarities with the kingdom of living creatures. Like all living creatures, the human body is also built up out of living cells. When we think about the biotic meaning of the many vital organs in the human body – organs such as the heart, lungs, brain – we realize that human beings take part, not only in a physical chemical substructure, but also in a biotic substructure. This biotic substructure is founded as a bodily structure in the physical-chemical substructure, since the human body could not be healthy without the necessary foodstuffs.

Both these substructures are in turn foundational for the sensitive-psychic substructure, which houses a person's complex sensory equipment and a person's equally complicated emotional life – which are both closely interwoven with the sensory and motoric nervous systems of human beings. On this level human beings are obviously very similar to animals.

In our discussion of the unique and distinctive characteristics of human beings it has become clear that they are in possession of numerous abilities which animals lack – even if we were to conclude on the common level of the substructures that human beings lack a bio-psychic specialization in comparison with animals.

When human beings act under the guidance of normative vistas they transcend animal abilities. Normatively correct or incorrect behaviour is only possible for humans. No animal can think logically or illogically, shape historically or unhistorically, act socially or anti-socially, be thrifty or spendthrift, just or unjust. The lack of specialization of the three substructures mentioned (physical-chemical, biotic, and psychic-sensitive) goes hand-in-hand with their directedness at the normative qualification of a person's bodily existence. Dooyeweerd prefers to speak of a person's act-structure. Since he limits acts to inner inclinations which must still be converted into external actions, it is probably necessary to find a broader term for this structure. Since the whole "normative instrumentarium" of a person not only indicates the distinctively human-ness of being human, but also qualifies the human being bodily in its entirety, it may be well to refer to this qualifying structure – following the preference of my colleague prof J. H. Smit – as the normative structure of being human.

When we want to refer to all four of these structures the best term would be **personality**. The term *personality* encompasses the particular nature of each partial structure of the human being, i.e. it encompasses the typical human tempo (bound to the physical substructure), the inclinations of a person (known as biotic dispositions – bound to the biotic substructure), the temperament (bound to the emotional-psychic substructure) and the character (bound to the qualifying normative structure of being human).

Since the variety of human expressions and bodily structures are concentrated in the human heart (which belongs to the central-total dimension of creation), we can typify a human being conclusively as a *religious personality*.

2.6 The value of a comprehensive philosophical view

At the end of this chapter on the unique nature of humankind we briefly reflect on the value of such a comprehensive philosophical view of a person. Medical science, for instance, is often accused of having lost a view of the whole and multi-dimensional existential reality of the human being – it easily reduces human beings to mere biotic organisms which can be manipulated as objects. Even from a nursing perspective this reduced view is sometimes accepted. The power of medical technique particularly grants apparent credibility to this reduction.

What is lost sight of is that a person is indeed human, that in inter-human relationships a person appears primarily and finally as a co-subject, and never in the first instance as a *manipulable object*. Of course there are many historical examples of societies which degraded human beings to mere utilitarian objects. We only need to recollect the institution of slavery which was still common practice in the West a mere 150 years ago.[31]

---

31 The well-known neo-Marxist writer from the Frankfurt school, Jürgen Haber-

To value and respect a human being **as** human in medical and nursing practice requires, before all else, recognition of the position of being human as *subject*. The human being as a religious personality is not finally qualified by any aspect of creation. While we can state with adequate proof that a material thing is qualified by the physical aspect of energy-working, or that the nature of plants is qualified by the biotic aspect of life, it would be meaningless to attempt to use any normative aspect as if it could qualify human existence.

Say we were to claim that human beings are a social creatures, that is, that our entire temporal existence is encompassed by the *social* aspect. That would imply that a person could only act in a social manner. What do we then do with those activities of peole qualified by *other aspects* of reality – such as economical activities, analytical activities, just or unjust actions, and so forth. It is exactly the complete freedom of a person to choose to act on different occasions under the guidance of any of the range of normative aspects which particularly distinguishes mankind's normative abilities.

One moment we can be engaged in the scientific analysis of a particular problem or phenomenon, the next we can act technically formatively by forming something, in creative freedom and with cultural creativity, which could not come into existence by itself, then we can buy something (economic activity), appreciate the beauty of a sunset (aesthetic evaluation) or simply relax with friends (a social activity). We even discussed in Chapter 1 that this differentiated multiplicity of normative expressions of life correlates with the many societal roles a person may play.

If we are to understand the multifaceted subjectivity of human existence in a meaningful way, it is essential to recognize that the human existence cannot be encompassed by or being limited to any single aspect of reality. None of these aspects can qualify or finally charac-

---

mas, has a clear awareness of the difference between subject-subject and subject-object relations – as is clear from i.a. the distinction he draws between "communicative actions" (regarding subject-subject relations) and "technical actions" (regarding subject-object relations). The late P.J. van Niekerk indicates that this distinction has deteriorated into a fundamental *dualism* in Habermas's thought – cf. his doctoral dissertation (1982:12-42, 82).

terize human existence. It is therefore not desirable to speak of the "kingdom" of human beings – "kingdoms" are limited to natural creatures: the kingdom of material things, the plant kingdom, the animal kingdom. This usage is linked to the specific qualification of each of these kingdoms by a particular aspect of reality.

Structurally this means that our temporal, earthly existence is characterized by the richly varied normative structure of bodies – a characteristic structure which is in itself unqualified by any particular normative aspect. Otherwise, a person would be able to act **only** socially, analytically, or economically, as we argued above.

The illness of a patient normally involves a defect in their biotic functioning. Provisionally we shall disregard the matter of multiple possible causes of this biotic dysfunction – illness can be the result of a shortage of necessary chemical elements, defects in particular biotic organs, or even psycho-somatic (tension, worry, excitement, and so forth). Primarily the duality illness-health has its origin in the biotic aspect of reality – physics does not even deal with these typically biotic terms.

> **Comment:** In a different context Von Bertalanffy uses the distinction between physical and biotic terms to indicate the limitations of (evolutionistic) attempts to understand living beings in physical terms only.
>
> He writes that physics cannot even indicate the difference between a living and a dead dog: "The laws of physics do not tell a difference. They are not interested in whether dogs are alive or dead". He continues on the same page that this remains true even if we take into account the most recent scientific advances: "One DNA molecule, protein, enzyme or hormonal process is as good as another; each is determined by physical and chemical laws, none is better, healthier or more normal than the other" (1973: 146).

The presence or absence of particular chemical bonds can without doubt have important implications for normal human functioning. Think of the important role of iodine in the nature and function of the thyroid gland. The thyroid gland (**glandula thyreoidea**) is placed around the lower part of the human larynx and the beginning of the wind pipe. It is responsible for the secretion of the important thyroid gland hormone (thyroxine) which, probably via an influence on the process of oxidation (oxidative phosphorilation) in the mytochondria[32] initiates the exchange of substances throughout the body's cells. This is essential for normal biotic growth as well as emotional and psychic health. Iodine itself[33] is qualified physically-chemically in terms of its own inner structure. While retaining this inner structure it is however enkaptically bound in the biotic functioning of the thyroid gland. Only the thyroid gland functions subjectively in the biotic aspect of reality (it is alive) while it depends on the enkaptically bound iodine for the production (internal secretion) of the thyroid gland hormone. This biotic function – with its influence on the physical-chemical substructure in the human body – is itself foundationally enkaptically[34] interwoven with the psychic-sensitive substructure and qualifying normative structure of the human being – as proven by its importance for the healthy emotional and normative life of a human being. A hyperactive thyroid gland causes excessive energy use which can lead to a faster heartbeat and a general unease, with accompanying heightened nervous sensitivity. It is clear that the interwoven iodine and thyroid gland functions within the integrated functioning of the entire human being. The theory of enkaptic structural wholes attempts to understand this enkaptic functioning of a human being as a whole, keeping in view the complex substructural interweaving also present in the structure of our bodies.

While all four of the human bodily structures have, apart from their enkaptic interweaving, a characteristic internal functional sphere, it is impossible to delimit any of them *morphologically*, i.e. to localize

---

32 It is one of the important 'organelles' in the cytoplasm of every cell which converts the energy in food into ATP – adenosinetriphosphate – to produce the necessary energy for various cell functions.

33 Concentrated by glandular cells out of the blood in which it circulates as iodide.

34 The term *enkapsis* was introduced by Dooyeweerd, following the biologist Heidenhein, to indicate cases where two differently-natured structures are interwoven in such a way that each retains its unique character. The constitutive substances of living things do not lose their physical-chemical qualification in living things. Thus we can say that such substances are functioning *enkaptically* – that is, retaining their physically qualified nature – in living things. Similarly both the material components and the biotic organs in a human being are enkaptically interwoven in the total bodily existence of a person.

them in a particular part of the body. The foot, hand or leg of a human being is never simply physical, biotic or psychic. The whole human personality, in all four of its enkaptically interwoven substructures, is expressed in every part of the body. For this reason exactly it is impossible for medical and nursing practice to try and work with a reduced "simply biotic human". This reduction can be directly linked to technicism, a force increasingly recognized by present-day philosophers as one of the dominant driving forces of contemporary Western cultural development.

During a guest lecture at the UFS (18 October, 1988) by prof. Egbert Schuurman – well-known Dutch engineer-philosopher – he referred to this pertinently. The danger of such technicism is that it reduces illness and health to mere scientific abstractions – losing sight of the totality of human existence. technique can only be of service if it escapes the limitations of this reduced abstraction:

> "When medical techniques are used in service of medical care, the physician's responsibility is enlarged while his or her attention is, next to the prevention and cure of illness, directed towards suffering, cosuffering, care and the meaning of all this.")

Manipulation of the human embryo in particular easily loses sight that this embryo is the minimal enkaptic structural whole of a person as a human being. Such manipulation consequently has consequences for all four structures of human bodily existence – consequences which, in the light of the limited medical knowledge available in this regard, cannot be foreseen on several vital points. Such experimentation does not only affect particular biotic organs with regard to their internal biotic functioning, but rather a person as a totality.

Apart from the limitations contained in the recognition of the enkaptic interweaving of the human body, medical and nursing practice also has to take account of the variety of societal relationships (DPP-relationships) in which every human being takes part. Whoever enters these professions must not only have an integrated encompassing philosophical view of a person, but also a balanced encompassing philosophical view of individuals within a society.

With this last excursion we have however arrived at the end of this chapter. The next matter under consideration shall be an ordered and systematic analysis of the temporal reality within which each of us exists concretely – with regard to all the facets and structures which we can discern therein. Against the background of a number of historically meaningful philosophical problems – such as the tensions between unity and diversity, we shall, within the context of a distinction between aspects and things, for the sake of continuity with the current chapter, focus attention in the next chapter on prominent aspects of a single concrete process, namely that of dying.

QUESTIONS FOR CHAPTER 2

1. What are the limitations enclosed within the combination of mutation and selection – the corner-stones of neo-Darwinism?
2. Reflect on the uniqueness of being human by considering his ability to conceptualize and to speak.
3. In what sense does the manufacturing of tools demonstrate something uniquely human?
4. What is the contribution made by the human experience of the world, the lack of specialization in the human bodily equipment and the remarkable biotic developmental nature of humans towards an understanding of the uniqueness of human beings.
5. Demonstrate the evading question: who is man? by discussing Buber's attempt to capture the essence of man in terms of *love* and contrast this approach by pointing at the three central relationships conditioning man's human nature.
6. Characterize the temporal appearance ('Gestalt') of humans as a religious beings.
7. Discuss the value of a comprehensive philosophical view with reference to the complex enkaptic interlacement present in the human body.

DIVERGENT TRENDS IN MODERN BIOLOGY

Trends	Aspects of creation	Nuclear meaning of aspects	Entities
Projection of freedom: Hans Jonas	Certitudinal/Faith	Certainty	H U M A N S
	Ethical	Love	
	Juridical	Fairness	
	Aesthetic	Beautiful Harmony	
	Economic	Frugality	
	Social	Social Intercourse	
	Sign	Symbolical Signification	
	Cultural-historical	Formative control/power	
	Logical	Analysis	
Pan-psychism (de Chardin, Rensch)	Sensitive	Feeling	ANIMALS
(Neo-)Vitalism (Driesch, Sinnot, Haas, Overhage), *Holism* (Smuts, Meyer), *Organismic* (von Bertalanffy), *Emergent evolutionism* (Lloyd-Morgan, Whitehead, Bavinck, Polanyi).	Biotical	Life	P L A N T S
Physicalistic evolutionism (synthetic theory)	Physical	Energy-operation	M A T T E R
Mechanistic trend (Eisenstein)	Kinematical	Uniform Flow/Constancy	
(Point of reference: holism)	Space	Continuous Extension	
(Point of reference: atomism)	Number	Discrete Quantity	

Chapter 3
Creation – Unity and Diversity

3.1 Our experience of reality

Without really being aware of it, the first feature of reality which we experience from childhood is the rich diversity of creation.

Within the growing awareness of the world in which a child lives such a child is increasingly fascinated by the *new things* one sees, hears and touches, by the new questions one asks and by the *new* discoveries one makes. This ever-expanding field of experiences is ultimately guided by the many-sidedness and multi-fariousness of creational reality *itself*. Our empirical world is not merely populated by the same *kinds* of things. There are not *only* flowers, *only* animals or *only* human beings. Even if we would abstract from all other kinds of entities and concentrate only on entities of a *specific kind* – like humans – our first awareness more often is not concerned with the *similarities* but with the *differences* between them. If, however, our attention is focused on entities belonging to different categories, we are compelled to disregard the uniqueness of different entities while lifting out that which is common between all of them. For example, if we want to distinguish between humans and animals – as was done in the previous chapter – we pay only attention to that which constitutes the *being-human* of each individual human being and that which constitutes the *being-an-animal* of each individual animal. In other words, in order to accomplish this we solely have to lift out the shared properties between different human individuals (resp. different animals). Only what is (universally) present in all humans as humans (resp. animals as animals) is then of importance.

In our actual daily life each person is constantly engaged in similar processes of lifting out by disregarding, i.e. with acts of identification and distinguishing. Actions like these demonstrate the basic analytical abilities of human beings, since the act of analyzing something entails the recognition (identification) of certain properties by distinguishing them from other features. This state of affairs is also described by the word abstraction. Whenever someone is engaged in an act of abstraction s/he has to lift out (i.e. identify) certain properties while simultaneously disregarding other properties (i.e. by distinguishing them from those identified).[1] From this it must be clear that analysis and abstraction are interchangeable terms – whoever analyses is *abstracting* and whoever is engaged in abstraction is *analyzing*.

In regard of the diversity in creation it is important to note that each activity of analysis or abstraction is always dependent on a multiplicity of givens which have to be identified and distinguished. It is precisely due to this inherent diversity present within the whole creation that we are able to analyze it. Formulated differently: analysis (abstraction) presupposes a given multiplicity transcending the limits of our analytical activity. In other words, was it not for the more-than-logical diversity within creation, it would in principle have been simply impossible to think analytically! The logical-analytical thinking of human beings presupposes the creational diversity.

3.1.1 Some problems in the history of philosophy

One of the remarkable features of the history of philosophy – as well as the history of the various special sciences – is that we encounter numerous attempts – and that by using our analytical ability to identify and distinguish – to deny this creational diversity. Mostly this denial

---

1   The same applies to identification and distinguishing (lifting out and disregarding) – both imply each other. Suppose we want to identify the pen on a desk. In order to achieve this we simultaneously have to distinguish it from the desk and other entities in its environment. The differences making this act of distinguishing possible in turn pre-supposes the *similarities*, since the *differences* could only be established on the basis of the given *similarities*. Due to the fact that both the *pen* and the *desk* are perceivable and tangible physical objects (the *similarity*) are we able to discern the differences between them.

is done in terms of the absolutization of one specific aspect which is elevated to the status of providing a principle of explanation for the entire universe.

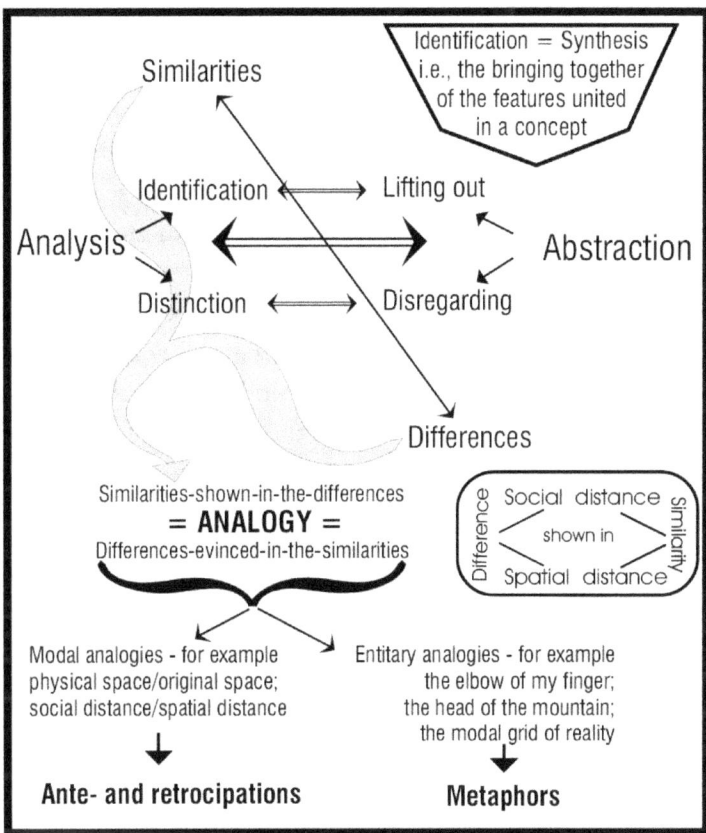

3.1.1.1 'Everything is number'

During the early phase of Greek philosophy the Pythagoreans realized the extremely fundamental place of number in reality. However, they were so impressed with this insight that they unjustifiably concluded that everything in reality is number.[2] Simple integers and the

---

2   In their doctrine of harmony the Pythagoreans discovered that musical harmonies are seemingly reducible to *intervals* which could be expressed in terms of natural whole numbers (1, 2, 3, 4). By adding these numbers they reached the number 10 – the *tetraktis* – which provided the scale for evaluating anything. The entire cosmos was to their mind a tremendous piece of elevated music – finding its foundation in relations of number.

relations between them (as expressed in fractions or rational numbers) are viewed as the key that can unlock every secret. However, the first 'undisclosable door' was given in the nature of space. There are spatial relations which cannot be accounted for merely with the aid of the rational numbers – for example the ratio between the diameter and circumference of a circle or the ratio between the diagonal and any side of a regular pentagram.[3]

The relationship between *unity* and *diversity* embodies one of the *first* problems confronting philosophy and the special sciences as such. Philosophical reflection is always concerned with the limits of our knowledge. Greek philosophy sometimes speaks about philosophy as being the science of the first principles (Aristotle). Even if we consider the admirable developments of the natural sciences during the past few centuries, it is striking that certain basic problems constantly recur. In view of these recurrent issues the Dutch philosopher, H. Van Riessen, prefers to characterize philosophy as "the science of border problems (*grensprobleme*)" (cp. 1970:11).

3.1.1.2 Persistence as opposed to changeability

Besides the problem of unity and multiplicity, Greek philosophy demonstrates various other enduring basic problems to us which still confront the practise of science in the West. Greek philosophers were first of all confronted with the *corruptibility* and *changeability* of humankind's temporal earthly existence. Amidst this awareness of the temporality and corruptibility of reality – from the titanic meaning-perspective closely linked with the changing seasons[4] – it is understandable

---

3   More or less in the year 450 B.C. Hippasos of Metapontum made a remarkable discovery – which implied an existential crisis for the pythagoreans since they elevated their arithmetical reductionism to the level of an ultimate religious certainty. Cassirer remarks that the counterpart of this crisis is found in the insight that although number does not constitute the 'essence' of things, it nevertheless provides the basis of rational knowledge of the world: "The claim that number grasps the essence of things was eventually given up; but at the same time the insight that number forms the basis of rational knowledge sharpened and deepened itself" (Cassirer, 1969:35).

4   On a sound basis Bos questions the accepted and influential conception devel-

that a deeply felt urge towards the incorruptable would arise. Although the oldest philosophers of nature focussed their attention on some specific *element* of nature which could serve as a *flowing* principle of origin of whatever we can perceive (like *water, earth, fire* and *air*), it soon became clear that the search for what is considered to be firm and *constant* turned out to be the implicit companion of the *dynamic* and the *changeful.*

Two of the earliest schools in Greek philosophy became, as it were, fixated on this bi-polar dilemma, i.e. on the relationship between that which is considered to be *persistent* and *constant* on the one hand and the supposed *dynamics* and *change* to which everything in the cosmos was subjected on the other hand. Heraclitus, the complicated thinker of Ephesus, said: "one can never enter the same river twice". Directly opposed to this approach Parmenides of Elea posited a reality excluding all *multiplicity* and *change* – whatever exists is simultaneously connected as one coherent whole in the present (B Fragment 8:3-6). Nothing becomes, everything *is*, everything participates in this *unchangeable static being.*

The best known theoretical antinomy in our Western scientific legacy stems from this reaction to multiplicity and movement. We encounter it in the argument of a philosopher belonging to the school of Parmenides – *Zeno.* Zeno argued that the big athlete of Greece, Achilles, would never be able to surpass the tortoise. In fact, a penetrating analysis would show that Achilles would not even be able to *catch up* with the tortoise! How did Zeno arrive at these conclusions?

Zeno argues as follows: suppose we assume that the tortoise starts with an advance of 100 meters. Then, obviously, Achilles first has to traverse this backlog of 100 meters. The time needed to accomplish

---

oped in one of Nietszche's early writings: *Die Geburt der Tragödie aus dem Geise der Musik* (1872). In this study Nietszche advances the conviction that Greek culture was dominated by a division between the Appolinic and Dionysian orientations. Cf. Bos, 1988:94 ff. In a later publication (*Dooyeweerd en de Wijsbegeerte van de oudheid,* in: Herman Dooyeweerd, Breedte en actualiteit van zijn filosofie, reds. H.G. Geertsema, *et al.,* Kok, Kampen 1994) Bos explains that though he questions the way in which Dooyeweerd accounts for the *rise* of the Greek dialectic, he believes that Dooyeweerd's analysis of the unbridgeable inner dialectic present in Greek thought remains sound (cf. p..220).

this enables the tortoise to move forward, say up to the 110 meter mark. Seemingly Achilles is on the brink of winning the race. But in vain: on arriving at the 110 meter mark, Achilles discovers that the tortoise once again moved on another 1/10th of the previous distance which it traversed – now being on the 111 meter mark! Suddenly the hopelessness of Achilles' attempt comes into view: every time he traverses the distance he is still behind, the tortoise takes the opportunity to establish a new advance – an advance which, each time, is only one tenth of the distance which Achilles caught up. In other words: Achilles will never be able even *to catch up with* the tortoise, since constantly one tenth of the previously traversed distance remains to be traversed – however small this 'tenth' may be! Zeno concludes: movement is an illusion – whoever uses his or her understanding to logically ponder on this situation would realize that everything is embraced by a *static rest*, by *being*, that what *is*.[5]

The confrontation of the schools of Parmenides and Heraclitus highlights various philosophical problems. We mention the following: if everything in reality is in a state of *static* (spatial) *rest*, then it is obvious that there cannot be any movement, i.e. that we have to deny the reality of movement. The influence of this emphasis on *static being* was so overpowering during the course of our Western philosophical legacy that we had to wait until modern times – in particular, the insights of Galileo (17th century) and Einstein (20th century) – to come to a clearer understanding of the nature of *movement*. To this point we shall return presently. The second issue is the question concerning that which is *constant* and *persistent* and that which is varying and changing. Apparently from our early childhood each one of us is confronted with this seeming tension between *constancy* and *dynamics*. Normally we connect it with our experience of *identity*. Afterall, my father and mother remain the same (constant/identical to themselves) in spite of the fact that they age all the time (i.e. *change*). My new jacket, beautiful shirt, lovely doll and enjoyable toy car also undergo the effect of use and

---

5   When I explained this argument once to a philosophy class engaged in studying Greek philosophy, one of the male students *took* the gap. He raised his hand and said: "Professor, if you happen to see me *moving* out of the class please don't worry, it is purely a deception of the senses!"

play – and amidst all aging that takes place the identity of these things is maintained – they remain the *same* clothes or toys. Whoever often looks in the mirror would realize that together with those changes that accompany maturation and ageing it is always possible to recognize one and the same person.

3.1.2 Plato's theory of ideas

Plato was first of all fascinated with our experience of identity amidst all change. On the one hand he was influenced by a pupil of Heraclitus named Cratylus and on the other hand he wanted to maintain the views of Parmenides. The convergence of these two lines of thought materialized in Plato's search for reliable knowledge of things in the surrounding world. The problems which he was confronted by, however, was that if one accepts the constant flux taught by Cratylus, no basis would remain for the claim that we know anything. At the very moment that I say that I have come to know this tree or that animal, the tree and animal concerned have already changed – implying that I do not know the new form they took on. The speculative answer which Plato constructed for this problem consequently accepts as constant basis of all change the so-called super-sensory ideas. Every changeable entity possesses a unique essence (αὐτός; τός; εἶδος). This essence could only be grasped by our understanding since it is contained in an elevated (transcendent) realm of ideas. Proceeding from a Christian world and life view one would look in a different direction for an answer.

The diversity in creation as well as the constant basis for all change could only refer to God's law-order for creation. This law-order not only guarantees the diversity in creation but also makes all change and dynamics as such possible. Consequently this cosmic law-order also lies at the foundation of our scientific reflection on the multifaceted nature of created reality. The question concerning the relation between *unity* and *diversity* which is closely connected with the relation between *constancy* and *dynamics* compels us to account for the different dimensions of reality.

In Chapter 1 we discussed the distinction between RCT and DPP. In Chapter 2 we characterized the RCT dimension as the *religious dimension*. The various branches of our human existence belongs to two other dimensions of reality, i.e. the dimension of *aspects* (properties and relations) and the dimension of *entities*. The forth and last dimension we can distinguish is the dimension of time – the whole creation is *temporal* – only God exists eternally.

3.2 Entities and their properties

Henk Hart opens his extensive work on our understanding of the world with the following striking explanation – an explanation focusing on the *things* we can experience, the *properties* (attributes) we can discern and the *relations* existing between these entities:

> "Our universe, the empirical world of time and space, is populated by little girls, white-tailed deer, yellow slippers, planets and many other things. We can attribute what may be called qualities, or functions, or properties to all of these entities in our world and we can say that they relate to each other. Little girls are cute and have mothers. White-tailed deer are fast and eat leaves. Yellow lady slippers have brown spots on their petals and need light. Planets move around the sun. We can record countless situations that always have these three elements: things with attributes in relation. Little girls feeling warm as they are cuddled by their mothers. White-tailed deer standing motionless as they listen to a sound. Yellow lady slippers hanging low as they bend under the weight of unexpectedly late snow" (1984:1).

Our experience of reality always concerns this trio of *entities, properties* and the *relations* between these things. The same applies to all events we can experience. Events are always *delimited* by the various dimensions of reality. Since philosophy is precisely that discipline which reflects on the *limits* of our experience, i.e. pondering on the *horizons* of our possibilities, we proceed by demonstrating the interwovenness of entities and their properties in terms of the many-sidedness of a *terminal event* appearing within the daily routine of the medical and nursing professions – the process of *dying*.

That the terms *health, illness* and *dying* first of all refer to the biotic aspect of reality was already shown in Chapter 1. Every living entity actively (i.e. *subjectively*) functions within this aspect. *Life* itself is not an entity – it is only an aspect of entities which also display – next to their biotic function – other facets. Living entities do not merely function in the biotic aspect, since they also function in the physical aspect (think about the metabolic processes taking place in every living entity), in the kinematical aspect of movement, in the spatial aspect (cp. the bio-milieu of living entities), and so on. Distinguishable from the original biotic meaning of the term *life* we naturally encounter many non-original (i.e. *analogical*) usages of this term: simply compare expressions like *psychic* life, *lingual* life, *social* life, *legal* life, and so on. It stands to reason that the term *death* could similarly be used in non-original (analogical) ways.

Normally the properties of entities refer to particular functions or aspects of those entities. As a result all scientific disciplines use *property-terms* or *concepts of function*. Biology uses concepts of function such as *growth, adaptation, procreation, survival, dying* and so on. Concepts of function in physics are, for example, the concepts *volume, pressure, entropy, mass*, and so on. Typical concepts of *entities* always form the counterpart of these concepts of function since every possible property which we can mention is always connected with certain entities. Plants, animals and human beings live, grow, procreate and die. Physics uses typical concepts such as atom, molecule and macro-molecule. Or to take a different example: *beauty* is an aesthetical concept of function which should be distinguished from an *art work* as a typical structural concept of aesthetics. Nowhere do we encounter *beauty* – though it is possible to experience beautiful entities.

Distinct from plants and animals, human beings also function actively (subjectively) in the normative aspects of reality, i.e. in the distinctly human aspects of logical thinking, (cultural-) historical formation, signification, social intercourse, frugality, aesthetic evaluation, the legal mode, the moral aspect and the aspect of faith.

3.2.1 The process of dying

Since *dying* is a process functioning simultaneously in different aspects of reality it is possible to approach this process from different angles. First we look at the legal aspect of the dying-event.

3.2.1.1 The bodily integrity of a person – a public legal interest

As a unity human beings not only function as *biotic subjects* but also as a *legal subjects*. The recognition of the legal subjectivity of persons was – historically seen – dependent on the rise and development of the modern state, since before this era Western civilization only knew realms (kingdoms). Realms or kingdoms were not *public legal institutions* since they were the private possession of the king concerned. As a result the status of citizens could not be evaluated as (public) legal subjects.

As maintainer of law, the government of a modern democracy is called to establish balance and harmony within a multiplicity of legal interests by legally undoing the infringement of legal interests whenever it occurs. This differentiated task also relates to the subjective legal interest which each legal subject has in connection with his or her *life*. In terms of constitutional law this legal interest is seen as a *public legal interest*. This means that the *public*, i.e. the *citizens*, have an interest in the protection of the *bodily integrity* (life) of each of its citizens.

> **Remark:** Please note that this subjective legal interest should not be identified as a supposed *subjective right* which one would have had on one's life. The distinctive feature of a subjective right is given in the relation to a legal *object* which, in a factual sense, the person may enjoy and dispose of – also implying the *competence* to get rid of the legal object. This *competence* to get rid of the legal object, however, must not be identified with the *factual disposition* over it. Precisely because human life belongs to the full subjectivity of a person, this *life* should never be objectified into a *legal object* (as in the case of slavery). One cannot put aside your 'life' as one can do away with a legal object. The conception that the *subjective legal interest* which a person has in connection with that person's life (the biotic subject function of an individual) should be viewed as a *subjective right* on it, is founded in the legacy of *natural law* dominant during the 17th and 18th centuries. Following Locke, a subjective right is even equated with that which is not forbidden by positive law. Of course, then an unlimited number of subjective rights on *life, freedom, sleeping, breathing* and so on "exist". Thon (a German jurist) once pointed out that we then have to accept the contradictory view that the life, breathing, movement, sleeping and eating of people who are considered incapable of legal acts would not qualify as subjective rights, whereas those of people who are capable of legal acts would qualify as the exercise of subjective rights. In order to exercise rights one has to be of legal capacity. The result

would be that people incapable of executing any rights cannot have any subjective right on their lives, implying that they could arbitrarily be (ab)used for organ transplantations without fear of committing any crime!

3.2.1.2 The dignity of being human

Of course the recognition of the *dignity* of being human does not only refer to the *legal aspect* of reality, since it also points to the coherence between the legal and the ethical aspects. The legal task of integrating diverse legal interests on the territory of a modern constitutional state under the rule of law (democracy) is, after all, deepened when the legal aspect anticipates (opens up its meaning) towards the *ethical facet* of reality. These deepened legal principles, which are also known as *legal ethical* principles or as *principles of juridical morality*, demand the recognition of the *dignity of the human personality*.[6] Next to the ethical aspect we can also take the faith aspect into consideration.

Seen from this aspect it must be clear that a person does not dispose of his or her own life. Juridically seen we say that no person has 'dispositional power' (*beskikkingsmag*) over his or her life since it would degrade his or her subjectivity into an *object*. Religiously seen we say that God determines the destiny and duration of human life.

3.2.1.3 Euthanasia

Of course, the process of dying is surrounded by a number of difficult questions. Most prominent is the question concerning the nature of the guidance which is given to the dying patient. In this context we have to consider the term *Euthanasia*. This can indicate (i) aid during the process of dying without any shortening of the life-span of the patient (unproblematic); (ii) aid with a possible (reasonably foreseeable) shortening of life (legally and in other respects problematic); (iii) actually causing the death of the patient, be it on request of the patient or not (for example in the case of unbearable suffering).

Even when the patient requests it, this form of Euthanasia is high-

---

6   Article 1 of the *Bundesgesetz für die Bundesrepublik Deutschland*, 1949 reads as follows: 'Die Würde des Menschen ist unantastbar. Sie zu achten und zu schützen ist verplichtung aller staatlichen Gewalt'. ('The dignity of a human being is unassailable. The obligation to respect and protect it is the final norm directing the use of all political force'.)

ly problematic from a legal perspective in most Western countries; (iv) the terminating of life which is considered to be worthless. This option was practised in primitive form by the Spartans and ancient Germans who applied it to malformed children, incurable diseases and aged people. In our modern time it recurred in Nazi Germany. This form of Euthanasia does not find any support in present day Western World.

3.2.1.4 The sensitive and biotic facets of the process of dying

In order to further proliferate the many-sidedness of the process of dying, we now look at the *sensitive* and *biotic* aspects of this process. Seen from a biotic perspective "suspended animation" differs from true death in the sense that only in the latter case do we encounter phenomena of decay. The self-demolition of an organism is accomplished by the functioning of its own cell-organs, known as *lysosomes*.[7] When the heartbeat and breathing cease, the situation is designated by referring to *clinical death*. However, it frequently happens that victims of accidents still function biotically although the activities of the brain are damaged beyond repair. In spite of continuous developments in this domain, we may refer to the practice which is described by dr Repko (cf. 1975) as an example of the way in which the moment of death is medically determined.

- (i) there must be no reception of or response to impressions;
- (ii) there must be no spontaneous breathing when the respirator is turned off for a period of three minutes;
- (iii) there should be no reflexes; and
- (iv) the EEG-test should not register any brain activity.

These four points must be checked – 24 hours apart – by two doctors. If both tests are totally negative, the patient is certified dead and only *after* this certification is the respirator withdrawn.

Because – as we have already remarked – *the integrity of the human body* constitutes a public legal interest which should be protected by

---

[7] They were discovered in 1955. Lysosomes are enclosed in a membrane and they are the seat of specific hydrolic enzymes which play a role, amongst other things, in the process of autolysis.

the government, it is important to the *legal security* of the citizens that the mentioned four points should be checked 24 hours apart. As far as human life and death is concerned there should not, in any sense, be any legal doubt. The confirmation that somebody is dead is therefore an administrative legal assessment which on the one hand refers to the sphere of competence of medical evaluation and on the other hand refers to public administrative law providing the administrative judge with the competence (for the sake of legal security) to perform an act of *marginal testing* (as it is called in Dutch law). In this act of marginal testing the principle of legal balance (the principle of legal economy) is applied enabling the administrative judge to move as it were up to the borders of the sphere of competence of the doctor in order to decide whether the doctor did indeed only act *within* his/her medical domain of competence or whether in fact s/he superseded these boundaries. Of course this meaning of the act of marginal testing presupposes an internal domain of competence for medical decisions by the doctor which in principle lies *beyond* the legitimate area of administrative law.

3.2.1.5 One 'moment of death'?

The variety of aspects discernable in the process of dying is further emphasized when we ask when a person has died: is there only one moment of death?

The way of posing this question ensures that our answer should refer to our awareness of *time*. However, if time is, as is generally and unjustly done, identified with *physical* duration (clock time), we would never be able to answer this question! Although physical time forms the basis of the determination of *biotic* moments of time, it remains completely external as far as the *internal biotic time* phases of birth, growth, maturing, ageing and dying is concerned. These biotic time phases are not at all homogeneous – in the case of all living entities the process of ageing always accelerates, in comparison with the earlier process of growth, when it is measured with external *physical* (i.e., *homogeneous*) clocks. After all, the biotic question: when has somebody died? does not pertain to the physical question: when (according to a normal watch) has someone died? If this was the meaning of the question concerning the moment of death, we would have become victims of a vicious circle: in order to determine the external physical moment of death one must already have decided on internal biotic grounds that the person is dead. This determination, however, requires from the doctors assessing the situation the necessary *medical interpretation* of the relevant phenomena ('symptoms') accompanying the process of dying.

The four check points mentioned above, nevertheless, call forth further burning questions. If *all* the points checked were *negative* but the respirator is not yet withdrawn, doctors easily use the following contradictory expression, namely that a person is 'dead' but is technically kept 'alive'. The contradictory affirmation and denial of two opposite predicates *living* and *dead* is seemingly relativized by placing in parentheses the term 'life'. In this context we must note that the four control points are not assessed in the same *circumstances*. Points (i), (iii) and (iv) are executed while the respirator is supporting the patient, while point (ii) is established without the aid of the respirator. In the case where all four points of testing are negative it is said that the patient is dead in spite of the presence of the respirator. Suppose that only point (iii) is not negative. In terms of the mentioned criteria the patient should then be called alive, even if it is on the basis of the aid of the respirator. In this condition the aid of the respirator enables the patient to display sensitive *reflex* activities as well as biotic activities. If, under the same conditions, a later state occurs where the sensitive activities (reflexes) disappear it would be, in a logical sense, completely justified to declare that the person is biotically still alive (even if it is with the aid of the respirator), since in the same sense during the presence of reflexes it was stated that (also with the aid of the respirator) there is still *psychic activity* present!

3.2.1.6 'Dead' but artificially 'alive'?!

This seeming contradiction could be solved by distinguishing between death in a *biotic* and a *psychic* sense.

It is not contradictory to claim that someone is *psychically* dead but still *biotically* alive. Thus seen it is also no longer necessary to use the term 'life' in quotation marks. Only after the withdrawal of the respirator does the person die in a *biotic* sense. In view of these insights we could ask whether medical personnel sufficiently account for the difference between death in a psychic and a biotic sense. If this distinction is posed within the legal question in the context of administrative law (marginal testing) there may turn out to be cardinal implications within the domain of penal law, which takes us to the Euthanasia problem of terminating biotic life considered to be worthless.

With regard to the moment of death, however, it is possible to conclude that since the process of dying functions within different aspects of reality there is not only one moment of death. Legally seen, a person is dead whenever the medical administrative legal assessment is made (for example after the second test after 24 hours elapsed). Since all four points should already be negative at the beginning of the 24 hour period, one can almost state with certainty that some time *prior* to the first test, the patient was dead in a *psychical* sense. Because the respirator is only withdrawn after the legal judgment is made at the end of the 24 hour period, the biotic moment of death is *after* the jural moment of death. In respect to this medical practice one can – i.e. in the case of brain damage and the need of the respirator – conclude that the moment of death is different depending upon the question whether we view the dying process from the *sensitive psychical*, the *jural* or the *biotic* aspects! Of course each one of these moments of death could be correlated externally with a particular *physical* moment in time – which once again confirms that the *physical concept of time* could never be used to determine the moment of death according to its *internal* biotic, psychical or legal sides.

Although we did not pay attention to *all* the modal aspects of the process of dying, our preceding analysis should certainly demonstrate that things and events in reality are not situated in isolation next to each other. Everything has *relations* with other things. Formulated in a more fundamental fashion: Everything coheres with everything else in creation. The question is: along which lines would it be possible to gain an insight into this fundamental *coherence* existing between everything created?

3.2.2 Establishing relations among diverse things

Say we were a primary school teacher trying to deepen and open up the numeral understanding of our pupils. We know well that most children going to school these days can do some counting. Their experience of counting, however, is bound to a considerable extent to particular things which they have learned to count: so many people, so many toy cars, so many dolls, so many sweets, and so forth. One way to use this experience is to present various different things to the children: say, a basket with four apples; a chair with four legs; a photo of a father, mother and two children; and a book with four dogs on the cover. The question to the children is to find the similarity among all these different collections of things. Keep in mind that the things which the children are seeing fall in widely different categories: they range from material things, plants (fruit) and animals to people and human relationships (a family). Judged in this manner it may appear to the children that there are only differences present. As soon as we draw the attention of the children to the question of **how many**, that is, how many entities are present in each little bundle, they would soon recognize that each contains *four* entities.

Something extremely important has happened. By means of the perspective of the aspect of number we could identify *a relation* among seemingly extremely divergent sorts of things. The aspect of number reveals a *universal relation among diverse entities* in reality. Numerical concepts are therefore *relational concepts* – such concepts reveal fundamental relationships among different things. These relations depend on the fact that each of the entities concerned *functions* in the numerical aspect of reality.

3.2.3 Dichotomous pairs in language

Even human language reflects the distinction between functions (characteristics) and things: nouns are linked to our awareness of things and verbs with the activities (functioning) of things. Linguists occasionally pose the question why certain lexical contents have immediately evident contrary oppositions (antonyms), such as "old"/"young", while others do not, such as "book"/"?". Geckeler is of the opinion that this problem has not yet been solved by linguistics (1971:242). W.J. De Klerk notes also that most adjectives occur in dichotomous pairs, such as short-tall, poor-rich, narrow-broad, ill-healthy, and so forth (1978:114).

This problem reflects the fundamental cosmological distinction between things and aspects of things. The thing-question we can call the **what**-question, and the aspect-question we can call the **how**-question. When a particular thing has been identified, we can always ask: **how** is this or that? is it many or few (numeric how), short or long (spatial how), fast or slow (kinematic how), strong or weak (physical how), is it healthy or ill (biotic how), painful or pleasurable (sensitive-psychic how), logical or illogical (analytical how), historical or unhistorical (historical how), lingual or un-lingual (semiotic how), friendly or ill-mannered (social how), thrifty or wasteful (economic how), ugly or beautiful (aesthetic how), just or unjust (jural how), loving or hating (ethical how), believable or unbelievable (faith how).[8]

3.2.4 The multi-faceted uniqueness of things

The **how**-dimension directs us to the way (mode) in which all things (entities) exist. We can speak of ways of being, ways of experience, or modalities (aspects). It is important, however, to realize that every entity still – just like the dying process analyzed above – functions concretely in every mode according to its typical nature. The concrete function in the biotic mode of a plant and an animal differs.[9] So also does the way in which a plant functions in the physical aspect differ markedly from the physical characteristics of non-living things. Karl Trincher[10] mentions four macroscopic characteristics strikingly illustrating the physical uniqueness of a living cell (1985:336):

1) The macroscopic spatial structure by which the cell is defined as a spatially limited surface;

2) the macroscopic temporal structure, which determines the finitude of the working cycle of the cell;

3) the isothermic character of the cell, which is responsible for maintaining the even temperature of the whole cell;

---

8   Note that we consequently chose the un-form from the logical experiential mode (aspect), although it is also possible to choose other forms, e.g. cheap and expensive, which is not necessarily equivalent to economic – un-economic.

9   In distinction from animal cells, plant cells have a clearly-defined cell-wall – which is connected to the absence of a nervous system in plants.

10 Dept. of Medical Physiology, University of Vienna.

4) the lasting positive difference between the higher cell temperature and the lower temperature of the surrounding external environment.

The modalities (ways of being) form universal contexts within which the various entities in reality (material things, plants, animals, cultural products, life forms, people and all sorts of happenings) exist and function. This functioning is evidence of the inherently dynamic nature of reality, which (as we have already observed) is reflected in all languages by the presence of verbs.

In view of these two dimensions of reality Geckeler's problem mentioned earlier becomes transparent. The reason why a lexical item such as book cannot be immediately bound to a contrary opposition as in the case of 'old' and 'young', is simply because the latter does and the former does not appeal to the **how**, which is distinct from the dimension of things (to which a word like 'book') appeals.[11] This state of affairs is probably linked with the tendency of certain languages (such as Persian) to structure reality 'substantively', while other languages (such as Classical Greek and German) prefers a verb-structure with numerous forms of the verb and numerous words developed on a verb-base.[12]

3.3 The diversity of aspects in our experience of reality

No single special science can escape the need to develop an explicit or implicit perspective on the diverse aspects. This theoretical view of the relationships among and coherence of the various aspects of reality form the philosophical core of every theoretical view of reality. While we shall mention views based on what we believe to be misconceptions of this given creational diversity, we shall first account systematically for the way in which this matter has been understood in the reformational philosophical tradition.

---

11 Other word types (than adjectives) can also act as indicators of the how-determination of reality.

12 Cf. Coseriu, 1978:43. We can say here that the formal dimensional conditioning of language formation determines the two extremes of an independent noun and verb structuring.

3.3.1 Characteristics of a modal aspect

To gain a brief overview we shall first mention the unique characteristics common to all aspects of reality.

a) It is necessary to emphasize again that aspects do not appeal to the concrete **what** of anything in reality. All concrete entities – planets, plants, animals, human beings, cultural objects, and even human societal forms (such as state, church, business or ethnic group) encompass our experience in a different way from the various aspects of reality. The limits or horizon of human experience is characterized by a number of dimensions. The dimension of entities always refers to the entire **what**-ness of things and differs as such from the dimension of aspects which refers to the way in which different things exist. These ways of being (Latin: modi) brings us into contact with a very important dimension of the human experiential horizon. The relation with the Latin expression *modus quo* enables us to refer to the dimension of aspects as the dimension of *modalities*. We shall also often refer *to modal aspects* to emphasize that we are concerned with fundamental modes of reality. There are numerous other terms available to describe this dimension of reality – *facets* (from the French), *sides* (a term with spatial connotations), *functions* and so forth.

In distinction from the *what*-question the dimension of aspects remains concerned with the *how*-question. In answer to *a what*-question we can refer to something: *this* or *that*. The entrance to the dimension of entities is offered to us by the dimension of modal aspects. Whenever something is indicated (e.g. a lounge chair) the modal dimension calls forth the how-question: how is the chair? is it large or small (its spatial way of being); cheap or expensive (economic function); weak or strong (physical aspect); beautiful or ugly (aesthetic modality)? The how question can be answered with: in this or that way, in distinction from the this or that which indicates the answer to the question about the concrete what of something.

b) A second distinctive characteristic of the dimension of modal aspects is the uniqueness of every distinct aspect. It is noticeable that every modal aspect is characterized by a central structural moment which actually presents three particular characteristics at the same time. This central moment, or core of meaning, is not only *unique* and *irreducible*,[13] but also *indefinable*. These characteristics have to do with the *sphere-sovereignty* of the aspects of reality.

c) The other side of the coin is the indissoluble coherence among the various aspects of reality. Every aspect reflects the whole diversity of aspects insofar as there are moments of coherence within the structure of every particular aspect which refers to the other aspects. This characterizes the *sphere universality* of the aspects of reality.

d) Since the aspects belong to the diversity of order in reality, we meet an *order* (law) *side* and a *factual side* within every aspect. God's creational law determines and delimits the existence of everything which functions factually in the aspects of reality.

e) On the factual side of every aspect we find factual subject-subject relationships and factual subject-object relationships. All physical entities (including atoms, molecules, macro-molecules and macro-systems) function subjectively in the first four aspects of reality (number, space, movement, and energy-working). The interactions during a chemical reaction are interactions among various physical subjects, and thereby demonstrate the nature of a subject-subject relationship. When we refer, however, to the role of a physical substance in the life of a plant (e.g. the vital water), it no longer has a subject function but an object function. Water is a physical subject, not a biotic subject – it does not live. Similarly the twigs with which a bird builds its nest does not have a subject function within the sensitive-psychic aspect, even though it is indissolubly involved in the subjective emotional life of the bird as an emotional object. In the normative aspects of reality we find similar subject-object relations – compare the nature of cultural objects.

f) The last characteristic we shall mention with regard to the aspects of reality is the particular relationship between the order and duration of time revealed in every aspect. In the biotic aspect we can

---

13 The example of Achilles and the tortoise at the beginning of this chapter demonstrates the absurd consequences which result from the attempt to theoretically reduce movement to static spatiality.

distinguish the biotic order of time in birth (germination), growth, maturation, aging and death. While every living entity (plant, animal and human) is subject to this order, the factual DURATION of life of every distinct entity differs widely – from annual plants to the long life expectation of people and certain animals.

We will illustrate these characteristics of the aspects of reality with a few examples and problems.

3.3.2 The unique nature of number and space

The aspect of number is identifiable as a distinct facet due to its core meaning of *discrete quantity*. Continuous extension, as the core of meaning of the spatial aspect, similarly enables us to identify and distinguish the aspect.

3.3.2.1 Arithmetizing mathematics

After the discovery of irrational numbers (currently more often referred to as real numbers) in Greek mathematics, an attempt was made to reduce number to space by seeing all of mathematics as geometry (Cf. Boyer, 1956:8 ff.). During the previous century Bolzano, Weierstrass, Dedekind and Cantor contributed to the apparently complete arithmetization of mathematics – an attempt to reduce space theoretically to number.

Already in 1872 Richard Dedekind published a work (on Continuity and Irrational Numbers) in which he explicitly declares that when the irrational numbers are added to the rational numbers (i.e. to the fractions), "the area of the numbers attains the same *completeness*, or as we can also say, the same *continuity* as the straight line" (Dedekind, 1969:9). A couple of pages later Dedekind mentions his "cut"-idea, in which he uses his final definition of continuity (Dedekind, 1969:17). Georg Cantor, who established the foundations of modern set theory, is also of the opinion that he is dealing with a purely arithmetical concept when he talks of a point-continuum (Cantor, 1962:192).

3.3.2.2 A stumbling block

In these supposedly purely arithmetical definitions of continuity, continuous use is made of a fundamental structural characteristic of the spatial aspect: the whole-parts relation. The concepts *whole*, *coherence* and *totality* appeal to the original irreducible meaning of the spatial aspect. The apparently "purely arithmetical" definitions of both Dedekind and Cantor deal with the idea of sets of numbers as infinite totalities, implying that the unique character of the spatial aspect is essential in the attempt to reduce space to number – an obviously circular argument! Paul Bernays says in another context regarding the *totality character* of continuity: "[it] undeniably belongs to the geometric idea of the continuum. And it is this characteristic of the continuum which would resist perfect arithmetization" (Bernays, 1964:283-4; cf. Bernays, 1976:74). The recognition of the reciprocal irreducibility of number and space is not only tenable in view of the current state of affairs in mathematics, since it is also confirmed indirectly by the history of mathematics and the nature of the current foundational studies in mathematics. With regard to the history of mathematics E.T. Bell writes: "… from the earliest times two opposing tendencies, sometimes helping one another, have governed the whole involved development of mathematics. Roughly these are the discrete and the continuous" (Bell, 1966:12). Fraenkel and others comment with regard to the foundational studies in mathematics: "Bridging the gap between the domains of discreteness and of continuity, or between arithmetic and geometry, is a central, presumably even *the* central problem of the foundation of mathematics" (Fraenkel et al., 1973:211). It is sufficient to realize that it is justified to keep in mind the irreducibility of the numerical and spatial aspects.

3.3.2.3 The whole-parts relation

There may be differences of opinion with regard to the placement of the whole-parts relation in the spatial aspect. Is it really true that our awareness of "wholes" and "parts" only comes to the fore in the spatial aspect?

A first possible candidate would be the concept "unity". Aristotle already realized, however, that units are discrete, that is, that numbers, as discrete units, do not possess a common barrier. Only when there is indeed a common barrier can we speak of a coherence (continuity) and of a connected whole (totality). This sort of continuous coherence is unique to spatial extension and indeed implies that the whole-parts relationship first appears in the spatial aspect of our experience. Exactly because every part of a spatial continuum coheres with every other part, the infinite further division of spatial continuity is necessarily linked to this. Spatial continuity founds not only the nature and original meaning of the whole-parts relationship, it also founds the infinite divisibility of such continuity.

A further problem is the prevalent use of the whole-parts relationship without asking whether such usage takes into account both the differences and similarities with its original usage in a spatial sense. The sort of problem which arises is evident already in physics.

It was initially thought that physical space, in analogy with the infinitely divisibility of spatial continuity, is also infinitely divisible. It soon became clear that this is by no means the case. The famous mathematician of the first half of this century, David Hilbert, referred in his commemorative article for Weierstrass (on infinity) to the "naive impression" according to which physical events and matter is continuous. Against the old dogma that nature shows no hiatus (does not make any jumps), the current investigation continues to show limits to the divisibility of matter, indicating that indeed, "nature makes jumps" (1925:81-82). Additionally he indicates that the presupposition of the infinitude of the universe rests on the implementation of Euclidean geometry which has been replaced by non-Euclidian geometries in the description of physical nature. Non-Euclidian geometries do not enable us to conclude an unlimited physical space on the grounds of its infinitude (1925:83).

In distinction from the original sense of space (with the implied whole-parts relationship), which is both continuous and infinitely divisible, physical space is both discontinuous and finite! Apart from these mentioned differences between spatial extension in the original sense and the nature of physical space, there are also similarities: both are *extended*. For that matter: in this moment of similarity we actually notice the difference between these two types of extension, since only insofar as both possess extension, the distinct natures of spatial extension and physical extension become evident.[14]

---

14 As we shall still see, this state of affairs demonstrates exactly what we have understood with regard to the moments of coherence among various *modal*

3.3.3 Perpetual motion

From antiquity there have been attempts to make a machine which, once set in motion, would continue this motion perpetually without using an external source of energy.

At the beginning of the seventeenth century Fludd designed a closed-circuit water mill. This initially appeared quite feasable, but every effort to actually make it work practically, failed.

Already in 1775 the French Academy for Science and Art decided to pay no further attention to purported designs of "perpetuum mobile". In England also all claims to the patent rights on such machines were subjected to the provision of a working model – to no positive effect. The question is: why doesn't it work?

To understand why this sort of perpetual motion machine cannot work, we must refer to the first main law of physics. The underlying idea of perpetual movement, after all, is that useable energy would be produced without using any energy. Practically, this means that energy would have to be created. What does this first law say?

Stimulated by German natural philosophy at the beginning of the previous century (especially the ideas of the philosopher Schelling), German natural scientists searched for a unifying law which would encompass all physical phenomena in a single perspective. The physicists Heimholtz and Mayer and the chemist von Liebig held the notion of the indestructible character of matter even before experimental evidence proved them right.

At the youthful age of 26 Helmholtz presented a formulation of his first main law of physics (actually thermo-dynamics) in 1847 to the Physics Society of Berlin. He began by pointing out that no-one had succeeded in building a successful perpetual motion machine. This was a logical consequence of the indestructibility of energy. Till the present physicists recognize this law as the law of energy conservation which means that energy cannot be created or destroyed.[15]

---

aspects. Such moments of coherence are also referred to as *modal analogies*. To explain this point of view we start of with a problem which has long stimulated human fantasy: perpetual motion.

15 This law does not exclude the fact that one energy form can be transformed

In view of the law of energy conservation it is quite clear today that the construction of such a machine is principially impossible, since it would mean that useful (newly created) energy would be released without using any energy!

Comment: A second such sort of machine had also been imagined – a machine which would draw heat from its environment and then convert this entirely into work. The impossibility of such a machine is evident in view of the second law of thermo-dynamics, that of non-decreasing entropy. Statistically this means that in any closed system the most likely situation would occur. Since there would always need to be a difference in temperature in the environment in order to convert heat into work, the second law implies the impossibility of this type of machine.

These two main laws of physics are fundamental insofar as they are universally applicable to all physical entities. Laws which indiscriminately count for all entities, must completely ignore all the typical differences between such entities. Such *modal laws* indicate the fundamental ways of being or modi of such entities. To deduce universal modal laws requires the scientific activity of analysis which we call *modal abstraction*.

3.3.4 Constancy and change

To grasp the physical modality (way of being) of physical entities, it is necessary to ignore their non-physical aspects – these are the two legs of abstraction. Amongst other things, this implies that it is essential to clearly distinguish between the physical aspect of energy-working and its founding kinematic aspect – that is, the aspect in which we refer only to uniform movement without referring to the cause of movement. Movement – as the mode of constancy – is an original given, just as number, space, the economic or the ethical. For this reason Galileo's law of inertia implies that we may at most speak of the origin of a *change* in motion! All change presupposes a continuing basis. If you do not remain yourself (constancy), you would not be able to age (change)! The importance of our understanding of constancy and change (dynamics), justifies a closer discussion of their nature and

---

into another energy form.

origin – which would also enable us to demonstrate further structural characteristics of modal aspects.

Since the development of Galilean mechanics and the formulation of his mentioned law of inertia, classical physics attempted to encompass all bodies exclusively under the aspect of *mechanical movement*. Since Newton until the beginning of the 20th century this attitude characterized the main tendency in physics. Max Planck (who discovered the working quantum h which presents the fundamental discontinuity of energy), typifies this mechanistic attitude as follows in 1910: "the view of nature which best served physics until today has without doubt been the mechanical. If we take into account that this position holds that all qualitative differences are finally explicable by movement, then we may well define the mechanistic view of nature as the conviction that all physical processes are fully reducible to the movement of unchanging, similar points or elements of mass" (Planck, 1973:53).

In the theory of movement all processes are principially reversible. Already in 1824, however, Carnot discovered principially irreversible processes – a discovery independently worked out by Clausius and Thomson in 1850 into the second main law of thermo-dynamics.[16] This law explains the principial irreversibility of natural processes: in any closed system the law of non-decreasing entropy takes effect – changes in a closed physical system can only take place in one direction, being irreversible. That is why Max Planck notes in his previously quoted work that "the irreversibility of natural processes besets the mechanistic view of nature with unbridgeable problems" (1973:55). Since the discovery of the decaying process of radioactive materials it has appeared that irreversible processes which spontaneously take place in one direction are also present in micro-structures. The irreversibility of the physical order of time (as encapsulated in the law of non-decreasing entropy), confirms without doubt that the physical aspect cannot be reduced to the kinematic aspect.[17]

---

16 In the year 1865, Claudius imported the term entropy. As mentioned the first law is the law of energy-conservation; cf. Apolin, 1964:439-440.

17 The order of time is reversible in the kinematic aspect. The constant tempo of a pendulum demonstrates e.g. the kinematic aspect of a physical pendulum movement. Seen purely kinematically, only the sign in a movement comparison

Initially Dooyeweerd did not distinguish between the kinematic and physical aspects. Since 1950 he does draw this distinction – amongst others since kinematics can define a uniform movement without reference to any causative force (as in the case of Galileo's inertia) (Dooyeweerd, 1969-II:99).

3.3.4.1 The core of Einstein's theory of relativity

We often hear mention of Einstein's theory of relativity. A physicist of his stature lends credit to the popular view linked to his theory, namely that everything is relative and changeable. Remarkably, Einstein's theory rests on a fundamental presupposition which is the opposite of all relativism. Einstein had to start of with the idea of an order which is uniform and constant – which means that everything which he has indicated to be relative is only relative in relation to this constant order.

That this is the case is evident from his postulate that the speed of light is constant in a vacuum. Einstein worked from the presupposition that a particular light signal would have the same constant speed (c) in relation to all possible moving systems. It was not even necessary for his theory for such a signal to actually exist. The fact that later experimentation proved experimentally that the speed of light does indeed conform to Einstein's postulate, is as the physicist Stafleu puts it, relatively irrelevant!

The crux of Einstein's theory of relativity is therefore to be found in the nature of the order of constancy which it presupposes.[18] We are familiar with the numerical order of succession which founds every counting activity: one, another one, another one, and so on. Just as

---

need be changed – and even then it produces a valid movement comparison. By changing the sign, we can, for example, see an expanding system change into a shrinking system – even if only the former is found in physical reality.

18 Spielberg and Bryon correctly emphasize that it is about "invariance" – i.e. constancy – although they unfortunately thereby confuse the terms absolute and unchanging: "Indeed, Einstein originally developed his theory in order to find those things that are invariant (absolute and unchanging) rather than the relative. He was concerned with things that are universal and the same from all points of view" (1987:6). The term unchanging is simply the denial (negation) of the change – a physical term. The term absolute cannot really be applied to anything in creation, that is, not if one wants to avoid the idolization of created reality.

familiar is the spatial order of simultaneity. In distinction from the numerical order of sequence and the spatial order of simultaneity, we experience the order of constancy in the kinematic aspect of movement.

This means that Einstein's special theory of relativity of 1905 is a purely kinematic theory.[19] Einstein therefore did not primarily develop a theory of relativity, but rather one of constancy.

Galileo already discovered the particular nature of the kinematic order of time, as it was revealed in his law of inertia. In terms of this law a body in movement would continue its movement without stopping unless something else (a force or friction) influences it. That means that our insight into the nature of movement does not depend on a causal power. The term "cause" belongs to the physical aspect of our experience where we come across the effects of energy-operation. It cannot be sufficiently emphasized that we can never talk of a cause of movement, but rather only of a cause of a *change* in movement.

The unique nature of constancy (that is, the irreducibility of the kinematic aspect) is the foundation of all references to dynamics or change. Without a constant basis all talk of change is senseless. For this reason physics cannot link any meaningful content to a discontinuous change of movement – change of movement (acceleration and deceleration) is always continuous, since a discontinuous change would require a physically impossible infinite force. Consequently, we can only establish change on the basis of something continuous.

3.3.4.2 An alternative formulation of the first main law of thermodynamics

This foundational position of the aspect of movement enables us to find a philosophical formulation of the first main law of thermodynamics which is true to reality.

The physical aspect must not only be distinguished from its foundational kinematic aspect, since there is also an indissoluble coherence between these two aspects. For this reason we shall find in the physical aspect a structural moment which reminds us of the foundational kinematic aspect. Constancy appears in the physical aspect as a structural

---

19 The irreducible nature of the kinematic time order is imported with the help of a subject which moves at a constant speed.

reminder of the meaning of motion. In philosophical terms we may say that we find an analogy of the kinematic aspect on the law side of the physical aspect.

A formulation of the first main law which intends to be true to reality would therefore have to refer to *energy constancy*. Strictly speaking the use of the term "conservation" is inadequate, since the activity of conservation itself requires an input of energy – as in the case of thermodynamic "open systems" (or "steady states"). The law of *energy constancy* illustrates not only the distinct uniqueness of the kinematic and physical aspects, but, taking into account the distinction between law side and factual side, also the indissoluble coherence between them: without the foundational position of the kinematic aspect in the order of the various cosmic aspects we would have no grounds on which to discern an analogy of the aspect of movement in the physical aspect, that is, the analogy of energy constancy.

3.3.4.3 The theory of relativity and relativism

In modern times there is virtually no science (including theology) not beset with attempts at historical relativism. Historicism, after all, claims that everything changes all the time, that nothing remains the same – moral standards, religious convictions, legal opinions, economic practices – all things continue changing.

The pitfall in this argument is already evident in the fact that every indication of change is inevitably accompanied by kinematic constancy terms – such as "continually", "still", "always", "incessantly", etc.

This implies that we may not identify constancy with something static, but that we should much rather evaluate it positively as the foundation of all dynamics! At the same time, however, we should leave aside the one-sided and excessive concern with *dynamics* which is set against all forms of *constancy*.[20] Such an approach only leads to an unjustified dialectical tension: that which is the condition and prerequisite of dynamic change – that is, something constant – is seen as its opposite pole and enemy.

---

20 Where a few a decades back one would still refer with the highest regard to a resolute or principled person, today it is fashionable to speak of a dynamic person.

The remarkable coherence between the terms constancy and dynamics not only enlightens us regarding the natural scientific basis for the use of these terms, it also emphasizes the insight that the way in which we talk about everyday occurrences can never escape the perspective of particular aspects.

The particular character of the different aspects of reality is strikingly evident in a sort of question with which we are intimately familiar as of childhood:

3.3.5 What is ... ?

From young every human being asks "what is ..." questions. "Daddy, what is that?", "Mummy, what is that?", and so on. Later on these questions deepen. Then it is no longer directed at some or other new or strange object seen, but concerns more abstract matters, such as: "Dad, what is courtesy/beauty/justice/frugality?"; or: "Mum, what is love?"; or: "Sir, what is life/number/...?". As natural as these questions may sound, just as misleading they may be!

Saturated in an age-old tradition in which the human intellect and ability to conceptually encompass reality has been overestimated, these questions are evidence of a desire to understand things conceptually which, by their very nature, cannot be understood conceptually. Most successful definitions of this kind of matter are little more than rerouted questions. Prominent biological schools of thought in our day answer the question "what is life?" with: "Life is nothing else than a highly complex interaction of atoms, molecules, and macromolecules". This supposed conceptualization appears to say much, but still misses its aim: "life" disappears from the horizon and all that remains are "dead" material things like atoms, molecules, and macromolecules – and even a neo-Darwinist like Simpson acknowledges that molecules don't "live".

Nothing alive exists apart or independently from constitutive physical substances. Without these substances there would be no life. This is not, however, sufficient grounds for defining "life" in simply physical terms. Things which live do not cohere only with the physical aspect of reality, since there would be just as little "life" in the absence of the spatial aspect. Think of the important role of biological environmental sciences today, or of terms like habitat (bio-environment) which unmistakably indicates the coherence between the biotic and spatial aspects of reality.

Even the numerical aspect contributes to this coherence, since the multiple members of a living thing needs to be bound together into a meaningful unity if its activities were not to disintegrate, causing death.

Such "what is" questions run into cul-de-sacs all the time. A Dutch legal scholar attempted to define the jural as an objective, trans-egotistic harmonization of interests – missing the unique nature of the jural aspect of our experience. Neither "objective" (in the sense of common or unbiased) nor "interests" say anything specifically jural. "Trans-egotistic" appeals to the ethical side of our existence (moral relations of love and trust), and "harmonization" refers to the aesthetic aspect of reality. Dooyeweerd comments rightly on this definition in his legal encyclopedia: it may as well be seen as a measure for the distribution of alms among the poor.

Such definitions do explain why whatever is original and unique is inaccessible to the very activity of definition: rather it forms the presuppositional foundation of definitions. Contradictory to the expectations of Western rationalism, people can only understand and define reality in terms which are not themselves open to a conceptual grasp or definition.

The irony of all apostasy is evident yet again: the opposite of the intended is achieved. Rather than gaining conceptual insight into something, the "what is …?" question leads to a denial of the unique character of the particular matter or aspect. This demonstrates clearly that human reason is not self-sufficient – even the simplest process of conceptual formation depends on terms which cannot be conceptually understood, and themselves make conceptual analysis possible. Western humankind has little resistance against intellectual hubris, and finds it difficult to deal with the realization that human conceptualization depends on the grace of an original creational diversity which also prescribes the contours of human thought.

3.3.5.1 The impasse of historicism

We have already mentioned that historicism attempts to sacrifice all of reality to historical change. Everything – legal concepts, moral standards, convictions of faith, and so forth – is simply subject to the ever-flowing stream of emergence, acme and decline. The first question to be directed at historicism is whether any grounds remain for speaking about *legal* history, *religious* history, or *economic* history?

Whoever ponders on this question soon realizes that we can only meaningfully talk of legal history because there exists both a historical and a jural aspect within the diversity of creation. Since law isn't history, it can have a history. If everything was history, as the historicist claims, then nothing remains which could have a history. This is the *irony* of historicism: that which is exalted to the *one and all* loses all meaning, since, if everything *is* history, nothing remains which can *have* a history, and we lose history itself!

This example also indicates that the meaning of history can only be understood in coherence with everything which isn't history. Every aspect is in an indissoluble coherence of meaning with all the other aspects. For this reason the historical aspect can also only reveal its meaning in coherence with all the non-historical aspects of reality. Without an inner interwoven coherence with the legal aspect we cannot gain insight into something like legal history. This is true for every aspect.

"Life", for instance, isn't something abstract which exists on its own, separate from all the other aspects of reality that co-constitute the realit yof a living entity. For this reason the famous physicist Schrödinger already in the fourth decade of the 20th century wrote a book about the *physical aspect* of the cell. More recent developments witnessed the rise of a number of biological subdisciplines exploring the coherence of the biotic and spatial aspects of reality – the *ecological* sciences.

The meaningful question we should ask in the place of the "what is ...?" question is "What is the meaning of ... justice? love? life? number? history? stewardship? trust?" Then we shall learn why love is considerate (retrospective coherence with the sensitive-psychic) and sacrificial (coherence with the economic), why justice establishes a balance between conflicting interests (retrocipatory coherence with the physical), why justice depends on the attitude of the actor and not only the consequences of the deed (anticipatory coherence with the ethical aspect), why historical understanding must have an eye for cultural treasures (which has grown as part of the traditional heritage) as well as for the demands of a new situation (reformation, sifting and selecting vibrant traditions for the future from among the dead wood) (retrocipatory coherence with the biotic aspect).

3.3.5.2 The meaning of faith

In the reformational tradition (cf. the Heidelberg Catechism) it is taught that faith is a certain trust and a certain knowledge. The latter indication is that of Calvin. Is this a definition?

Some exegeticists are of the opinion that we find a "definition" in one place in the Bible, namely Hebrews 11, where the nature of faith is supposedly "defined". In reality it only states simply and strikingly by means of repetition that faith has to do with something about which we are convinced with confidence:

> "Now faith is being sure of what we hope for and certain of what we do not see."

As with every other aspect of creation we are confronted with the limits of concept and definition – every attempt to further define this unique meaning of faith by means of merely repetitive confirmation runs the risk of being reductionist. Then we only say what faith is in terms of what it isn't.

The unique nature of faith becomes apparent in coherence with the other facets of our existence – therein lies the meaning of faith. What value has faith without works (cf. James 2:14)?

Faith implies and demands fidelity in faith and sacrifices of faith, together with knowledge of faith – correct faith distinctions (as emphasized by Calvin), faith sensitivity – not the same as faith directed by feeling. It requires a dynamism of faith, perseverance in faith and integration of faith, it brings about a harmonious and balanced faith, requires correct interpretation of signs of faith (e.g. that the bread and wine in communion does not really turn into the flesh and blood of Christ), it brings about community in faith which leads to joint worship, praise and exhortation in the meeting, it requires contemporary forms and expressions in response to the new problems and tasks arising out of changing historical circumstances. At the deepest level faith unifies our lives and directs them at the loving service of God and the neighbour with our whole heart.

In the previous paragraph we made a subtle transition. Initially we emphasized the meaning of faith which coheres with other facets of creation, while in conclusion we closed with an appeal on the root of our faith which requires and implies total obedience. Does this mean that the word faith is used in different senses in the Bible?

Indeed, since while it is used to indicate the total and all-encompassing heart relationship of the reborn Christians with God – for which reason the term Christian refers to their entire existence – it is also used to indicate one of the rays in the colour spectrum of our lives. The same is true for the word love.

In the previous chapter we saw that the heart, as the religious centre of human existence, is at the root of all the expressions of life. For this reason Christ requires a reborn heart – the wellspring of life. When faith or love is used in this radical sense, it cannot refer to merely one aspect of our experience of reality – then it refers to the fullness of our covenant relationship with God in Christ. This is evident when we speak of the central commandment of love or of faith as a heart commitment to God.

These radical usages are not in conflict with those texts where the words love and faith are used in a *differentiated* sense next to each other, since these references are not to the root, but the divergent expressions of life.

Compare for instance Gal. 5:22 where love is used next to and with joy, faithfulness and self-control as a fruit of the Spirit, or I Tim 6:11 where a Godpleasing person is asked to pursue righteousness, faith and love, among others.

The heart is the root of faith, the reborn heart determines the direction (towards God) of our faith, the creational order founds the normative structure of faith – thus no unbeliever can escape from it since even atheism is a form of (apostate) faith – and the Bible (as the genuine and trustworthy Word of God) determines the *content* of our Christian faith.

The structure of God's creation is so astounding that everything coheres with everything else. Nothing is self-sufficient. The diversity of meaning in creation, which is placed in an indissoluble coherence of meaning, exists from, through and to God and is created in, through and for Christ – the fullness of meaning of creation.

3.3.6 Provisional reflection

Up to now we have explored various characteristics of modal aspects in terms of a number of examples and problems. With reference to early Greek philosophical views of reality – particularly the view of Pythagoras that everything is number – we looked at the unique nature of aspects, amongst them those of number and space. The problem of *constancy* and *dynamics* enabled us to pay attention to the fantasy of *perpetual motion*, the foundational coherence between the kinematic and physical aspects, the general character of Einstein's theory of relativity and a formulation of the first main law of thermodynamics which is true to reality (i.e. *energy constancy*). The latter example demonstrates the value of insight into modal analogies since *energy constancy* expresses a *kinematic analogy* in the structure of the physical aspect. Subsequently we discussed the indefinable nature of the cores of meaning of the different aspects with reference to the common "what is?" questions. The meaning of the biotic, jural and faith aspects were discussed in this regard from the perspective that everything in created reality can only be understood when their coherence with other creational phenomena is taken into account. The irony of every absolutization of something created is exactly that it robs the absolutized aspect of its meaning – as in the case of historicism which tries to historify everything but runs into the impasse that nothing remains which can have a history.

If we have a perspective which attempts to escape in principle the relativism inherent to historicism it implies that we must pay attention to *principles*. The question, however, is:

3.3.7 What are principles?

From all sides we hear every day about "principles". Political parties like to declare their continued commitment to "basic principles", churches refer to christian and scriptural principles, young people are raised to guard sensitively against all that conflicts with the "principles" according to which they were raised, in arguments it is often concluded that an unbridgeable "difference of principle" exists.

When we dare to ask a critical question: what exactly is a principle supposed to be? we are mostly sent off without an answer. Can someone's principles change? Or are they unchangeable and static?

Are principles universally valid? In other words, is it part of the nature of a principle that it is valid at all times and in all places? If so, does any space remain for human freedom to adapt to new situations? Universally valid principles have an obvious concrete significance – what then of the equally familiar thought that principles must be concretized (be made valid)? If alternative applications of a principle is considered acceptable, can such applications change along with historical circumstances?

These are surely enough questions to lead anyone reflecting on the nature of principles into a virtually impassible labyrinth!

3.3.7.1 Principle and application

We are often informed that something like the death sentence is a principle. In reality, however, the death sentence refers to the underlying disclosed Western principle of criminal law which requires that the punishment should fit the crime (taking into account fault, both in terms of intent and negligence).[21] This principle of punishment relevant to fault is a deepened legal-ethical principle fundamentally different from the strict responsibility for outcomes evident in undisclosed legal systems (e.g. the talio-principle in the Old Testament, known as the "eye for an eye" or "tooth for a tooth"-principle). In the talio-prin-

---

21 Following a suggestion of Alan Cameron, the current editor of Dooyeweerd's *Encyclopedia of Legal Science* (it forms part of the Collected Works of Dooyeweerd), we translate the Dutch and Afrikaans word "schuld/skuld" with the word "fault.". It could be translated either as "fault" or "guilt." Although, in English-speaking Common Law jurisdictions, "fault" is normally reserved for civil wrongs (*torts*) while "guilt" is used for criminal wrongs, we will capture both these meanings with the term "fault" taken in the mentioned broad sense (not specific to any particular category of legal wrong), encompassing both civil and criminal delicts.

ciple the ethical aspect of moral love had not yet deepened the meaning of the jural aspect of reality, since the attitude of the actor was neglected, and only the consequences of the act were taken into account. In an ethically deepened, or disclosed,[22] legal system the death penalty can only be considered as an application (positive expression) of the underlying principle of punishment according to fault. Other applications of the same principle could be e.g. life imprisonment or an even shorter term, depending on the degree of mitigating circumstances which may be present.

God's creational will for humankind approaches the latter in the form of constant points of departure (Afr. "begin-sels"), and humankind's calling is to give concrete effect to these points of departure as cultural shaper, according to the unique historical circumstances of a particular cultural period. Without foundational constant principles it would be impossible to speak of adaption, dynamics, concretization, application or positivization. Only in the light of the Scriptures does the Christian realize that God set his creation-wide law for being human (his Law-Word) and that the central unity and fullness of this law is given in the law which demands that we must love God and our neighbour with all our heart.

3.3.7.2 Are principles valid for all time?

As constant points of departure all true principles have an appeal for all times and places – they are universal in the sense that no human being anywhere, ever, can escape their claims. Contemporary "situation-ethics" attempts to make the uniqueness of every situation determinative, elevating the situation itself to a norm. This is nothing but complete *normlessness*. This universality (that is, the point of departure for action in all situations), however, does not mean that any principle is valid in itself. In order to become valid, to be made effective, human intervention and activity is essential – the human being alone is empowered to give concrete expression to principles in a particular unique historical situation.

---

22 Notice that this disclosure regards the "opening up" of anticipatory analogies in a particular aspect. Guilt here refers to the anticipation of the ethical aspect from the jural aspect.

The mere distinction between principle and application is linked by Hart with those attitudes towards life referred to as legalistic, conservative or traditionalistic. According to him extreme and excessive traditionalism or conservatism is the result of an inability to understand the meaning of this distinction. He explains his claim in terms of the various expressions of respect in social habits of greeting. While the fundamental principle of social respect remains, the concrete expression given to it in greeting changes:

> "In certain cultures men may express respect by taking off their hat to each other. Let's say that after some time people no longer actually raised the hat all the way, but just lifted it slightly. Still later we see people just touching the hat. In the end all that remains is raising the hand. We can distinguish between a principle (i.e. expressing respect) and actual patterns of behaviour (i.e. various actions with the arm relating to headgear). ... In spite of all that varies, something 'in principle' remains invariant through all this historical development" (1984:59). Three pages further he explicitly rejects the extremes of conservatism and chaos: "Either only lifting one's hat all the way counts as greeting, or anything I choose is greeting. The recognition of 'greeting in principle' makes it possible to avoid both conservatism and chaos" (1984:62).

There exists an old tradition in the history of Western science in which it has been wrongly claimed that principles are effective in and of themselves. This took shape especially in the writings of 17th and 18th century legal scholars – the natural law school – who were of the opinion that there is an eternal and unchangeable legal order containing positively valid and positively applied legal norms for all situations at all times.[23] At the beginning of the previous century the historicist school of Von Savigny opposed this position. This reaction rejected entirely the constant nature of principles as universal points of departure for concrete historical action. This rejection emerges out of an absolute negation of our biblical faith in an underlying creational order.

Several contemporary theological currents have, as a result of this

---

23 Hugo de Groot, for example, saw the demand that contracts must be kept – "pacta sunt servanda" – as such an eternal and positively valid principle of natural law.

historicist emasculation of the biblical creational faith only the future in view (hence their eschatological emphasis), without any sensitivity for the creational points of departure out of which our obedience should be directed towards the future. Olthuis observes, "The current eschatological orientation in theology which tends to seek even the beginning in the end will need revision. The Bible begins with Genesis and Genesis begins with creation. The Scriptures see the Gospel as the link connecting creation and consummation. And this link between past and future is revealed as the Word which connects the end with the beginning, the consummation with the creation. 'I am the Alpha and the Omega, the first and the last, the beginning and the end' (Rev. 22:12). A proper vision of the consummation requires a proper appreciation of the beginning. Without this understanding, the fulfillment lacks substantial content and tends to evaporate into pious words about hope. A non-robust view of creation emasculates the gospel, for it is the creation which is brought to fulfillment in Jesus Christ even as it began in him" (Olthuis, 1989:32-33).

While the appeal of the central commandment of love is without doubt also present in the commandments of the Old Testament, as confirmed by the fact that Jesus, in his reply to the Pharisees, uses the formulation of Deut.6:5 and Lev.19:18, it is equally true that God's covenant will for Israel was presented to Israel in the form of numerous concrete regulations. These are a diversity of positivized principles – which are as such, i.e. in their positivized form, not universally applicable. Consider the following example.

3.3.7.3 The historical distance between positive expressions of principles

What is the meaning of the covenant word: you shall not commit adultery? Suppose we were to put this question one Sunday morning to a number of churchgoers at the church down the road. Most likely they would all reply: I understand it to mean that a man must be faithful to his wife and vice versa. They may therefore not have any love relations in the marital sense with other men or women, since this would be adultery. In response we would be able to ask: does your minsiter understand it in this way? And what about the members of the congregation? How do they understand this commandment when they hear it? To this also, the answer is most likely to be: yes. Now, however, comes the critical question: is this what Old Testament Israelites understood the commandment to mean?

Not at all! In the Old Testament situation a man was not only allowed to have more than one wife and more than one concubine, he was even allowed to have sexual relations with an unmarried women as long as he was willing to take her as wife or concubine after his involvement with her! Without doubt the positive content of this covenant word was different from the way in which we give form to the ethical relationship between husband and wife today. On what grounds, with what criteria, can we judge our different and adapted approach? The Old Testament positive form cannot be used, except if we were to pursue the absurd casuistic path of elevating a particular positive form to a universal norm for all times. Such an attempt would lead to the following problematic situation. If what we understand under this commandment today is the meaning and content of the Old Testament covenant word, then virtually any situation would be justifiable in its terms. How would we counteract claims that the intention of the covenant word quite justifies one man to have three wives, or one wife three husbands? In this way any arbitrary situation would be justifiable by claiming that contemporary practice is according to the commandment. This would lead to complete normlessness.

What happened when Jesus was approached by the Pharisees with regard to divorce? Christ held that what God has put together, no prson may put asunder, to which the Pharisees replied by asking why Moses prescribed the use of a letter of divorce? Jesus replied, "Moses permitted you to divorce your wives because your hearts were hard. But it was not this way from the beginning" (Matt. 19:8). Jesus appeals to the beginning – in the beginning God created the heavens and the earth (Gen.1:1). This is an appeal to the original creation: in principle (Afr. "begin-sel") no-one may divorce, even as a person's sinful heart and its antinormative acts (cf. Matt. 15:19) requires it factually.

3.3.7.4 Central appeal and contemporary expressions

Only with an appeal to the creational principle of marriage do we gain a measure which liberates us from the arbitrariness with which virtually any situation could be seen as conforming to the Old Testamental commandment.

The central unity of God's law and the religious fullness of God's claim on whole-hearted loving service is expressed differentially in the diversity of creational structures – linked to the historical level of development (differentiation) and disclosure in effect in a particular civilization (cf. the example of the death penalty discussed above). This explains again why we cannot biblicistically consider a particular positive form of the differentially expressed central commandment of love as valid for all time.

In the ten covenant words of God the central commandment of love is given contemporary expression. The commandment: you may not commit murder, has an Old Testamental positive expression which must be understood in view of the relative undisclosed and undifferentiated legal system of the time. Disclosed, deepened jural-moral principles (fault, fairness, and so forth) were not prominent in this system.

The sabbath commandment is perhaps the most obvious in this regard, since it is completely interwoven with the Old Testamental tabernacle and temple orders of worship, with the particular position of the high priest, all of which is part of the whole people of Israel, which is supposed to be holy as God is holy (cf. Lev. 19:2). The holy cultic days did not exist to make the people holy, since Israel was supposed to be a royal priesthood in all her covenantally obedient activities. Thus the people had to regularly recall cultically (including a variety of festivals) God's mighty deeds of care and redemption. Once Christ, priest-king in terms of the order of Melchizedek, sacrificed himself (differently from the high priests who always sacrificed both on their own behalf and on behalf of the people) (Hebr. 7:27), a change in priesthood required a change of law (Hebr. 7:12). This is why we celebrate Sunday, the first day of the week, since the new covenant is no longer bound to the celebration of the sabbath (the seventh day of the week). In Christ there is a sabbath rest for the chosen people of God (Hebr. 4:9), a restoration of the paradise-order of peace and obedience in all activities of life in God's kingdom come, and coming.

In the New Testament we find a continuous central appeal to the commandment of love, even as the diverse concrete situations and commandments of which we read provide us with positive expressions.

From this perspective the covenant history of the Old and New Israel can be understood within the context of the all-sided dynamic and disclosure of meaning of God's creational order. Conversely we cannot deduce the differentiated principles for our richly nuanced contemporary life from the covenant words of the Old and New Testamental positive expressions, which were true to their particular times. The common point of reference remains God's universal order of creation within which God gave his Word revelation and speaks to us in a central religious sense.

Of course, the religious heart appeal of the Bible is normative for all Christian expressions of life, and not only the narrower life of faith. Only in the Bible do we come into contact with the radical (cutting to the root) religious content of the central commandment of love, while the factual content of our Christian faith is only brought to us by the Bible, in Christ through the working of the Holy Spirit. It would be clearer, however, if we were to say that the Bible *determines* the content of our Christian faith, rather than that it is the *norm* for our faith. The Bible itself, as we have seen, refers us to the principles of divine creation (cf. Christ's mentioned reply to the Pharisees) and is given within the order of creation.

In this regard it cannot be emphasized enough that no insight into the existence of creational principles, nor any actual theoretical analysis or discovery of these principles can ever take place independently of the Bible, since only the Bible reveals to us that God created all things, which subjects a person to the normative law which was set over us. Only when the radical and total authority of the Bible is recognized, can we attempt theoretically and fallibly to uncover creational principles.

The arbitrary and indiscriminate way in which certain positive expressions in the Bible are biblicistically elevated to universally applicable "principles" is well-known to most of us. Without realizing the inconsistencies of such an approach, an appeal could for instance be made to Deut. 22:5 that a woman may not wear male clothing and a man not women's clothing, while all other expressions in the same context are ignored.[24] At the same time the question isn't asked whether the prohibition could have had something to do with certain heathen cultic practices from which Israel, as a holy nation, had to distance herself.

This sort of abuse of particular positive expressions follow a particular "exegetical procedure": when it appears in any way as if a particular positive expression in the Scriptures has any similarity to any contemporary positive expression (e.g. monogamous marriage), it is immediately concluded that we are dealing with a "scriptural principle".[25]

All positive expressions which may differ obviously and considerably from our contemporary situation, is mostly simply ignored, without closer justification, even while we are still supposedly bound by positive expressions already invalidated from a New Testamental perspective (such as the mentioned difference between keeping the sabbath and celebrating the Sunday).

Without extensive discussion we conclude this section on the nature of principles with a brief typification:

> a principle is a universally constant point of departure which only becomes effective (is given positive expression) through the actions of a competent person or institution which has a responsible free will which enables them to reach a normative or antinormative application of the particular principle in unique historical circumstances.[26]

---

24 You may not sow two types of seed in your vineyard (verse 9) and you may not wear mixed materials – wool and linen – at the same time (verse 11). Where would this leave modern farmers and women?

25 Even the way in which a modern marriage comes into existence or to an end is absent from the New Testament, since it is dependent in our times on the differentiated civil and non-civil private law (to which we shall return at a later stage), which had not as yet crystalized at the time of the New Testament.

26 Notice that this formulation implicitly uses the gateway of a number of aspects – which signifies that the term principle is a complex or compound fundamental scientific concept – in distinction from the elementary fundamental concepts in science which appeal to a single particular analogy in the structure

3.3.8 Problems with the "new mathematics": Is a line a set of points? (the spatial subject-object relation)

While the idea is ancient, modern Cantorian set theory again came up with the conviction that a spatial subject such as a particular line must be seen simply as an infinite (technically, a non-denumerable infinite) set of points.

If the points which constitute the one dimensional continuity of the line were themselves to possess any extension whatsoever, it would have the absurd implication that the continuity of every point is again constituted of smaller points than the first type, but which would necessarily also have some extension. This argument could be continued *ad infinitum*, implying that we would have to talk of ever-diminishing points. In reality such diminishing points do not at all refer to real points, since they are supposed to indicate the nature of continuous extension, which as we have seen, is infinitely divisible. Such points build up space out of space.

Anything which has factual extension has a subject-function in the spatial aspect (such as a chair) or is a modal subject in space (such as a line, a surface, and so forth). A point in space, however, is always dependent on a spatial subject since it does not itself possess any extension. The length, surface or volume of a point is always zero – it has none of these. If the measure of one point is zero, then any number of points would still have a zero-measure. Even an (enumerable) infinite set of points would never constitute any positive distance, since distance presupposes an extended subject.[27]

---

of an aspect of reality. Cf. e.g. Strauss, 1988c. The nature of modal analogies, seen together with the distinction between law-/norm-side and factual side, enables us to trace down many principles philosophically. Every analogy on the law-side of a normative aspect provides us with a fundamental modal principle.

27 The following classical "definition" of a line is well-known: *A straight line is the shortest distance between two points.* A straight line is a factual spatial figure extended in one dimension. The measure of this extension, however, is indicated by the numerical analogy of distance (magnitude). In a particular instance we can say that the length (i.e. the numerical analogy) of a line is so much. The so much of a line, however, is not the line. In other words, the extension of the line cannot be defined by the indication of its length. The length of a line presupposes the factual extension of the line – from which it remains distinct. For

In the mathematical theory of measures a little trick is used in an attempt to overcome this limitation. Cantor had proved that the real numbers cannot be counted one by one, that is, they are non-denumerable. Then it is no longer possible to define addition, since in order to add, a set must be denumerable: only then can one and another one and another one be added. In such a case it is said that the non-denumerable set of points between two points x and y has a measure larger than zero – in order to define a line as a set of real points.

In this mathematical argument implicit use is made of a disclosed idea of infinitude. Our original awareness of number depends on a temporal order of one, another one, and so forth. This order of succession we can call the *successively infinite*. When we consider a sequence of numbers as if all the elements of the row are observed *at once* – as the points on a straight line are in view at the same time – we come across a deepened sense of infinitude, the *at once infinite*. Without the nature of spatial simultaneity this supposition of an *at once infinite* set has no foundation. The *at once infinite* is a numerical anticipation to the spatial aspect. It is an anticipatory analogy in number of space. Thanks to this analogy the arithmetical order of succession is directed in anticipation towards the spatial order of simultaneity.[28]

The *at once infinite* presupposes the irreducible, unique nature of the spatial aspect and cannot be used subsequently to reduce space to number (a distinct number of points) in terms of a non-denumerable set of real points. This reductionist attempt is *antinomical* and implies the following *contradiction*: space can be reduced to number if and only if it cannot be reduced to number (i.e. if and only if the *at once infinite* is used, which presupposes the irreducibility of the spatial aspect)!

A point always functions in an objectively limiting way with regard to a spatial subject. If it is a one-dimensional subject, points serve as its beginning and end. If it is a two-dimensional figure (such as a square),

---

this reason Hilbert imported the term *line* as an undefined term in his famous axiomatic foundation of geometry (cf. 1899).

28 In Aristotle's discussion of Zeno's antinomies – i.e. that of Achilles and the tortoise – the distinction between these two types of infinity is indicated as the potential infinite and the actual infinite. Historically other terms have also been used, such as incompleted and completed infinity.

points serve as the corners, and so forth. A line, which is a subject in one dimension, can also function in a limiting (objective) sense in higher dimensions – e.g. limiting the surface of a square, or acting as the edge of a cube. In similar fashion a surface can act as a limiting object in three dimensions, as when it delimits the volume of a cube. In general it can be stated that whatever is a spatial subject in n dimensions, is an object in n+1 dimensions. A point is a spatial object in one dimension (an objective numerical analogy on the factual side of the spatial aspect), and therefore a spatial subject in no dimension (zero dimensions). In terms of the principial difference between a spatial subject and object, it is impossible to deduce spatial extension in terms of spatial objects (points). Consequently it is unjustifiable to see a line as a set of points. (The sketch on page 81 gives a brief overview of the interrelations between number and space.)

3.4 Conclusion

In this chapter we have given attention – with reference to a handful of problems and examples – to the various structural moments common to the general nature of a modal aspect. We indicated that every modal aspect has the following characteristics: a unique, undefinable and irreducible core of meaning; an indissoluble correlation between the law-/norm-side and the factual side; a reflection of the cosmic coherence of meaning with other aspects of reality in (retro- or anticipatory) analogies; a position in the irreversible cosmic order of time which appears in every aspect in the correlation between the order of time (law-side) and the duration of time (factual side); in all the post-arithmetical aspects there is a correlation between the factual subjectivity and factual objectivity (a subject-object relation).

In conclusion we provide a short summary of the various points raised which would be useful in the identification of distinct aspects.

(1) In the historical course of Western philosophy there has always been recognition of the diversity in reality – an indirect indication of the distinct aspects.

(2) In non-scientific ("naive") experience we also find this diversity – as reflected in the common human analytical awareness of this diversity.

Creation – Unity and Diversity | 123

(3) The great variety of isms found in philosophy and the special sciences, which each absolutizes a different aspect of reality to be the all-encompassing theoretical foundation, also indirectly implies the distinct aspects.

(4) Reflection on the various kingdoms in nature (matter, plant and animal), as well as on the various human societal forms (such as the state, church, sports club, school, cultural society, theatre group, marriage, business firm or language association) directs us towards the various modalities (aspects) which provide access to the qualifying aspect of each. This helps with the distinction and identification of aspects.

(5) The method of exposing antinomies helps us to avoid the identification of aspects with each other.

(6) The development of independent special sciences, delimited in their area of study by a particular aspect of reality, indicates the variety of aspects of reality.

(7) Another aid in the identification of a particular aspect is that which appeals to our immediate intuition (experiential insight) when reference is made to the meaning of any distinct aspect.

(8) All the special sciences use typical entity concepts (such as: atom, molecule, plant, animal, table, painting, murder weapon, engagement ring, church building) as well as functional concepts unmistakably appealing to the modal aspects of reality (such as life, volume, control, agreement, exchange, threat, love, integration, sensitivity).

(9) An indirect method of analysis, the indication of an analogy in the modal structure of an aspect, can lead to the identification of the original, non-analogical nature of a particular aspect. The *fact* that something like jural agreement and disagreement – legitimacy and illegitimacy – exist, refers to the logical aspect in which agreement and disagreement first appear.

(10) In the case of the normative aspects of reality a negative indication, or even the negation of a negative indication, can sometimes help to express our insight into the nature of a core of meaning (note, not to comprehend it, exactly since every core of

meaning is conceptually indefinable!). The core of meaning of the economic aspect, for instance, can be indicated with the expression of "avoidance of excess", i.e. to act in a non-excessive manner. The negation of this negative formulation indicates that it refers to the way of having enough (and how many large businesses, with their incredible striving for excessive profits know when they have enough?). Without obedience to the modal demand of having enough a person simply ignores his or her responsibility for economic stewardship.

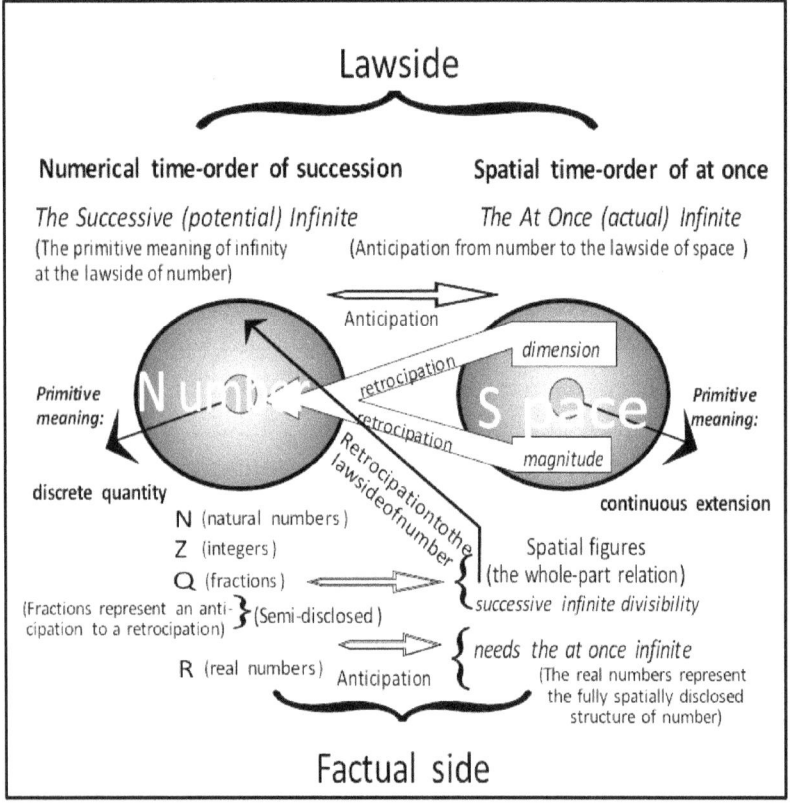

The mutual coherence and irreducibility of number and space

QUESTIONS FOR CHAPTER 3

1. Explain how human experience of reality is confronted with a unity-in-diversity on the basis of our analytical ability to identify and distinguish.
2. Discuss the following two fundamental issues in philosophy with reference to examples from the history of philosophy: unity and diversity; and constancy and dynamics.
3. Explain concisely the difference between entities and their properties.
4. Analyze the multi-faceted nature of a concrete process such as dying – with particular reference to the question whether we can speak of a 'single moment of death'.
5. Discuss in overview six aspects of a modal aspect.
6. Analyze the unique nature of number and space and 'place' the whole-parts relationship.
7. What do understand under constancy and change? Illustrate your answer with reference to the problem of perpetuum mobile, the cul-de-sacs of classical mechanistic physics, and the core of Einstein's theory of relativity, and conclude with a philosophically founded alternative formulation of the first law of thermo-dynamics.
8. Use the "What is...?"-question to illustrate the indefinable nature of the cores of meaning of the various aspects of reality.
9. As a substitute for the "what is...?"-question, we should ask: "what is the meaning of...?". Explain this perspective with reference to the inner untenability of historicism, the nature of 'life' and the meaning-coherence between aspects.
10. Explain the meaning of faith by giving simultaneously account of the root-uses of the terms love and faith in the Bible.
11. Analyze the nature of a principle with reference to the distinction between principle and application and in view of the question whether principles are valid for all times.

12. Indicate the historical distance which exists between various positive expressions of principles and distinguish between the central appeal of the commandment to love and its different contemporary expressions.
13. Use the perspective of the spatial subject-object relation to expose the untenability of the accepted notion of a line as a 'continuum of points'.
14. Which ten perspectives can help us in the identification of irreducible aspects of reality?

Chapter 4
Creational Reality – Kingdoms and Societal Forms of Life

4.1 From aspects to things

IN CHAPTER 3 WE LOOKED AT the aspects of concrete things. In this chapter we want to explore the inverse of this initial approach and through the gateway of aspects attempt to find more clarity about the nature of the different entities which we encounter in reality. We have already seen that the things, events and societal relationships which we experience, belong to the concrete, i.e. to the dimension of entity structures. The concrete existence of something like a chair – to take a school example – functions in its own way within each aspect of reality – whether as subject or object.

Such a chair possesses four legs (numerical: the interest of mathematical arithmetic); it is large or small (spatial aspect; mathematical geometry); is a wheelchair or not (movement aspect: kinematics); it is strong or weak (physical-chemical aspect); it is usable in human life (although as biotic object because a chair has no life – biology studies reality from the biotic aspect); it is comfortable (sensitive-psychic aspect: psychology); it is identifiable and distinguishable (analytical aspect: logic); it is culturally formed (historical aspect: historical science would be interested in, for instance, the historical development of different chair styles); it has a name (a verbal sign – the sign aspect; general semiotics and linguistics); it is used in the interaction of people (social aspect: sociology); it has a price (economic aspect: economics); it is beautiful or ugly (aesthetic aspect: aesthetics); it belongs to someone who has a subjective right to it (a competence to dispose and enjoy it – juridical aspect: legal science); it is or isn't someone's favourite seat (ethical/love aspect: ethics); and it is reliable – everyone believes that the chair will carry them if they sit on it (faith aspect: viewpoint of theology as science).[1] The aspects of such a lounge chair form the constant universal context (spheres) within which it functions. Even so, the individuality of every entity possesses a structure that could never be explained by the variety of aspects within which it functions. Although a study of the nature of the aspects of reality must ignore the typical structure and individuality of entities in reality, at the same time, we must recognize that the individuality of things is still recognizably expressed within the universal structure of the various aspects. The way in which a solid, a liquid and a gas behave in the physical aspect, differs in such a way that we can speak of the typical structure of each. In order to speak about entities, we cannot but use the gateway which the aspects of real ity offer. The two parts of the joining word "total structure" both appeal, for example, to the original meaning of the spatial aspect. Furthermore the concrete functioning of an entity is particularly coloured or specified by two prominent functions: these are known as the *foundational function* and the *qualifying/directive* function. To explain the meaning of this distinction, we begin with examples from the qualifying function of an entity structure.

When we speak, for instance, of the typical way in which a state and a business function within the economic aspect of reality, we actually mean that the uniqueness of the state is marked or qualified by its juridical function – that is why we speak of the state as a collective juridical societal entity.[2] In other words: only states belong to the (entity-) type state. The juridical qualifying function of all entities which belong to this type qualifies the way in which the state functions in all the other aspects of reality. Think only of the economic aspect:

---

1 Such trust must not be confused with trusting faith in the religious sense – except of course if someone were to make an idol of the particular chair!

2 Since the Dutch and German term "Verband" does not have a suitable translational equivalent in English, we will employ variations of the phrase *social collectivity* to capture its meaning.

to maintain the public legal order, the state budgets for the essential expenditures which must be covered – for example by means of the collection of taxes.[3] In other words, the qualifying juridical function of the state colours (i.e. specifies) the way in which the state as organized life form, functions in other aspects of reality.

With reference to common daily objects of use, one can easily see how determinative this qualifying function is for the nature of an entity. To get onto the track of the internal qualifying function of such a household article (cultural object), we need only ask: it was made to …? e.g.: tools are made to …? to make something else – its objective cultural-historical directive function; money is made to …? to buy with – its economic qualifying function; a book is made to …? to read – its qualifying sign function; a painting is made to …? to be aesthetically appreciated – its objective aesthetic qualification; etc.

A tool can also be used to beat someone to death. Is it then used according to its internal qualifying function? Certainly not, just as little as a painting is used according to its internal qualifying function when it is bought and sold.

4.1.0 The disclosure of the object functions

At this point we meet a further meaning of disclosure.

(i) Any thing from nature which was not made by a human being, can be objectified in some or other normative aspect – then a particular normative object function of that thing is disclosed (opened). These object functions are latently present in all natural things – they are only made patent by objectivation, active disclosure. One can, for instance, appreciate a sunset aesthetically, as something beautiful – then one is making patent the aesthetic object function of the natural phenomenon. When one identifies and distinguishes the sunset from the clouds, one unlocks the analytical object function of the same natural phenomenon.

(ii) Because cultural objects are made by human beings to … it means that every cultural object makes a kind of double disclosure possible:

---

3 Other sources of income also exist, i.a. since modern governments sometimes establish non-state enterprises.

(a) according to its internal qualifying function – then it is used true to its nature (e.g. a book is read) and

(b) correlating to another objective function – then it is used without the internal qualifying function being patented (disclosed) (e.g. when a book is used as an ornament or status symbol in a lounge).

The directive function is not the only function which is determining for the individuality and typicality of an entity (note: determinative for, not deductive from). Think of the nature of technical tools. We said in Chapter 2 that tools were made by human beings in order to make something else. They were made – i.e. it originated through the technical controlling formative labour of human beings: the cultural-historical foundational function of tools. At the same time they were made in order to make something else – their historical qualifying function. Tools represent a specific kind of entity, because their entity structure possesses a historical foundational and qualifying function! H. Van Riessen, already in his thesis: FILOSOFIE EN TECHNIEK, developed this characterization of tools (technical objects) (cf. 1948:509). In reality, all human-made objects of use possess a technical foundational function.[4]

4.2 Natural things

4.2.1 Material things

Although the history of philosophy and the natural sciences have tried for long to find a qualifying qualification for material things in one of the first three aspects of reality, it was only at the beginning of the 20th century that general natural scientific consensus was reached concerning the energetic qualification of material things (elementary particles, atoms, molecules, macromolecules, macrosystems). The Pythagoreans wanted to reduce everything to number. The discovery of irrational numerical relationships led in the school of Parmenides (to which Zeno with his arguments against movement and multiplicity also belonged) to the geometrization of Greek mathematics and to

---

4 With regard to the relations between being human as subject and a variety of utensils we sometimes use the term technical as the equivalent of cultural-historical.

the conviction that all physical things are spatially characterized. This spatial orientation lasted for more than two thousand years! The father of modern philosophy, Descartes (1596-1650), divided reality into the two spheres of an extended and thinking "substance" (*res extensa* and *res cogitans*): "the nature of body consists not in weight, hardness, colour, and the like, but in extension alone" (Principles, Part ll, IV). Even in the great German philosopher of the 18th century, Kant, this view exerts its influence unchanged. He says that when we remove everything which the mind conceives of in the representation of the body (like substance, strength, divisibility, etc.) as well as everything which belongs to our awareness of the body (like impenetrability, hardness, colour, etc.), then all that remains is extension and form (*Ausdehnung und Gestalt*) (1787, B:35). In connection with the nature of constancy and change we saw in Chapter 3 that the main tendency in classical physics (since Newton) was *mechanistic* – in other words, it was of the opinion that all physical processes can be reduced to (mechanical) movement. The last great representative of this mechanistic approach was probably Heinrich Hertz – the German physicist who did experimental work about electromagnetic waves more than a hundred years ago.[5]

It is clear that every attempt to find an arithmetic, spatial or kinematic qualification for physical entities necessarily runs into theoretical antinomies. Besides the given arithmetic function which an atom has, it also possesses a clear spatial function: it is characterized by a particular spatial configuration – the nucleus of an atom with peripheral electron systems. According to wave mechanics, we find quantified wave movements around the atom – the kinematic function of the atom. Already in 1911, in Rutherford's atomic theory, the hypothesis was posed that atoms consist of a (electrically positive) nucleus and negatively charged particles which moved around it (a view which was inspired by the nature of a planetary system). In the following year (1912), Niels Bohr set up a new theory which contained two important new ideas: (i) the electrons move only in a limited number of discrete orbits around the

---

[5] This work not only established him as the founder of wireless telegraphy and the radio, but also immortalized his name in the unit of frequency (Hertz) named after him.

nucleus and (ii) when an electron moves from an orbit with a high energy content to one with a low energy content, electromagnetic radiation occurs. In 1925, Pauli formulated his exclusion principle (Pauli-exclusion).[6] According to the division of charges of electrons, corresponding electron-shells exist, and in each peel there is room for a "maximum" number of electrons. This maximum number is given by the simple formula: $2n^2$. In the first peel (known as the Kpeel) there is room for 2 electrons; in the following L-peel, there is room for 8; in the M-sheel for 18; in the N-sheel for 32; and so on. Within a sheel with a quantum number n, (where there is room for $2n^2$ electrons) sub-orbits are identified so that each sub-orbit with a quantum number l has room for $2(2l+1)$ electrons.

It is already obvious from these facts that the distinct number of elementary particles in the internal atom structure are joined into a typical spatial order of electronic orbits which configure the atom as an individual physical-chemical micro-totality. The special spatial configuration which is manifest in the internal build of an atom, reflects the typical foundational function of atoms.[7] In connection with the problem of the structural interweaving of entities, Dooyeweerd developed a theoretical approach which accounts for the retention of the internal nature of entities which are interwoven (cf.1969-lll:627 ff., 694 ff.). When the internal nature of an interwoven entity is retained, Dooyeweerd speaks of *enkapsis*. When the structure of one kind of entity is foundational for the structure of another kind of entity, it is referred to as a one-sided enkaptic foundational relationship.

In Chapter 3 we noted that, with regard to the infinite divisibility of a spatial whole, there are important limits in the unqualified use of the spatial whole-parts relation. The nature of enkaptically interwoven forms illuminate further limits in this regard. The interweaving which exists, for example, between the Sodium and Chlorine atoms which are found in table salt, is in no way given account for with the help

---

6   It applies to fermions, i.e. elementary particles with a semi-integral spin (1/2, 3/2, 5/2, etc.) for which the statistical laws of Fermi-Dirac are formulated.

7   Dooyeweerd initially thought in 1935-1936 that natural things do not have a typical foundational function. In 1950 he relinquished this position (Cf. 1950:75 note 8).

of a whole-parts perspective. Every division of table salt must – that is if we still want to be working with real parts of salt – still possess the same chemical structure (NaCl). The critical question is whether Sodium and Chlorine have each individually got a salt structure? Are Sodium and Chlorine true parts of salt? The answer is obvious: No, because neither one has an NaCl-structure on its own!

This simple example already uproots the unqualified way in which, especially in modern system theory, literally everything in reality is spoken of in terms of a whole and parts (systems and subsystems) (cf. my criticism of this in Strauss, 1985).

Within the kingdom of physically qualified entities, we encounter different geno-types.

Atoms are, for instance, geno-types within the radical type (kingdom) of material things. Within different bonds the same atom displays a number of variability types. When an atom engages in chemical bonding, we encounter a characteristic of enkaptic totality: (i) besides an entity's internal structural working sphere, an (ii) external enkaptic working sphere (in which the enkaptically-bound structure is serviceable to the enkaptically encompassing totality).

A water molecule can, as a structural whole, exist e.g. on the foundation of the geno-type of the bond of the oxygen and hydrogen molecules. Without atoms, there can be no mention of a molecule – thus the indication: unilaterally founded. Does this imply that the atoms totally become part of the chemical bond which exists in the molecule? Not at all, because the bond applies only to the bonding electrons and not to the whole atom. Besides, the atom nucleus is not just a specific characteristic of the atom, but precisely that nuclear part of an atom which determines its physical-chemical geno-type (compare the atomic number = the number of protons of the nucleus), as well as the atom's place in the periodic table.

The fact that the atom nucleus remains structurally unchanged in the chemical bonding, guarantees the internal sphere of operation of the atom. Because the electrons cannot be disengaged from the atom nucleus, the atoms function as a whole in the Water molecule. Note that we cannot say that the atoms function in a chemical bond. The bonding does not encompass the atomic nuclei. Nonetheless the atoms (with their nuclei, electron shells and bonding electrons) are present as a whole in the Water molecule which encompasses them enkaptically. The indication: *enkaptically encompassed*, shows that the atoms, retaining their internal nature, is externally serviceable to the Water molecule as a whole. The enkaptic interweaving of the atoms in the molecule does not make them intrinsically part of the molecule, since this would abrogate the internal sphere of action of the atoms.

The external enkaptic function of the oxygen and hydrogen atoms in the Water molecule indicate the functioning of the atoms in the molecule as totality via the chemical bond. This presents us with three facts:

(i) First of all, we must distinguish the internal sphere of action of the atom.
(ii) Secondly, we find the chemical bond which leaves the atom nucleus unchanged because it only reaches the outer electron shells, so that the atom nuclei can in no way be part of the chemical bonding.
(iii) Thirdly, we find the enkaptic structural whole of the Water molecule which enkaptically encompasses the atomic nuclei and bonds and ascribes to each its structural typical place.

4.2.2 Living things

In Chapter 2 we made acquaintance with the different biological points of view. Apart from the prominent physicalistic tendencies in modern biology – of which neo-Darwinism is certainly the best known and most influential – we also find other tendencies and viewpoints. Think only of holism, neo-vitalism, organismic biology, panpsychism and emergence-evolutionism.

The best known heritage from this variety of viewpoints is probably what we find in their way of referring to living matter. It is encountered even at school.

In a textbook from the New Syllabus of 1985[8] – we read, for

---

[8] Senior Biology, Std. 8, written by Du Toit, Van Rensburg, Du Toit, Botha, Van der Merwe, Volschenk, Van der Westhuizen, De Kock and Niebuhr – Third Edition, Second impression, Aug. 1985 Goodwood.

example, that all "living organisms" are "built from matter" but that these chemical constitutive substances "do not themselves possess the characteristics which are associated with life": "The phenomenon of life is only revealed by the activities of the matter from which it is built" (p. 84).

Further on, we often read of "living material" or of "living matter". However, a bothersome problem lies hidden in this expression: As far as physicists and biologists are concerned, there is no doubt that atoms, molecules and even macromolecules are NOT living – nevertheless "living matter" is still spoken of. If matter is not living, how is it possible to have something like living matter!?

Apparently this consequence is avoided by the statement: "A knowledge of the chemical make-up and physical nature of living matter does not yet explain the phenomenon of life. Even if these chemical substances were combined in exact amounts in structural units, they would still not be living. Life is only revealed through the activities of these substances. Matter is only seen as living and obtains biological meaning if it can fulfill the following tasks" (*op. cit.*, pp. 88-89 – and then functions like metabolism, growth, fertilization and the maintenance of a constant state with the environment are named).

What an amazing story! Chemical matter (matter) is not alive – but yet its activities are described as living! It is comparable to the following statement: certain entities cannot speak, but their activities we call language. Matter – i.e. material things – are physical by nature, not biotic (living). Things which are alive are not entirely absorbed in the biotic aspect of creation, since they unmistakably have functions in other aspects as well. Living things are only marked or qualified by the biotic aspect – in distinction from material things which are qualified by the physical-chemical aspect of reality. Therefore we speak of the kingdom of material things and the plant kingdom.

This perspective in no way excludes the fact that living entities exhibit their uniqueness physically in a particular way. In the previous Chapter, we said that Karl Trincher identified four macroscopic characteristics from which the physical uniqueness of a living cell is evident. Trincher argues, also on the grounds of this physical autonomy of living things, that the living cell could in principle not be artificially manufactured. He believes that the opposite position, namely that living things are merely a developmental product of nonliving matter, is responsible for the moral irresponsibility of contemporary natural sciences. He prefers to speak of a duality of matter, while we would prefer to speak of the irreducibility of the physical aspect and biotic aspect as two facets of the God-established order-diversity in creation.

4.2.2.1 Mechanistic reduction of the identity of living things

Already the indication: *living things* shows the active functioning of such entities in the biotic aspect. The fact that living things must be viewed in a thermodynamic way as open systems, shows that every living entity, distinct from the qualifying biotic aspect of it, also unmistakable has a physical aspect. This is the subject of the well-known book of E. Schrödinger: What is life? The physical aspect of the cell (1955). We already know that a living entity also possesses subject functions in the first three aspects of reality. Important distinctive significance is often attached to the question of whether living things are self-moving or not, especially with regard to the difference between plants and animals. (This question appeals to the typical function of plants and animals in the kinematic aspect.) The continuity of life (durability) in a plant can definitely only be constituted in coherence with the kinematic function of living entities. Besides the proportions of spatial form of living things, their spatial function is also prominent in expressions like bio-milieu or *Umwelt*.[9] Finally, we have seen that a living thing is a unit in its various organic activities – when these numerous activities of life are no longer bound together the living entity disintegrates and dies.

We have already noted that living things, seen thermo-dynamically, maintain a flowing equilibrium through which order is drawn from the environment (Schrödinger calls it *negative entropy*). In other words, living things maintain themselves in a state of high static improbability – in a growing process ever more and more internal order is built up. This cannot, however, be seen as the distinctive characteristic of

---

9   The term *Umwelt* became known especially through the work of the biologist J. von Uexküll (cf. e.g. Von Uexküll and Kriszat, 1970).

living things because various lifeless entities exist which represent thermo-dynamically open systems (like a flame or glacier).

Only when the qualifying biotic subject function of living things is taken into account does it reveal its distinctive characteristic in comparison to material things. This qualifying function determines the *biotic identity* of a living entity. According to the mechanistic approach in biology, living entities are only "complex physical-chemical systems of interaction" in which, according to the nature of an open system, continuous metabolic processes (ana- and catabolism) are taking place. From this it follows that a living thing must, on mechanistic opinion, possess a physical-chemical identity which are constituted by its atoms, molecules and macromolecules. Which of these physical-chemical components are truly constitutine for the supposed physical-chemical identity of living things? Is it those atoms, molecules and macromolecules which are presently there, those which were there in past years, or those which will be there in the years to come? When living things are reduced in the physicalistic sense, through the mechanistic viewpoint in biology, to their constitutive matter-ingredients, then it goes without saying that the biotic identity is lost out of sight – the supposed elements of identity *continually changes*.

However, if the biotic function of living things is accounted for, it can even be said that a living thing, seen biotically, exists in a *stable state* (referred to as *healthy*), while at the same time – and without any contradiction – it can be said that it exists in an *unstable state*, seen physically-chemically (with regard to the fluctuating equilibrium of the constitutive building components). If the physical-chemical substructure of living things approach a state of higher static statistic probability, biotic instability steps in as a signal of the final process of dying.

From his organismic biology (cf. Chapter 2 above), Von Bertalanffy strikingly indicates the dead-end path of the mechanistic viewpoint which eliminates the biotic function of life processes: "These processes, it is true, are different in a living or sick or dead dog; but the laws of physics do not tell a difference, they are not interested in whether dogs are alive or dead. This remains the same even if we take into account the latest results of molecular biology. One DNA molecule, protein, enzyme or hormonal process is as good as another; each is determined by physical and chemical laws, none is better, healthier or more normal than the other" (1973:146).

4.2.3 An alternative structural theoretical approach

Although the habit of speaking of "living matter" is placed within another context by the different tendencies in modern biology, it still reflects the unsolved problems of each of the viewpoints.

For the mechanistic (physicalistic) approach, everything is in principle material, physically determined, which implies that any terms which appeals to the actual biotic aspect of things are problematic. Conversely, it is exactly vitalism which searches for the actual nature of "life" in immaterial life plans, formative factors or central instances. It also makes it difficult to speak of living matter in this viewpoint – a problem which a vitalistic biologist like Haas admitted with his accentuation of the fact that the physical substances maintain their "being and working" also "subsequent to their assimilation" in living things. Understandably, therefore, Haas is also critical of the habit of speaking of "living matter" – according to him, the biochemists and cell physiologists do not know of any "living matter" with "secret vital characteristics" (1968:24). He prefers to speak of the material substratum of organisms (1968:20-40).

This approach of Haas rejects what he sees as Aristotle's "monistic vitalism" – and at the same time he draws conclusions about his own approach: "The organisms therefore consist essentially of two realities which are distinguished from each other, a material and a non-material component, it consequently possesses, viewed ontologically, a dualistic constitution" (1968:39).

In a striking way, Hans Jonas once gave a typification of the monistic forms of vitalism and mechanism. A monistic approach does not, like the dualist, reduce reality to two basic principles, because it wants to find ONE all-inclusive all-clarifying principle. That is why we can speak of *pan-vitalism* and *pan-mechanism*. Already in the earliest Greek philosophy of nature, we find *hulèsoism* (*zoè* = life; *hulè* = matter): one of Thales's indirectly preserved statements would be that everything lives. From this point of view it is unthinkable that "life" is not the normal, governing rule in the universe. Jonas points out: "In such a world view, death is a puzzle which stares humankind in the face, the antithesis of the natural, self-explanatory and understandable, that which is the common life" (1973:20). The paragraph in which Jonas makes this remark is about: Pan-vitalism and the problem of death (1973:19 E.V.). Those, however, who think pan-mechanistically, stress the thought that phenomenon of life is actually a borderline case in the encompassing homogenic physical world view. Quantitively negligible in the immeasurability of cosmic matter, qualitatively an exception to the rule of the material characteristics, epistemologically the unexplained in the explainable physical nature – that is how life has become a stumbling block for pan-mechanism: "Conceiving life as a problem here means that its strangeness in the mechanical world, which is reality, is recognized; explaining it means – on this level of the universal ontology of death – denying it, relegating it to a variant of the possibility of the lifeless" (1973:23). This paragraph deals with: Pan-mechanism and the problem of life (1973:22ff.).

We have already repeatedly stressed that a first step from this problematic situation has been given in the distinguishing of different modalities. The fundamental modal nature of the physical and biotic aspects remains only a functional condition for concrete entities which still function in this (and other) aspects of reality in a typical way. What is of importance in this regard, is the basic distinction between the aspects and the dimensions of entities – a distinction which has always been evident in the different trends in biology because modal functions are time and again spoken of as if they are concrete entities (that is where the expression of "the origin of life" came from, instead of "the origin of living things"). As an aspect of reality, life pertains to the how of entities and not the concrete what.

In addition we must stress that life phenomena are always connected to living entities which can, precisely as entities, not be totally enclosed in the biotic aspect. Especially in the vitalist tradition – which sees life as independent variations of an immaterial life force – this becomes a problem. That the biotic aspect of living entities cannot be seen on its own, i.e. separated from the intermodal coherence in which it is fitted, is still confirmed by the inherent analogies in the structure of the biotic aspect. Even the expression life force, which is so often chosen by vitalism (but remarkably enough, has been replaced with other terms like *Gestaltungsfaktor* or *Zentralinstanz* in the last few decades), can never indicate or typify the separate existence of the biotic aspect – simply because it unmistakably represents a physical analogy in the modal structure of the biotic aspect. In Chapter 3 we saw that force is a term which finds its original (i.e. non-analogical) modal home in the physical aspect of energy-operation.

With the help of the theory of an enkaptic structural whole, this problem is placed within a new context. The physical-chemical structure of the constitutive physical components of living things is foundational for their enkaptic (i.e. biotically directed) functions. When this perspective is accepted, the task of organic chemistry can be seen similarly to be foundational for biochemistry, which ought to focus on the disclosed enkaptic functions of the material structures which are exposed by organic chemistry. This foundational relationship confirms the close interweaving of the structure and functions of the constitutive substances of living things. Today it is a virtually universal practice for the biochemist not to limit himself to an analysis and study of the biotically directed functions of macromolecular material structures, seeing that the biochemist is mainly concerned with the exposure of these structures themselves.

Within the context of the ordered (centred) structure of the cell, we find (seen from a biotic angle) the different organs (organelle) of the cell which are parts of a living whole. Because the cell is built up of non-living material ingredients, we cannot simply say that the organelle are parts of the cell. To explain the biotic life functions within the cell, we will in the future preferably use the following term: *cell-organism*. In other words, the different organs in the cell are all parts of the cell-organism. The different organelle in the cell exist naturally only on the basis of their physical-chemical constitutive substances – i.e. in the sense of a unilateral enkaptic foundational relationship.

The cell organism is consequently a specifically *biotically* qualified structure, which can only exist on the basis of the enkaptically-bound physical-chemical constitutive substances. Because these physical-chemical substances are not biotically qualified, but still function in the living cell, we are obliged to also distinguish a structural TRIO if we want to give an account of the complex structure of the living cell.

(i) Firstly, there are the physical-chemically qualified constitutive substances which already represent enkaptic structural wholes.

(ii) Secondly, we find the cell's living organism as biotically qualified part structure which can only function on the basis of the enkaptically-bound building material.

(iii) Thirdly, we find the cell body as structural nexus which enkaptically embraces both above-mentioned part structures.[10]

4.2.4 The animal kingdom

Although we approached the relationship between a human person and animal from a specific angle in Chapter 2, we conclude this discussion of the nature of natural things with a succinct reference to the structure of psychic-sensitive qualified entities.

From our daily life we know that something is either material, vegetable or animal. For any scientist who is in search of "transitional forms" bridging this discontinuity the troublesome implication of this is naturally that there is no *third* possibility: if something is *either* material *or* vegetable, then all candidates in between drop out. Therefore the question whether something like viruses are "living" or "non-living" cannot provide a transitional form. It does happen that through our scientific inability, we have no certain answer with regard to the systematic classification of particular entities. Sometimes it turns out that our classification was incorrect – like in the case of Acrasiales – a group of amoeboid animals which were previously classified as plants. From this perspective, we must appreciate the position of protista.[11]

---

10 In paragraph 23.2 we will explain the distinction between concept and idea actually needed to explain a seeming ambiguity in this context. The idea of enkapsis is used as a substitute for the whole-parts relationship, but we still referred to *part structures*. Within the framework of the theory of enkaptic interlacements the spatial whole-parts relation is no longer employed in a conceptual sense, but in the stretched sense of an idea-usage, referring beyond the limits of the spatial aspect to the structural integrity of enkaptically interwoven structures.

11 The protista is a group of living things which are grouped apart as a result of their simple biotical organization. It includes algae, bacteria, fungi, slime and protozoa.

What is remarkable in this regard, is that within the protista, a distinction can be made between those that possess vegetable characteristics[12] and those that possess animal characteristics.[13]

Not only are there divergent classifications in the animal kingdom, but there are also clear differences in perspective. Without going into detail in this context, we mention only that the tension between *nominalism* and *realism* – which has stayed alive in Western scientific history since Plato – even caused the paths of modern biological theories to separate. The realistic approach has been known as the idealistic morphology since the 17th century (following thinkers like Ray and Linneaus).[14]

While nominalism proceeds form the assumption of a structureless continuum (each organism is wholly unique and cannot be forced into some or other universal ontic form), idealistic morphology accepts "primal types" (e.g. a primal leaf, a primal plant, or a primal animal) which serve as genuine platonic models with reference to which any empirically observed living thing or fossil has to be judged.

The idea of an entity structure which acts, as a typical total structure, as the law for the entities which are subject to it, represents a structural theory which wants to overcome the one-sidedness present both in a realistic (idealistic) and nominalistic approach. The structureless continuity of a nominalistic vision simply does not allow for relatively-constant structural types. Just as a modal-physical law can't be identified with any subject function or concrete subject, the structural types of plants and animals cannot be identified with particular concrete plants or animals. However, entity structures are types which are embedded in the cosmic dimension of time and which still find their correlate in the succession of transient individual living creatures which appear on the paleontological horizon during the course of the

---

12 E.g. those who gain their energy by means of photosynthesis, including algae like Chlorophyta, Euglenophyta and Pyrrhrophyta, as well as plantlike protozoa of the class Flagellata.

13 E.g. protozoa feeding by means of absorption or ingestion.

14 Out of the pen of W. Troll an encompassing and authoritative botanical textbook appeared (3d impression 1973) written from the perspective of the idealistic morphology.

history of the earth.

The psychic-sensitive qualifying function of animals is expressed in the total life orientation of animals. Portmann typifies animals well when he says that they exist *instinctually-secured* and *milieu-bound* (1969:86).

4.3 Interaction in human society

Actual interaction between people still functions in some or other specific way in the full structure of the social aspect. By way of this concrete functioning, the universal modal structure of the social aspect (with the analogical structural moments which are present in it) is specified differently in every instance. This specification has various possibilities with regard to distinct analogies. For instance, when we look at the nature of the *kinematic analogy*, we can distinguish between the ways of interaction which are of shorter and longer *duration*. This applies, in other words, to social interaction with a changeable durability – one kind of relation can show a rather long continued existence, while another relation can be quite *incidental*. The meaning of these possibilities are only approximated when the precisioning of other analogies are accounted for. As analogies of thermodynamic open systems (i.e. the physical analogy in a precise sense) some show such durability in social relations that the mutual exchange (coming and going) of individuals does not abolish the existence or identity of that specific social relation. The expression: inter-action signifies a combination of the spatial and physical analogies – and it goes without saying that just the incidental social interaction cannot constitute a durable whole which continues regardless of the exchange of participating social subjects.

This remark refers us to the alternative specifications which the spatial analogy can receive. Social interaction can occur, for example, within a life form which is integrated into a genuine whole (totality), or it can occur on a less rigid basis of standing-over-against-one-another/facing-one-another. The standing-alongside or co-ordinate nature of certain forms of social interaction faces in turn those forms where the definitive relations of sub- or superordination are found. This particular expression of the spatial analogy refers us directly to the historical analogy on the norm side of the social aspect, because this analogy applies to the competence (power) of a specific bearer of authority over certain subjects. This is not the only context where the term competence is used – inter-individual relations which are on an equal footing presumes a certain social maturity or competence, even if it applies to something like little children playing. This competence for social exchanges constantly requires the ability to correctly interpret the response of other social subjects (analogy of the sign aspect), because without it the mutuality of interaction would become dispirited.

From these examples it is clear that a classification of the different underlying ways of interaction will have to keep in mind the meaning which a particular expression of all analogically structural moments in the social aspect acquires. Because a complete analysis of this would take us into an analysis of the *complex* (or: *composite*) basic concepts of sociology as scientific discipline, we just briefly mention the result of such an analysis.

What it comes down to (in the light of our previous remarks) – besides the question in which way are specific analogies in the structure of the social aspect specified – concerns the following two characteristics: (i) a *solidary unitary character* and (ii) a *permanent structure of super- and subordiantion* (i.e., of authority).[15]

When a societal form (referred to in the future as a *life form*) possesses both a solidary unitary character and a permanent authority structure, we call it a *social collectivity*. Examples of societal collectivities are the state, the church, business, the school, the university, the family, the art club, the sports club, the cultural club and the language club. The state possesses a durable sub- and superordination of authority and subject (i.e. a permanent authority structure), while the unity and identity of a state is not abolished by the exchange of its citizens (either office bearers or subjects). The same applies for all the other societal collectivities that we named in the list of examples.

When life forms possess only one of these characteristics, we call

---

15 From our brief analysis of the difference between modal and entitary analogies (the latter are designated by *metaphors*), we have to note that here we highlight irreplaceable modal analogies within the modal structure of the social aspect. Consequently, we have to object to a 'postmodern' stance that would claim that we have to do away with terms like these to account for inter-human relationships.

them *communities*. A *nation* ('volk') as ethnic entity and the *extended family* both possess a solidary unitary character (that is why there is continuity between a nation of a hundred years ago and today in spite of of changes), but no permanent authority structure can be indicated. The marriage community does possess a permanent authority structure, although a solidary unitary character is absent. In terms of these distinctions neither a state, nor a province, nor a rural town is a community. With reference to the state-side of the given facts, we are working with (higher or lower) forms of *governmental authority* – and therefore with subordinate and superordinate relations which are absent from the community as we have described it. In reality a city and a town exhibit an enkaptic interweaving of diverse societal collectivities, communities and coordinational relationships. Coordinational relationships have neither a permanent authority structure, nor a solidary unitary character – they concern the inter-relations of individuals and organizations on an equal footing with each other.

The approach which we have followed here is only aimed at the social aspect, that is to say on the different ways or functions of interaction in the social aspect. It means that the typical total structure of life forms is ignored in such a way that account is taken of neither the foundational, nor the qualifying function.[16]

4.3.1 The correlation between collective and communal relationships on the one hand and coordinational relationships on the other hand

In a differentiated society various life forms exist which bind together individuals for all or only for a part of their lives, independent of their own decisions. Think, for instance, of the state – a life form which does not (as the humanistic behavioural theorists think) originate from

---

16 Dooyeweerd links the nature of communities directly to their (natural-biotic) *foundational* function and then states that historically founded (i.e. organized) communities can be referred to as societal collectivities (Dutch: *verbande*). Natural communities, on the other hand, are unorganized (cf. *New Critique*, 1969-III:178ff.). This approach causes Dooyeweerd not to distinguish meaningfully between a *marriage* and the nuclear *family*, since he sees both as natural (i.e. biotically founded) and ethically qualified communities. In terms of our distinctions *marriage* is a community and the family is a social collectivity.

a mutual agreement (contract), but which nevertheless organizes its citizens in various ways independently of their will (e.g. with regard to tax obligations). Dooyeweerd calls such life forms institutional (1969-III:187). Marriage exhibits an institutional nature because it is meant to constitute the spouses' marriage relationship for the duration of their lives. A person is born within a family and circle of relatives and grows up in it without any choice. Like this life form, the church is also institutional because baptizing (as a sign and seal of the covenant) is done independently of the child's will.[17]

Not all societal collectivities possess an institutional character. Think only of a business firm, a university or a sport club – all examples of societal collectivities which rest totally on voluntary membership. Yet it is impossible for any person to let his or her life be taken up completely in any of the various societal collectivities and communities in which s/he functions – simply because such a person also takes part in various other interrelations. Two families, for example, stand in a (inter-collective) co-ordinational relationship; two married couples in a (inter-communal) co-ordinational relationship. Furthermore, every individual is, in a differentiated society, taken up in countless inter-individual co-ordinational relationships where that individual relates informally to fellow human beings in co-ordinate relations. Conversely, no person's life is ever completely absorbed in co-ordinational relationships, because at the opposite side we find institutional and non-institutional communities in which that person is involved. The variety of DPP-relations (referred to in Chapter 1) is therefore nothing more than the multiplicity of *social collectivities*, *communal* and *co-ordinational relationships* in which human beings are socially involved.

In contrast to this, we look at the nature of an undifferentiated society.

4.3.2 The nature of an undifferentiated society

The first general characteristic which can be pointed out, is given in the indication which we have chosen: its *undifferentiatedness*. This undifferentiatedness marks both its foundation and its qualification. When

---

17 Sects denying paedobaptism thus deny the institutional character of the church.

we dealt with natural things, we saw that such entities still possess a univocal foundational and qualifying function. In an undifferentiated society, such univocal radicaltypical functions are absent. All activities in such a society are bound together in *one undifferentiated organizational form*.[18] In a differentiated society, each independent life form possesses its own organizational form, which coheres with the fact that each life form also possesses its own and univocally differentiated qualifying function.

Since undisclosed societies have a part in an undifferentiated organizational form, there is no possibility for any differentiated qualifying functions. The variety of life forms which come to the fore later, in the course of a gradual process or cultural-historical differentiation and disclosure, are bound together in an undifferentiated manner within such a society. That is why such a society does not only exhibit an economic aspect, because the *whole* acts as something which is recognized on a differentiated cultural level as an *economically qualified business* (whether it be of a hunting-, agricultural or cattle farmer type). An undifferentiated society exhibits not only a juridical aspect, because as a whole it acts as fulfilling the functions which are performed by an independent state on a differentiated civilizational level. The same applies to the faith aspect – the undifferentiated society acts as a whole in cultic-religious capacity similarly to a differentiated collective faith community. Within the undifferentiated total organizational form, we therefore find a variety of structurally typical "evaginations" which time and again brings its totality to activities which are performed by independent life forms within differentiated societies.

This state of affairs implies that the correlate of an undifferentiated foundation (viz. one total organizational form) is given in an undifferentiated *qualification*. This means that there can be no possibility of a univocal qualifying function, because *one* of the enkaptically interwoven *structures* has taken the lead.

This is obvious from the nature of the most basic type of undifferentiated society. This type of society, which binds parents, children and grandchildren together in a patriarchal unit, puts the patriarch and the

---

18 Cf. with regard to this entire issue the striking analysis of Dooyeweerd – 1969-III:346-376.

oldest son in such a position that it cannot be exclusively derived from the blood relationship which exists between them – for that a specific kind of historical organization is required.

The *extended family* does not only evince a *family* structure, because in its undifferentiated total structure, other life forms are also interwoven. The presence of the political structure is clear from the (political) force with which the patriarch maintains internal order and peace. Equally clearly the economic enterprise can be distinguished by the way in which the *subsistence economy* functions. The question is: which one of the enkaptically interwoven structures takes the lead in the undifferentiated total structure?

The role which the (fatherhood-related) family structure plays in the extended family is truly of a central leading nature – despite the fact that the interwoven family structure does not inherently possess a permanent authority structure.

The sib (clan or *gentes*), which apparently only occurs when agriculture and livestock farming partly or completely replaces hunting as the basis of economic life, is an coordinationally organized larger group of relations (where either only the father's or the mother's line of descent is taken into account). Normally, membership is dependent on blood relationship, that is to say ‚it rests on natural birth. However, the sib is so large that it is no longer (as in the extended family) to assume direct descent from a communal father – although such descent functions as a *fictitious presupposition* or *mythological conception*. Besides activities like the ancestor cult (typical of an eventually differentiated cultic institution), carrying out revenge (which at a higher level of development is carried out by an independent state), and the presence of forms of division of labour, also the family structure is interwoven into the sib. In reality this interwoven family structure takes on the undifferentiated leading role within the sib – a leading role which rests on a particular historical form of *power organization* (just as in the case of the *extended family*).

It is only the stronger organized tribe that displays such a prominent political organization that the interwoven family structure cannot any longer take the lead in it. Nonetheless there is not yet any mention of a durable monopolistic organization of the sword power in this leading political structure (as in the case of a true state), because even fights between members of the tribe do not provoke any tribal punishment – only a relative of someone who is killed in such a fight could consider revenge.

Further examples of undifferentiated societies are, i.e., the *guilds* of the middle ages (with structures similar to those of the extended family and sib, but without any real or fictitious common descent), the *pre-feudal* and *feudal communities* (villas and domains) and *lordships*.

4.3.3 The structure of a some societal life forms

The classification of the diverse ways of interaction in a society does not contain a closer indication of the specific differences among the various societal collectivities, communities or co-ordinational relationships. In order to establish that, we must look at the analysis of typical total structures – as they function simultaneously in all aspects of reality.

4.3.3.1 The state

Before the emergence of the modern state a dominant form of historical political organization was the monarchy, which was the private property of the monarch. In the undifferentiated structure of late Medieval society (that is, the non-church society), government authority was an item of trade (a *res in commercio*) over which the sovereign lords could freely dispose. When private persons or corporations gained this authority, it was their inviolable right. Government authority was not as yet seen as a public office standing in service of the public welfare (the *common good – res publica*). Especially the undifferentiated nature of the guilds, encompassing all the spheres of life, stood in the way of the realization of the collective bond characteristic of a genuine state.

The state characteristically possesses a *public legal character*, typically different from the monarchy as private property of the monarch. For this reason the state is typically a truly *public matter*. In this *public legal sense* of the term the sovereign state can emerge when the process of civilizational development allows a sufficient measure of differentiation and unfolding within human society – such that a variety of unique societal life forms can emerge in an integrated manner, each with its own internal organizational form and domestic sphere of competence and of legal relations. In such a process of differentiation and crystallization the state cannot emanate on its own – a range of other distinct non-state societal forms should also emerge. Structures such as the church, the school, the university, the business and many more arise through the course of the *historical* process of differentiation.

The public legal bond characteristic of the state implies, strictly speaking, that every individual state is a *republic*, that is, a *public legal institution*. For this reason we should not see a republic as a particular *form* of government – as, for instance, in distinction from a *monarchy* (cf. Van Schoor and Van Rooyen, 1960: 16). The *republican* character of the state does not tell us anything about its particular organizational form. A state could be organized as a *totalitarian* state (an absolute dictatorship), as in the case of traditional communist states. The communist "people's republics" were therefore really totalitarian republics! On the other hand, we find a range of *constitutional republics under the rule of law*.[19] South Africa is, for instance, a *parliamentary democratic* republic, in distinction from the Netherlands which is a *monarchial* republic.

If we use this perspective consistently, we would have to refer to a democracy as a *'constitutional-state'*-republic.

By placing the state in the context of the principle of sphere sovereignty, we in principle avoid the two extremes of a *totalitarian* whole and *individual* freedom.

From ancient times the history of reflection on the nature of human society and the state is characterized by these two opposing points of view: the presupposition of some or other *societal whole* which integrally encompass a human being, as opposed to the conviction that human society is nothing more than the sum of a number of free and *autonomous individuals*. While there was something in Greek civilization referred to as a *"democracy"*, this was by no means what we would understand by the term. In the Athenian democracy of Pericles (5th

---

19 We can state provisionally that political freedoms exist in such a state – both *civil* freedoms and *societal freedoms* within the non-state forms of life. In a totalitarian and absolutist state none of these freedoms exist. This distinction will become clearer when we pay attention at a later stage to the nature of the diverse *legal spheres* in a differentiated society.

century before Christ) the legislative institution could make laws which regulated the lives of Greek citizens in a totalitarian manner. This was coherent with the Greek view of human society.

The sum of Greek wisdom with regard to the state is to be found in the ideal of an all-encompassing, self-sufficient state. Both Plato and Aristotle see the state as the capstone of human society. Plato sees the state, with its three estates, as a high and encompassing whole which strives towards the good, but which allows no real space for distinct non-state societal relations. Aristotle's organological (teleological) view denies in principle the possibility of unique non-state life forms. In his view the state grows organically out of the nuclear family via the extended family and village into the supposedly self-contained total state.

This frame of reference was continuously in use, with minor or major changes, during the Middle Ages. In this period the Roman Catholic church, as relatively differentiated superstructure, dominated the undifferentiated societal substructure. Troeltsch referred to this situation with the term "ecclesiastic unified culture", indicating the total way in which the church dominated society – the so-called *societas perfecta*.

In theoretical terms the unfettered glorification of the autonomous individual only appeared during the Renaissance. Apart from the reconsideration of classical Greek and Roman culture, we find in the Renaissance the point of departure of a new spiritual attitude, placing the human person, the *humanitas*, in the centre. Modern humanity considered itself free of all papal authority and attempted to take its fate in its own hands by setting a self-generated law for itself. Rousseau worded this fundamental inclination of modern thought as follows: "obedience to the law which we prescribe for ourselves, is freedom" (Rousseau, 1975: 247). This marked the emergence of the desire for *autonomous freedom* in modern anthropocentric, humanistic thought.

In the individualistic approach personal freedom and/or equality (and unlimited discretion) of the supposedly autonomous individual was/were elevated to the highest good. A reaction to this one-sided individualism was to be expected. This reaction, unfortunately, was excessive in the opposite direction – some or other societal whole was overemphasized. The recent heritage of reflection on the nature of the state and society in terms of a *large encompassing whole* with *parts* has its origin in the post-Kantian freedom idealism of the beginning of the previous century, when we first came across the modern *universalistic (holistic) community ideology* (Schelling, Fichte and Hegel). The opposite approach has an even earlier origin in the thought of the Enlightenment which attempted to provide an *individualistic* (atomistic) and rational explanation of the existence and nature of the state by means of the hypothetical "social contract" between autonomous individuals.

The effect of these two opposed traditions (the universalistic and individualistic) is also evident in the political history of South Africa.

Consider the extremes in contemporary South African politics. On the one side is those groups who are concerned above all with the rights, interests and self-determination of "groups" and on the other extreme those who advocate the absolutely free interaction between individuals. A position apparently in between these extremes is taken by those supporting the theory of consociative democracy, in terms of which we have to take into account the two extremes of "state" and "individual", as well as the *intermediate groups*, even if these are considered to be part of the state. Practically this refers particularly to different ethnic groupings, which leads to the question whether we can justifiably promote non-state relationships like membership in an ethnic group to an integral part of *citizenship* in a state?

To escape this impasse we ought to acknowledge the distinct societal life forms which are not part of the state, but which are nonetheless *interwoven* with the state as public legal institution.

4.3.3.2 The nature of the state as public legal institution

The state is as public legal institution is called a social collectivity – called to maintain balance and harmony among the multitude of legal interests present on its territory. It must act in a legally restorative manner whenever legal breaches of rights occur. Government and subject are fitted in a collective relationship. As such the state, as one of the life forms in a differentiated society, is founded in the governmental monopoly over the power of the sword (land, air, sea and police forces). It is directed by the idea of *public justice* which demands that all subjects on the state territory must receive what is justly theirs.

The government of a state is set over the citizens within its territory and must as such be distinguished from the state itself which encompasses both government and citizens. In a constitutional state government is put into office by the enfranchised citizens according to the applicable public legal election regulations.

A differentiated society does not only present itself to us in diverse unique (–sphere sovereign) life forms (church, state, business, family, school, etc.), but also in three indissolubly coherent legal spheres. What legal spheres can we identify in a differentiated society?

(i) The sphere of public law

This sphere encompasses the relations within the state between government and subject, as well as the legal order among nations (international law), with its co-ordinational nature. As such it encompasses *international public law*, *constitutional law*, *penal law*, *penal procedural law*, and *administrative law*. The political rights of citizens are circumscribed by this legal sphere: the right to political assembly, organization and opinion, as well as the rights to criticism and protest, with the right to elect as the capstone.

(ii) Civil private law

Civil private law abstracts from all non-state relationships in which a subject may take part. This legal sphere protects citizens in their position as *free individuals* within the differentiated legal interaction and as such it is the guarantee for *individual personal vindication* in legal life. In distinction from constitutional law in which there is a relationship of super- and sub-ordiantion between government and subject, *civil private law* maintains a *co*-ordinational legal relationship among individuals and institutions. Both public law and civil private law are *jurally* qualified.

(iii) Non-civil private law

This is the sphere which encompasses the internal law of the various non-state societal life forms. This means that in every instance such law is *differently* qualified. Internal business law is qualified by the economic function of business; internal church law is characterized by the certitudinal function of the church as a faith-qualified social collectivity, etc. This sphere of law delimits the legal competence of the state *externally* – that is, apart from the internal delimitation of government action by the juridical qualification of such action.

If these fundamental differences between the various legal spheres are ignored, it would be impossible to value in an constitutionally correct manner the diverse legal interests within the territory of the state.

This approach emphasizes above all else the *jural* task of the state, as a public legal institution, called to maintain the a public legal order. Only in this way can proper care be taken of the *legal protection* to which all citizens are entitled, knowing that the government is called to protect their particular (state and non-state) legal interests, and to harmonize all these interests in one *public legal order*.[20]

4.4 Marriage – divorce or living together?

When one says that marriage was ordained by God at creation as a two-in-one community of love for life, the response (especially among modern young people) is often a bored shrug. Living together seems to be more convenient and less troublesome, according to the increasingly influential counterargument. Can we still understand marriage particularly as a *love* relationship with a particular relationship of authority between husband and wife, in which no unity exists apart from the particular marriage partners – i.e. if either party should fall away the marriage no longer exists.

The central question is whether fundamental norms (principles) have been given for marriage life. From the perspective of the worldview presented in Chapter 1 the answer would have to be in the affirmative: along with all typically human activities and life forms marriage is normatively structured – the nature of marriage places certain claims on both husband and wife, requiring obedience, but which are all too often ignored by fallen human beings. The structural principle

---

20 If more attention were to be paid to this perspective on the nature of the task of the government we would in principle be liberated from the misplaced emphasis on ethnic conflict – a non-state perspective which could then be replaced with the necessary demand for a truly public legal integration of a multiplicity of legal interests, such as the government of a constitutional state under the rule of law ought to establish and maintain.

of marriage requires of man and wife that they should love each other.

The lasting identity of marriage does not depend only on the subjective love relationship with each other (which can differ from moment to moment, experiencing both highs and lows), since both marriage partners are subject to the divinely instituted structural principle of marriage as a love relationship. This normative structural principle provides the guarantee for the *durability* of the marriage, and is the touchstone by which the couple must measure their subjective love relationship and towards which their common love must be directed.

That marriage is characteristically monogamous has been disputed especially by evolutionists. Their view is that the original forms of marriage were polygamous and polyandrous, which slowly evolved into monogamy. Remarkably, some of the oldest known cultures – certain pigmy societies – practice monogamy! The normative structure of marriage is by no means suspended in situations of polygamy or polyandry. These are simply *antinormative* attempts by one person to be engaged in more than one marriage relationship *at the same time*. In a society in which monogamous marriage is honoured as an institution, it could happen that one person legally enters into more than one marriage relationship, one after the other.

A central question, also asked by modern young people, is whether two people who really love each other aren't already "married" in God's eyes and may share in the intimate privileges of marriage before acknowledging their external societal responsibilities. This question reflects a tradition which came to the fore at the beginning of the nineteenth century (the Romantic period) and in terms of which the marriage bond depends entirely on the continuation of the mutual subjective love of the marriage partners.

If this was true, marriage would have no structural durability or identity, since there would be numerous occasions on which one or the other of the marriage partners do not show enough love (say, during a domestic quarrel), temporarily suspending the marriage! It is clear that this approach does not acknowledge the *ethical imperative* of marital love (in terms of the structural principle of the marriage). It suggests that two people who once loved each other may as easily be released of their love responsibilities in marriage, even by the mere declaration that they no longer love each other.

While marriage calls the marriage partners to mutual and durable love, marriage is not only about this love relationship. As an institution marriage is interwoven with church and state. Internally marriage is qualified as a love relationship, but externally it is interwoven with all other societal life forms.

For this reason marriage does not only possess an internal legal sphere. Marriage is also interwoven with "thirds" – a side belonging to the sphere of civil law. Additionally, both marriage partners also have public legal interests – since the protection of their lives and property represent public legal interests which have to be protected by the government in its public legal order.

The civil law-side of marriage emerges in the marriage contract which regulates the relationship of the marriage partners to *third parties*: it is in the interest of legal interaction (e.g. eventual creditors at bankruptcy) that marriage is organized within an applicable juridical arrangement. Apart from these external civil legal arrangements, the wedding has a public character which serves the interests of the public legal order of the state. As a result of these interwoven relations between marriage and other life forms (in which each form retains its sphere sovereign unique internal character), getting married and divorced can never be left entirely to the decision of the marriage partners.

Marriage has its foundation in the biotic function of life. It is in this function that the *gender difference* between man and woman is originally expressed. But sexual interaction between man and woman it not exhausted by this foundation. Since marriage is qualified by a typical *love* relation, the sexual interaction between the marriage partners is internally directed and deepened by the marital bond of love, and should therefore only be given expression in the institution of marriage (as a monogamous relation for life) in a disclosed, differentiated society. What happens, however, when marriage partners divorce?

The public form of the wedding (in which an interweaving of marriage, state and church takes place) nonetheless presumes the internal bond of love between husband and wife. No civil or ecclesiastic order can guarantee obedient expression of the love internal to marriage. This can only come about when the love relation between husband and wife complies with the normative demands of the marriage.

When marriage partners live in continual strife, or as strangers or enemies, it is evident that the *internal* marriage bond between man and woman has already fallen apart, even if the marriage still functions *formally* as a unit in societal interaction to the outside. If steps are taken in a civil court to dissolve a marriage, the judge cannot present "grounds" for the dissolution of the marriage, since the judge does not have the power to maintain or dissolve the *internal* bond of marriage. He or she can only affirm from the *outside*, from the *external perspective of civil law*, that the marriage partners will no longer act in legal interaction as married people, because of the already existing continuing disrepair of the internal bond of marriage. As a result of this disrepair the civil judge can therefore find grounds for the formal divorce. Whoever takes these external civil grounds of divorce for the internal grounds of divorce in the marriage, turns the matter upside down, exchanging *cause* and *effect*: marriages cannot end on the decision of a divorce court, but are ended in the divorce court because the internal bond of love no longer exists.

Apart from the internal and external legal relations of the ethically qualified marriage relationship, marriage also exists in a number of other nuances characterized by love. The internal troth and trust in marriage is strengthened by common faith convictions – thus the striking Dutch proverb: *twee geloven op een kussen, daar ligt de duivel tusschen* (two faiths on one pillow, between them lies the devil). The fellowship of husband and wife in marriage ought to be characterized by a particular loving harmony and balance which is refined by a loving interaction based upon an own love symbolism and love style supported by the basis of a considerate love feeling which creates the calm atmosphere for a dynamic and lively realization of that intimate two-in-one community which a marriage continuously ought to be. As such the choice of a marriage partner finds its easiest vantage-point in the lifestyle of someone who comes from the same cultural community, though a successful marriage even between people from different cultural communities is not excluded.

The structure of marriage has been given to humankind *in principle* and not in an *already positively realized form*. For this reason every married pair, also in a differentiated society, has a calling to give *concrete* and *positive* shape to their love relationship with full love responsibility.

4.5 Church and Kingdom

Since we have already extensively discussed the relation between the one encompassing RCT-relation of human existence (being a Christian or not being one) and the diverse DPP-relations in which people partake at the same time (from the perspective of the foundational role of worldview decisions in life and science in Chapter 1), we shall now only emphasize a few central distinctions.[21] Of particular importance is a clear picture of the *continuities* and *discontinuities* between Old and New Testament. A meaningful perspective in this regard cannot escape the question of the relation between the "old" and the "new" Israel. Just as little can the relation between "church" and "kingdom" be ignored.

4.5.1 Continuity and discontinuity

In the Old Testament, Israel was the people of God. As covenant people Israel was a holy people (cf. Lev. 19:2) chosen by God to be his own (Deut. 7:6). God claimed complete obedience encompassing the entire life of Israel. Consider the numerous economic regulations,[22] regulations for dealing with rebellious children, for the different forms of judicature,[23] for love relations,[24] and for a variety of cultic-religious matters.[25]

---

21 A more comprehensive treatment is available in Strauss, 1980:238-263.

22 Such as the remission of debts every seventh year, the ban on interest from fellow Israelites, the honouring of the sabbath year and the year of jubilee, the responsibility to take care of the poor, etc.

23 The elders who sit in the city gates, adjudicating various applicable punishments.

24 E.g. the letter of divorce, the levirate, regulations regarding chastity and matters of marriage and the family.

25 Consider the various festivals, sacrifices and the pilgrimage to the place selected by God to establish his Name.

This life-encompassing covenant appeal provides the background for the blessing and curse in Deut.11:26 ff. (cf. Deut.28), "the blessing if you obey the commands of the LORD your God that I am giving you today, the curse if you disobey the commands of the LORD your God ..."

In the midst of this appeal to total obedience we must keep in mind the Old Testament *veil-order* which implies a distinction between *holy* and *less holy* (not unholy!): the sabbath (which must be honoured) against the other six days of the week; the tenth against the other nine-tenths; the Levite against the non-Levite; clean against unclean animals; man as opposed to woman (only men could become high priests), the eldest son (receiving a double inheritance) against the other children, and last but not least, the people of Israel against all other nations.[26]

The incarnation of Christ, and particularly his crucifixion, has torn the veil (which delimited the most holy, which the high priest could enter only once a year with a blood offering) from top to bottom. The writer of the epistle to the Hebrews states clearly that a new and living way has been opened up for us "through the curtain, that is, his body" (10:20). The rift of the curtain indicates that the death of Christ opened the way to God for whomever God chose in Christ. Paul even says that "he chose us in him before the creation of the world to be holy and blameless in his sight" (Eph.1:4).

Those elected in Christ are no longer limited, as in the Old Testament with its particular covenant, to an identifiable nation (the old Israel), since it indicates the elect out of all nations – something which Paul and Luke, among others, emphasize (cf. Eph.2:11ff, Gal.5:1ff and Acts 15). The symbolic character of the Old covenant is now fulfilled, and with it the veil-division between Israel and non-Israel, since in Christ we are all baptized into one body, whether we are Jews or Greeks, slaves or freeman (1 Cor.12:13, cf. Gal.3:28).

Peter refers to the new elect humanity in Christ in Old Testament terms: a *spiritual house*, a *holy priesthood* (1 Peter 2:5), a *chosen people*, a *royal*

---

26 The Roman Catholic dualistic view of nature and grace (secular and sacred) is i.a. an imitation of this facet of the Old Testamental veil-order.

priesthood, a *holy nation* (verse 9) (cf. Ex.19:5-6).

In the way that the old Israel had to live obediently to God in all expressions of life, so the new people of God, the new Israel, have to stand in the service of God with all of their lives, within God's Kingdom – whether they eat or drink, or whatever they do (cf. 1 Cor.10:31 and Col.3:17). The Old Testament veilorder has ended, there is now full life in Christ, God's Spirit consecrates whatever it works within, setting it apart and dedicating it to God who is present in Christ and through the working of the Holy Spirit – *all days* of the week, *all places* on earth, *all ten tenths* of our income, in *all life forms* (not only in the church institute) within which we may live in Kingdom service of God.

4.5.2 The Kingdom of God

We have already seen that having citizenship in the Kingdom of God depends on being born again in Christ. The term "Kingdom of God" is understood in a few slightly different ways:

(i) First of all the *Kingdom* refers to the creational government of God in Christ over all that is – God did, after all, create everything in Christ (cf. John 1:1ff, Col. 1:15ff.); Christ to whom all power in heaven and in earth has been given (Matt. 28:18).

(ii) Secondly, since the fall the *Kingdom* indicates God's government over both the old (fallen) humanity (in Adam) and the new Israel, becasue fallen creation is still *maintained* in Christ (the second Adam) (Col. 1:17). Since God maintains creation in Christ *both* believer and non-believer can still live within the possibilities which God has given for being human at creation.[27]

(iii[a]) By means of God's saving intervention in Christ he rules in Christ and by means of the work of the Holy Spirit in the heart and life of every believer, to whom he was given as head above all other things (Cf. Eph. 1:21 and Col. 1:18).[28] Wherever the elect citizens

---

[27] Sin acts as a parasite on these possibilities, twisting it in an idolatrous, God-disobedient *direction*.

[28] Notice that Eph.1:21 refers to what has been discussed under (ii) above – the creation-wide government of God in Christ which extends also over apostate humanity, while Eph.1:22 (and Col.1:18) refers to the creation-wide government of Christ over the citizens of the Kingdom, over those who share in the

of the Kingdom are wholeheartedly obedient to the creational will of God – in whatever facet of life – there the Kingdom of God has already come.[29] The present *Kingdom* indicates simply the degree to which reborn people obediently can (or did) give expression to their divine calling in every avenue of life and on every terrain of life.

(iii[b]) Since we are still only saved *sinners* in this order even our best works are still despicable in God's eyes – cast through with the sin which still accompanies us, but, by the grace of salvation in Christ, no longer governs us. The creational history beginning in the Garden of Eden, has been deepened by the vicarious intervention of Christ which allows a future hope on the new Jerusalem, the coming Kingdom.

Creation inherently contains the structural principle of a faith institution bound together as a consociation – i.e., as a super-individual and super-arbitrary point of departure which can receive closer positive expression either directed towards God or away from Him. The church institution is nothing more than such a God-oriented expression of the normative structure of a collective community of faith. This implies that the church is by definition qualified by faith – in distinction from the various non-christian social collectivities qualified by faith – like a Mosque or Synagogue.

Christ is the root of both common and particular grace (as Kuyper calls them) – Christ acts as mediator both in the maintenance and salvation of creation. Claims that the church can only be Christian do not prove that the church belongs to a supernatural order of "recreation" or "salvation", but are mere tautologies: a Christian faith institution (the church) can only be Christian! It is contradictory to claim that

---

  total, radical and integral meaning of their salvation and to whom he has been given as Head.

29 Whether it is in the manner in which the christian farmer expresses his or her economically diected stewardship, or the obedience of the marriage and family to the demands of God for in timate love relations, or in the way in which christian citizens respond to their political calling, or even in the way in which members of a church form the church-institute into a sincere and sympathetic community of faith which serves to strengthen faith by means of the ministry of the Scriptural Word in common praise and worship.

such a thing as a non-Christian church could exist, since this means literally: there exists a non-Christian Christian faith institution! Just as little as the church can be non-Christian and remain church, can a mosque be Christian and remain a mosque!

Suppose we called a Christian state *X* and a Christian university *Y* – then it is equally tautological that *X* and *Y* can only be Christian like the church, since all three are typical terrains of God's kingdom equally rooted in the body of Christ. The fundamental antithesis: for or against Christ, cuts through the heart and all other sectors of life and not merely through the *ecclesiastic* sphere of faith.

The word *ecclesia* is undoubtedly used at times in the New Testament to indicate the central relationship with Christ (cf. Col.1:18 and 24 as well as Eph. 1:22-23). In the first case the body of Christ and *ecclesia* are used as synonyms, in the latter it is stated that the *ecclesia* is the body (soma) of Christ.[30]

The life-encompassing kingdom service which is to be rendered by the people of God, explains why both Augustine (cf. *De Civitate Dei*, 9) and Calvin (Cf. Institution, IV, 2, 4: "the church is the kingdom of Christ") identified *ecclesia* with *basileia* (kingdom). Herman Ridderbos comments in this regard that the New Testament nowhere refers to the people of God ("church") as "kingdom" (1950:296ff.). When kingdom refers to God's government over all creation by means of his creational Word, the kingdom does indeed encompass the *ecclesia*. We have already referred to the distinction between the coming kingdom and the kingdom come – only the latter indicates those terrains of human life in which the people of God obey God's kingdom will with all of their lives. It is indeed mistaken to identify *ecclesia* and *basileia*. One facet of the view of Augustine and Calvin, however, must be retained when we distinguish between the kingdom (*basilea*) and the citizens of the kingdom (*ecclesia*): the calling of the citizens stretches across the kingdom and cannot be delimited to one expression of the kingdom only (e.g. of a cultic nature).

---

30 Even when the use of the word ecclesia refers to the relatively undifferentiated fellowship of the people of God, the meaning of being elect, or called-together, cannot at its deepest refer to *human organization*, since our election in Christ is independent of *any* human organization.

It is noticeable that reformed theologians, when distancing themselves from the Roman Catholic position (namely that the kingdom in this world coincides with the church), mostly simply emphasize that the kingdom stretches further than the church – without rejecting the traditional Roman *identification* of the citizens of the kingdom (the body of Christ, the ecclesia) with the church as institution! The gospel of the kingdom of God always calls forth its correlate – the new people of God, the citizens of the kingdom, the *ecclesia* in this RCT-sense.

The biblical antithesis between *ecclesia* and world is co-extensive with that between the *kingdom of God* and the *kingdom of darkness*. The unbiblical Roman dualism of *nature* and *grace* is evident in an understanding of the antithesis as being between the church as institution and the various non-church terrains of life. This view is simply a consequence of the church-centric *mis-indication* of the nature of the citizens of the kingdom which we have already referred to critically in Chapter 1.

4.6 Societal forms – the "internal" and "external" coherence among aspects

In terms of the distinction previously drawn between societal collectivities, communities and co-ordinational relationships it was not yet possible to indicate the *foundational* and *qualifying* function of any of these. Only these unique, differentiated foundational and guiding functions of particular life forms typically *specifies* their meaning. This means, however, that we are moving beyond the limits of the modally-delimited (elementary and composite sociological) basic concepts. The total nature of such life forms can never be justified only in terms of the various ways of interaction, simply because they function concretely in **all** aspects of reality.

This concrete functioning in the various modal aspects of reality must be described carefully, because it may be difficult to indicate some *original modal functions* of various life forms. It is obviously not difficult to understand the biotic functions of the marriage – after all, sexual interaction between husband and wife is founded in the biotic side of our existence. But how could we understand the original biotic function in the state? To function originally in the biotic aspect requires the presence of genuine *biotic subjectivity*. How can this be ascribed to the state without reverting to a mistaken biologistic view of the state – seen as a peculiarly biotic organism?!

To understand this problem we must remember that all life forms typically organize all human subject functions in the particular form of life under the guidance of a radical typical qualifying function. Only the indissoluble coherently distinctive nature of the two radical functions (foundational and qualifying/directive) of a form of life can guarantee its internal structural unity. The structural typical unity and identity of any form of life can only express typical functions in all aspects of reality in the entity structural manner in which the subject functions of all the members are bound together. It is only from this perspective that a justifiable understanding can be formed of e.g. the objective-biotic living space and the subjective-biotic living together of subjects and government in a state within a delimited territory – indicating clearly the original biotic function of the state as a form of life. That is, the state has no biotic function *apart* from the citizens whose lives therein are bound together juridically in the typical way of the state.

These insights cohere with the distinction which we can draw between the *internal* and *external* coherence between a particular aspect and other aspects of reality. The internal coherence between aspects indicates the various analogies which we can distinguish and identify within the structure of an aspect. The external coherence only comes in view when we study the dimension of things (entity structures) and give attention to the way in which one or another entity qualified by a particular aspect functions in other aspects of reality.

This can be illustrated by the nature of any objective cultural thing. A work of art, qualified by the aesthetic aspect, has, apart from the analogies in the qualifying aesthetic aspect, also original concrete functions in the various nonaesthetic aspects of reality. The economic analogy in the structure of the aesthetic aspect can be indicated by the moment of *aesthetic economy* (guarding against aesthetic excesses). This economic analogy in the aesthetic aspect obviously differs from the *original economic function* of a work of art – evident in i.a. the *price* it can command in the market. In the same way we can distinguish between the *semiotic* (sign) analogy in the aesthetic aspect (aesthetic signification, significance and interpretation) and the original sign function of the work of art (the *verbal sign* or name we give it). The *aesthetic sensitivity* (psychic analogy in the aesthetic aspect) with which a work of art depicts, verbalizes or entones something aesthetically is distinct from the *sensory perceptibility* (original psychic function) of a work of art. The *aesthetic effect* (analogy of the physical cause-effect relation) of a work of art can be distinguished from the (enkaptically encompassed) *material* from which it is made. In this way a complete analysis of the distinction between the *internal* and *external* coherence between the aesthetic aspect and other aspects of reality is possible. A similar analysis is possible with regard to various life forms – as we shall now illustrate with reference to the state and the institutional church.

The state exists as a unit amidst the multitude of citizens who are juridically ordered in the relation of government and subjects. The nature of the state territory, as a spatially delimited (cultural) area, obviously indicates the spatial function of the state. The concrete existence of the state as an arrangement of life has a certain durability – not only in the organization of the sword power or function state buildings (an objective durability), but also in the continuous manner in which the citizenry of a state are juridically integrated in terms of their kinematic subject functions. Physical power necessarily forms the foundation for the exercise of the typical sword power of the state. (We have already referred to the state's biotic functioning). The *feeling* of solidarity among the citizens of a state rests on the structural unity of the state and illustrates the *sensitive-psychic* function of the state.

Public *opinion* represents the manner in which the state functions in the *logical aspect*, while the organization of sword power (the foundational function of the state) indicates the *historical function* (also consider the *history* of a state).

The *sign function* of a state is evident not only in its *name* (verbal sign), but also in *national symbols* such as the national flag, anthem, emblems, and the significance of public holidays. Referring to a state as a social collectivity already indicates the specific sort of interaction (social aspect) taking place within a state – not forgetting inter-national interaction. The state household (including the various sources of state income and the budget with regard to expenditures) represents the original *economic function* of the state. The aesthetic aspect of the state is expressed in the beauty or ugliness, the stylish grace or lack thereof, with which the state meets its typical responsibilities. We can recognize the function of the ethical aspect in the greater or lesser degree of *patriotism* characteristic of the citizenry, while the function of faith is evident in the *trust* citizens place in the integrity of the government, or in the sense of *security* all citizens have that the government is indeed governing in service of the *public interest*. Sometimes certain typically religious activities are occasionally interwoven with state activities (e.g. the opening of parliament with prayer).

Note that the existence of a Christian state is not subject only to the state's function in the aspect of faith, since only when the activities of government and subjects are obedient to the many-sided *typical structural principle* of the state as a social collectivity can there be a God-oriented positive expression of these principles – resulting in a *Christian* state. Christianity does not ever mean sinlessness or perfection – a Christian political understanding and practice can therefore never fall back on the Roman Catholic teaching of the "societas perfecta" (*the perfect society*).

With regard to the church we must mention first of all that the institutional church finds expression in the unity of the *local congregation* – in opposition to the Roman Catholic view which sees this unity primarily in an *institutional hierarchic totality*. While the institutional church is organized in local congregations, the church does not have an own *territory*, like the state. Every member of the congregation is *personally* bound to the faith authority of the church – wherever s/he may find himself or herself.

Only on this basis are the many members of the institutional church bound together in a durable unity which continues regardless of changes in membership. The powerful way in which members involve themselves in the church, identifying with the kingdom appeal of the ministry of the Word in the church, does not only presume mature motivation and discernment among the members, but also refers to the covenantal, loving interaction in the congregation. This interaction should express a particular harmony which coheres with the way in which the congregational offerings are administered. Since the veilorder of the Old Testament is past, there are no longer grounds to cling to the giving of the tithe. All ten tenths of the Christian's income must be used (on all terrains of creation, according to their particular requirements) in the service of the kingdom.

The function of the institutional church in the *sign aspect* of reality is evident in the *name* used by a local congregation or a denomination, as well as in the various signs and symbols playing a role in the normal functioning of the congregation – e.g. baptism, the bread and wine used in the Eucharist, the cross, and so forth. The mutual love among members, practically expressed in the diaconate, which is responsible for charitable service, presupposes the common faithfulness to the confessional statements of the church.

When we consider the typical functioning of the church as an institution (qualified by the Christian faith)[31] in all the aspects of reality in this way, it is clear that we are not dealing with structural characteristics of the church as a form of life which are merely external or accidental, since these are normative *entity-structural conditions* for the very existence of the church. Every attempt to discern a dialectical contrast between the eschatological nature of the new Israel and its creational kingdom calling, will transform the church into a superficial, supernatural unstructured spirituality which devalues all human responsibility, since there is no space left for the responsibility to obey normative structural principles.

---

31 That is, qualified by the aspect of faith and founded in the historical organization of the ministry of the Word and the sacraments.

QUESTIONS FOR CHAPTER 4

1. Explain the nature of material things concisely.
2. Why is it problematic to speak of 'living and dead matter'? In your explanation refer to the supposed mechanistic reduction of the identity of living things.
3. Discuss an alternative approach to the unique nature of biotically qualified entities in view of the theory of an enkaptic tructural whole.
4. Briefly discuss the nature of the animal kingdom.
5. Classify the various ways of intercourse in human society with reference to the distinctions among associational, collective, and coordinational relationships.
6. Typify the nature of an undifferentiated society.
7. Analyze the structural principle of the state as a public legal bond.
8. What is meant by refering to marriage as an ethically qualified two-in-one (biune) community?
9. Analyze the continuity and discontinuity existing between Old Testament and the New Testament dispensation.
10. Discuss the unique nature of the church as an institution against the backdrop of the perspective provided by the Bible on the kingdom of God.
11. Distinguish between the 'internal' and 'external' coherence between various aspects of reality.

Chapter 5
The University

5.1 The emergence of the university

IF WE LOOK AT THE DEVELOPMENT of what has been called the university since 1200, it is soon clear that the university cannot be seen in isolation. Initially, the form which the university took was linked with the relatively undifferentiated society of the Middle Ages in which the church played a dominant role. This situation was partly responsible for the fact that the university of the Middle Ages was geared to establishing scientists as academic lecturers. Although there was an appreciation for the increase of literacy generally, it was still closely linked to the relatively undifferentiated structure of the society of the Middle Ages. The church was seen as the over-arching grace-institute, with the state as its serving subject. The rest of society appears undifferentiated as "society" – cf. the well-known (especially evident in theological writing) distinction between "church, state and society". The relatively undifferentiated nature of late medieval society is reflected in the meagre harvest of "faculties" which we find at the end of the 13th century: the propadeutic faculty of "free arts" (*artes liberales* – later named *facultas artium* or *philosophiae* – the origin of the present faculty of the arts); the theological faculty (*sacra pagina*); the faculty of law (which included both the so-called Roman world law and the church canonic law); and the medical faculty. During the 16th and 17th centuries this moderate differentiation served as basis for the justification of the "social service" of the university: the university provided preachers for the churches of most protestant countries, lawyers for the state and doctors for "society".

Besides the influence of the relatively undifferentiated Middle Age society, we must also focus our attention on the influence of the general process of technical and cultural disclosure. The limited, and often exclusive, availability of handwritten (or: hand copied) books led, under others, to colleges emerging at universities which had exclusivity because of their unique collection of books. In England this heritage from the Middle Ages had a durable influence – as it is reflected in Oxford and Cambridge.

Can we still claim that these expressions (and countless others not mentioned) of universities through the centuries, really did have a common and underlying constant structural principle?

From the history of the Western university, the modern university has emerged as an institution in which structural continuity exists with the origin of the first university of the Middle Ages around the year 1200. Provisionally, we can link this structural continuity to the simultaneous presence of two particular facts:

1) The organization of the university into a specific societal institution;
2) The bringing together of teachers and students with the aim of carrying over scientific knowledge by way of scientific teaching (cf. Huizinga & De Rijk, 1974: 784). Although this provisional description is thoroughly dependent on the way in which scientific practice is typified, it is useful to point out something essential in the Western university. It is useful to take account of the historical fact that the term "universitas," according Huizinga & De Rijk, (1974: 784), did not refer to an institution where the all the sciences were lectured (universitas scientiarum), because it had a societal connotation ("een sociologische betekenis"):
"It represented 'communality', 'connectedness' and served to designate various collectivities, whether it concerned a municipal community or a guild, or even (as in this case) a corporation of teachers (magistri) and students (scholares), who organized themselves in service of their reciprocal protection

and with the aim to demarcate themselves rightfully from other societal institutions, including the worldly and church authorities."

Only after the emergence of modern humanism and the breakthrough of the reformation do we find a special striving to use only Latin at university. A result of this was that the term *universitas* was forced into the background because of the prominence of the term *academia*. The gain of this heritage is that we do not need to refer to the university only as a form of society where science is practiced, because we can shortly describe the university as an academic bond – in which science in teaching and research capacity is practiced within the context of a particular organizational form (Faculties and Departments) in which the academic interaction between lecturers and students occurred. Venter points out that the unity of the masters and students was known as a *studium*. A *studium generale* indicated a situation where masters in the *artes*, in *canonic law* and in *civil law* were present (Venter, 1987:1). He even points out that what we understand under the term "university" today, externally looks the most like *studium generale*. If we keep up the Middle Age use of these terms, it means that we must see the *Lyceum* of Aristotle as a university, because research and teaching in a variety of sciences had occurred (Venter, 1987:2). This academic nature of universities has a particular commonality or universality regardless of the variable ways in which specific universities express it in a concretely organized form (consider the diverse ways in which universities' different faculties are organized).

If the critical question, where is the unique distinguishing characteristic of science found (cf. Strauss, 1980:1-8), is asked, we focus our attention on the following viewpoints.

5.2 The uniqueness of scientific thought

Common characteristics – like methodology, "verification", systematics, subject-object relation and abstraction – are not conclusive because all these characteristics represent similarities between scientific activities and nonscientific activities. If we do not define exactly what science/theory formation precisely involves, a description as follows does not really help us: "The practice of science is the cultivation of the process of knowing with basic characteristics like economical thought, logical systematic pattern of theoretical construction formation" (Venter, 1987:11). The cardinal question is what distinguishes science/theory formation from all non-scientific (non-theoretical) activities? Maybe the abacus with which most of us used to learn to count in primary school, is the best aid to explain the nature of scientific-theoretical thought.

Beforehand, we must say that we are dealing with scientific thought leading to scientific knowledge – and we said in Chapter 2 that the nature of thinking is marked by a person's ability to classify, i.e. to be able to divide up on the basis of similarities and differences which are identified. We identify and distinguish on the basis of similarities.[1]

From this it should be clear that the mark "abstraction" itself is insufficiently precise to qualify as the distinguishing characteristic of science. All usual everyday concepts are based on abstraction: certain universal characteristics are elevated and combined in the unity of a concept (e.g. the concept *human being, tree, horse, motorcar*, etc.). That is to say that the uniqueness of each individual human being, tree, horse, or motorcar is ignored and only the universal characteristics of humans, trees, horses or motorcars are concentrated on. Although everyday concepts are based on abstraction, no one would claim that the mere formation of such concepts is sufficient for the justification of the uniqueness and distinctiveness of scientific concepts. What can we learn from the example of the abacus?

When we learn to calculate with the help of the abacus, we begin by involving different aspects of reality: we take into account the colour, the movement, the shape and the quantity of blocks on the abacus. Gradually we have to ignore the colour, movement and shape, and concentrate on the quantity, i.e. we must elevate the numerical aspect in order simultaneously to ignore the nonnumerical aspects, (namely, the spatial, the kinematic and the physical aspects). With that we have moved to theoretical thought – i.e. we abstracted certain aspects of reality. Note – abstraction as such is useless here because we have utilized a closer precisioning: aspect abstraction (modal abstraction). By

---

1   We have already indicated that abstraction and analysis are actually exchangeable terms.

naming modal abstraction the unique distinguishing feature of scientific thought, we have in no way built in a limit in terms of concrete things of our everyday life, because the different aspects of reality still act as the gateway to our experience of the different things within reality. Therefore we can never say that a special science (i.e. a theoretical discipline which is delimited by a single aspect of reality) is restricted to a "section" of reality. The full concrete reality of our everyday life experience falls within the field of study of every special science – with this single qualification: seen from its modally-abstracted angle.

The well-known demands of prediction and explanation are linked by Stafleu with the coherence between the logical-analytical aspect and the foundational meaning of the kinematic and physical aspects of reality:

> "Prediction is the first and most obvious aim of any theory. This is a consequence of the deductive character of a theory, i.e., its kinematic foundation, deduction being the logical movement from one statement to another. We shall characterize prediction to be 'kinematic' function of a theory, to be distinguished from its 'physical' function, which is to explain. Explanation is tied to a cause-effect relation of some kind" (1987:31).

Given the factual illustration regarding the distinguishing nature of scientific practice, it goes without saying that more attention must be given to the other facets of the contemporary development in scientific theory if we want to understand the particular nature of the university.

Science practiced at university stands within the context of particular special *scientific traditions*. Only compare the influential view of T.S. Kuhn about "paradigms" or the "disciplinary matrix" which can be dominant in different disciplines. These theoretical frameworks of thought do not float in the air but are based on deeper central convictions which appeal to a central vision concerning the nature of human beings, their place in reality and history, and also to the meaning of scientific practice (cf. the related views of Popper, Kuhn, Polanyi, Feyerabend and Stegmüller). We could refer to these central convictions as the "ultimate commitment" of science or of the institution or discipline because it is also directive for the practice of science at university. The encompassment of scientific practice in such a central vision expresses the *directional choice* which is unavoidably present in all scienctific activities. The distinction in Chapter 1 between *structure* and *direction* gives us a perspective with which we can understand the most fundamental nature and functioning of the university as academic life-form.

Actually, precisely the question about the relationship between structure and direction reveals the deepest point of divergence between life- and worldview orientations as such. The standard criticism against the university, viz. that it exists as an *ivory tower* in the midst of social needs and demands, evaluates the university precisely from a peculiar central directional perspective – namely a perspective which does not measure the university in its own right because it is the victim of a narrow utilitarianism which evaluates the university only in terms of its serviceability to external practical societal goals. In order to confront this complaint – i.e. through the nature of a university's mission statement – it must be done on the same directional level.

What we are trying to say here is that the justification of the intrinsic value and relative merit of being a university already requires a central direction choice. Therefore the appeal for the continuation of the university as an academic institution flows from a vision of society which gives recognition to diverse and differently natured life forms in human society which each exist in its own right, no matter how they may be linked. The "use" of being a university for society lies precisely in the fact, namely that it must be obedient to its structural calling.

Concluding this section we give a succinct defition of philosophy:

Philosophical thought is *theoretical thought* directed towards the integrally coherent *creational diversity* in its totality – guided by a theoretical *total*-view accounting for the *coherence of irreducibles* and directed by an *ultimate commitment* operative in the *deepest core* (i.e., the *heart*) of *being human*.

5.2.1 The uniqueness of the university

In order to see the relative durability and identity of concretely existing universities we have to approach them in the light of the normative structural principle of being a university. This requires further justification of the structural typicality of the university as institution.

The organization of the university (historical foundational function) and the nature of the university as an *academic* institution (qualification) determines the unique way in which the university as life form functions in other aspects of reality. Venter suggests the following description of the university:

> "The university is a community of people in which people interested in science (as a supporting skill to gain wisdom in career and life) through participation in the scientific process, under the guidance of advanced scientists, are introduced in a particular tradition regarding the scientific cultivation of humankind" (1987:15).

At this point we must refer back to the distinction between the internal and the external coherence between the different aspects of reality where we stopped at the end of the previous Chapter.

The qualifying theoretical-analytical function of the university has both an *internal* and an *external coherence* (interweaving) with the different facets of human society. The *academic mission* (task and credo formulation) of the university, reflects, for example, the external coherence between the qualifying (disclosed) *logical* function of the university and its faith aspect. This regards, in other words, the concrete function of the university in the faith aspect of reality. The confession of faith of a *political party* makes it into a church. Similarly, when a university formulates its peculiar *academic* confession of faith it is not transformed into a church. In distinction from this function of the university in the faith aspect of reality (external coherence) the theoretical-logical aspect also has an *inner* coherence with the faith aspect, particularly in the anticipatory analogy of *logical certainty/trust* – sometimes with regard to scientific practice also designated as the *intellectual credibility* of scholarship (inner coherence) (cf. Van Huysteen, 1986:4,5,48,129).

The unavoidable structural functioning of the university in the faith aspect of reality illuminates the necessity for mission formulation. If it does not occur explicitly, the university is still (mis-)directed through some or other implicit mission choice. An unwillingness or inability to account for this directional choice in practice often boils down, to a greater or lesser extent, to *disintegration* in the scientific practice of the university. Before we go into this, we will concentrate on a few other functions of reality in which the university functions as a social collectivity.

Every university reflects a particular *university ethos*. Often it reflects an unwritten common task-orientation and relation of mutual trust which exists between colleagues and students (the function of the university in the ethical aspect, or, in other words, the external coherence between the analytical and ethical aspects of reality) – but without it there can be no mention of a healthy intellectual integrity in a university (the internal coherence between the two aspects just mentioned).

Every university will unavoidably, i.e. according to its cosmically multifaceted structural principle, have a function in the jural aspect of reality. Since the Van Wyk de Vries-Report in the seventies, the following false contradiction lives in the South African reflection on the nature of the university, viz. that the university must be seen as a legal entity which is a complete state creation (through the relevant private law) and that it must be seen simultaneously as an autonomous societal entity which exists independently of the state. The concrete functioning of a university in the jural aspect of reality however, has many sides, including an internal and external civil jural side.

The internal law of the university as life form appeals to its academic freedom. This academic freedom locks in the competence of each university to determine its character. This "character determination" does not only include the choice of a particular style of scientific practice, but also explicitly includes a particular central *directional choice* of a university.[2]

The recognition of the academic nature of a university (as a social collectivity) implies at the same time that inherent structural borders (limits of competence) exist for the academic activities of the university as institution: the university is called to the formation of academic power and cannot act as an economic institution, political action or religious grouping at the same time – however much each of these

---

2   The underlying distinction between *structure* and *direction* that this concerns has been discussed several times already through the course of this book.

expressions of life can be reflected upon academically. According to its nature, the university must bind itself to the characteristic (–sphere sovereign) limits which the deepened (disclosed) theoretical-logical qualification thereof sets and which should express itself in its typical teaching and research activities.

Once a university has exercised a particular choice of direction which is faithful to the internal structural principle of the university, it deserves *legal* recognition and protection – which is referred to as the *external civil-legal side* of a university. The university, considered according to its *internal* sphere of competence, belongs to the sphere of *private law*. The state grants lawful recognition to a particular university in a way reflecting the external civil legal side of a university. This recognition does not indicate a second type of entity – a legal entity, which is distinguishable from the university as academic institution, because it only points to the external civil-legal function of one and the same entity, viz. the university as an academic institution.

We must also say something about multiculturism – the relationship between culture and university. The view exists that the *transcultural* value of knowledge – not being culturally relative – means that a university in its knowledge expansion and distribution must act "culturally free". Besides the relationship between the university and different ethnic communities, the university as a life form also has a concrete function in the *cultural-historical aspect* of reality. For that reason practicing science requires from the university a particular *academic cultural style formation*! Cultural style formation appeals to specific *ways of doing* which are typically distinguishable in all standard Western universities and which are expressed in the academic organization at different universities – a difference which is remarkable in South Africa if Afrikaans and English campuses are compared with respect to their respective *academic* styles (i.e, not ethnic styles!). The inevitability of having an *academic style* presupposes the constitutional requirement of non-discrimination against the cultural (racial or gender) background of any student. The supposed concern of science and university-endeavours with universal structures/laws (as well as the transcultural appeal of the kind of knowledge which is acquired there) does not mean that every existing university cannot continue this in an academic cultural style-specific way – two universities are therefore never identical.

5.2.2 Structural typicality and university aims

It is very important to realize that the structural nature of a life form like the university cannot be characterized or defined in terms of particular *aims* or *goals*. In order to strive for a certain goal, the particular life form must already have a *typical structural nature*, because only the recognition of this foundational structural principle offers a criterion which puts us in a position to distinguish typical (university) aims from non-typical (outer-university) aims! All aims presume the structural-typical principles of the University as life form which must found and delimit the nature of each aim!

The structural principle of the university requires from every life form which wants to qualify as such,[3] that concrete expression must be given to the fundamental normative structure for being a university. Every already existing university is a concrete historical answer to the normative requirements encapsulated in the structural principle of the university as a social collectivity – no matter how this expression falls short of the normative starting-points for being a university.

Every justified university strategy of any existing university can therefore only be seen as a *purposeful* attempt from within the accepted fundamental direction of being a university to come to a better (and more normatively obedient) structural organization of the university as life form in the unique historical circumstances in which the university might find itself.

These insights imply that we must also question classical organizational theory, which, linked with general systems theory, has particularly influenced business economics and industrial sociology. Besides the problematic way in which the whole/part scheme must be brought into relation with the means/ends scheme, the most fundamental problem

---

3   A Teachers' Training College and a Technicon are respectively focused educationally- professionally and educationally-technically, and as such lack the essential, scientifically- deepening, *research* character of the university. These distinctions does not restrict the *scope* of scientific investigation, since the University is competent as an academic institution to reflect academically on literally everything in reality – the encyclopedia of science reaches as wide as all of creation.

with some of these directions is that they depress the unique nature of the university by making its functional meaning serviceable to the structural demands of the "societal whole" – compare the theory of instrumental organizations which can be conveniently used to see the university as a means in service of non-university aims (compare Luhman, 1973:55ff.). This approach cannot take account of the sovereign unique nature of the university as life form and in principle runs into a complete leveling of the typical academically-marked structural principle of the university. For the education of mature members of society an insight in the nature of the limits of competence of the different societal forms is essential. The nature and structure of education itself requires illumination.

5.3   The structure of education

In the first place the disclosure of the normative structure of being human (cf. Chapter 2) shows the deepened (anticipating) way which a person functions subjectively in the different normative aspects of reality.

A disclosed normative structure does not only indicate the open nature of the different normative subject functions of the human body, but over and above that the linked diversity of life forms in which the disclosed personality must live himself/herself out, as well as on the variety of objective cultural products in which humankind finds itself in the variety of life relationships.

A disclosed legal awareness cannot, for example, be expressed without a state which maintains balance and harmony in the multiplicity of legal interests as a public legal collectivity (amongst others under the guidance of the deepened principles justice) having crystallized in its territory. Such a political order requires all kinds of objective cultural things (like weapons, administrative buildings, courts, etc.). The same can be said about every other life institution, life form and cultural product.

The deepening of human normative structures, which is indissolubly interwoven with an educational process in which a person is brought to mature disclosure, is therefore fundamentally a total, religiously-determined process of development and education to an encompassing maturity in all expressions of life, sectors of life and the use of cultural goods.

Education possesses a differentiated (5) normative structural (3, 4) character, which, owing to its normative (1) richness in variation (2) is in itself unqualified (3). We discuss the indicated central terms shortly in numerical order.

(1) The term *normative* refers *positively*, as we have already seen, to the freedom of expression which a person has as the one who forms culture, and *negatively* to the transgression of all principles which exist at the norm side of the post-psychical aspects and which are given positive form in an antinormative sense as a result of the fall.

(2) The expression *richness of variation* indicates the multiplicity of normative aspects in which a person can function – we have seen that one moment one can be analytically occupied with a scientific problem, then be with a transgressor who must be punished and after that interact socially with one's friends.

(3) The expression *normative structure* refers to the fourth bodily structure of a human being which marks (qualifies) all bodily substructures.

(4) Precisely because education appeals to the characteristic normative structure of a person, and because this normative structure can never be enclosed in one specific aspect – that is to say can never be qualified by a specific aspect or be completely exhausted by it – education itself is *unqualified*. Imagine that education was qualified by the *social aspect*, then it would mean that only social education would be possible – which implies that a person could never undergo any *economic, jural, ethical* or *religious* education. Education appeals to each one of these normative possibilities of human beings and therefore cannot, just as little as the normative (bodily) structure, be qualified by any modal aspect.

(5) The term *differentiated* places further accent on the unqualified nature of education, since, precisely because education itself is unqualified, it must possess a modally-differentiated realization structure. This general anthropological insight into the nature of education can be made fruitful on different sides and in different

directions. We refer firstly (a) to the coherence of the above perspective with the nature of a person's emotional disclosure and secondly (b) to the nature of education in the context of an undifferentiated society.

(a) By way of a person's sensory equipment, that person is able to orientate himself/herself in the surrounding world. Our senses enable us to be aware of our environment immediately: we see the movement of the dove that flies from the branch, we hear the roar of an approaching vehicle, we feel biting cold in the winter wind and we taste salt water when we swim in the sea. Although we can focus our attention on specific things in our sensory environment, the basic functioning of our sensory orientation is free from reasonable deliberation.

On the basis of this sensory equipment, we are capable of meaningfully slotting into the different normative dimensions of our socially differentiated existence. We read the result of an examination which fills us with happiness or sorrow; we hear of a planned social happening and we feel excited about everything we can possibly experience and enjoy, etc.

De Graaff (1980) even distinguishes between our *feelings* and *emotions*. According to him, all the different types of feelings reflect an own distinctiveness, extent, durability, intensity and vitality which is simultaneously open in terms of the normative subject functions of human beings. He believes that our feeling reactions are a direct response to that which we observe sensorially. In our awareness of something we experience pleasure or discomfort, we like it or disapprove, experience acceptance or rejection and even the good and bad. That is why he holds that to feel is intrinsically linked to *appreciation*. When we taste something bitter, we feel rejected, when we enjoy a nice warm bath, we feel relaxed, etc. In distinction from our feelings, he argues that emotions show the total bodily agitation which we experience as our reactions to a particular situation: "emotions are immediate, spontaneous, overwhelming, intense reactions that deeply affect our entire physical and organic functioning. They mobilize the whole person and make us pull away from or move toward someone or something. In our emotions we live out here and now and surrender bodily to how we feel in a particular situation".

Emotional openness is linked closely by De Graaff to the way in which we react in emotional disclosure within the context of a differentiated diversity of normatively-marked societal contexts. The joy which we experience is not, for instance, purely psychic-sensitive by nature. It is the joy with which we approach an old friend at a meeting (social joy), or it is the joy which we experience when we listen to a good musical performance (aesthetic joy), etc. Similarly the anger we experience is not just a psychic phenomenon because it is always about the feeling of injustice of someone who is wronged, or the bodily scar which someone inflicted on you purposefully, etc. That these different emotional reactions are always imbedded in the normatively-differentiated human reality is evident in our inability to react in an appropriate emotional way. Someone who laughs in reaction to the serious warning of a friend is considered to be irresponsible; someone who bursts into tears when hearing a good joke is considered socially abnormal, etc. In reality it is a fundamental requirement for every person who is educated to differentiated maturity, to possess the full spectrum of emotional reactions. Actually, it is often a first sign of emotional-psychic disturbance if a person is no longer able to experience the full spectrum of human emotions. Each person's emotional health is not only dependent on the possibility of the emotional spectrum of fury, anger, offense, feeling touched, feeling neutral, feeling excited, experiencing happiness, reacting positively, exultant and even having an ecstatic experience, but also to the active living out of all these "escape valves". Disclosed maturity cannot do otherwise but to lean on and be supported by a healthy emotional disclosure and the appropriate emotional reactions which are coupled to it.

(b) The description of education which we have given above, did not describe the moment of disclosure as a constitutive element of education. This is so because a typification of education must firstly be able to indicate both disclosed and closed education. If education brings no disclosure about in a truly differentiated society (no expression of life is deepened, the life forms are not differentiated and the cultural state is still undifferentiated), and if our description of education contains disclosure as a constitutive building element, it would in principle be impossible to speak of less developed education.

In the given description of the structure of education we stressed that which marks (qualifies) education. The entity structure of education also contains a foundational function, namely the historical function. Through education, the educator gains a certain educational power over the one being educated – a power coherent with educational competence as it is expressed in the various life forms. Still, this educational power and competence is aimed at what we indicated above as the encompassing, unqualified character of all education.

Terminologically, it is essential that we notice the difference between *forming* and *disclosure*. The incredible influence of the Greek view of education as *forming* is conquered by this description. The entire Greek culture is cut apart by the consequences of the idolatrous religious ground motive of form and matter.

In his famous dialogue *Politeia*, Plato deepens the expression of the form-matter motive by giving a specific totality character to his ideal state with its three estates (philosopher, soldier, worker) – the formation of the Greek into a mature state citizen includes all spheres of life. Besides the fact that this ideal state of Plato has no inner borders (grounded in the creational order which guarantees the sphere-sovereignty of every life form), education is also reduced in its qualification to the *cultural-historical aspect* in which the (subject-object) relation between *formative control* and a given *material* is original: people merely become material which the state must form into mature state citizens.

Education does bring certain formative skills to human beings – firstly in a truly cultural-historical sense because humankind has a cultural task grounded in creation: to fill, subject and control the earth through formative cultural power. These controlling formative possibilities will therefore stand central in all concrete subject-object relations in which a mature person eventually finds herself: in modern Western society one must have a reading (lingual subject-object relation) skill, be able to get about in a motor car, be able to handle a variety of eating utensils, be able to clothe oneself decently, be able to use public facilities in a civilized manner, and so forth. One must be educated so that one skillfully can handle all normal utensils (objective cultural things) with which the educated person interacts on a daily basis. Does this mean that education is formative?

Not at all, because the conveyance of certain style figures with regard to objects of use (that is formative skills) does not have to be a formative activity itself, unless education is (wrongfully) per definition equated with formation.

In this context we must point out in closing that education, precisely because of its differentiated mark, can occur within differently qualified life forms. Besides family education, education also occurs, in the encompassing sense of the word in the church. Just as family education appeals to all facets of the education situation and not just to the ethical aspect as qualifying function of the family, so the education situation in the church appeals to the full spectrum of the creational aspects, i.e. because the preaching itself effects a creation-wide appeal on the listener to come to obedience to God in all sectors of life.

Our last stretch of thought in this Chapter is given to a few matters which in our opinion are of fundamental importance for philosophical education of every philosophically interested reader. Three matters are discussed: the relation between *analogy* and *metaphor*; the distinction between *concept* and *idea*; and the nature of *nominalism* (to which we only referred in passing in Chapter 4) as well as the influence of nominalism on the development of modern philosophy and contemporary postmodernism.

5.4 A few closing philosophical distinctions and insights

5.4.1 Analogy and Metaphor

Similarities and differences exist between things (if differences were absent we would not have to deal with similarity but identity – regarding the same entity). There are also differences and similarities between the characteristics of a particular entity.

The remarkable figure which since Greek philosophy captured the attention of thinkers, regards the following situation: two entities or two characteristics exhibit a similarity with regard to the way in which they differ (alternatively: they differ with regard to the way in which they are similar!). Think, for example, of the characteristics spatiality and conviviality. Differences exist between the spatial aspect and the social aspect of reality. These differences can never dissolve the coherence between both aspects. This is evident in the difference between these two aspects as it reveals itself in the similarity between them. Friends can only interact convivially because they are socially close to each other – large age or social status differences usually hamper social interaction because the social distances between people are too great and distancing takes place quickly. The size of the social distance which is at issue here reminds us of our awareness of spatial extension, even while no-one would confuse the two – two people who are socially far apart can on occasion – that is spatially seen – be right next to each other (think of the President and his/her bodyguard). Without a grasp of *spatial extension* (distance) we will not be able to form a concept of *social distance*. Exactly in the moment of similarity of "distance" the difference comes to the fore: *spatial* distance is different to *social* distance!

This given, in which the difference between two aspects (modalities) shows itself in the moment of similarity, we have identified as a modal analogy.[4] The qualification "modal" indicates that there are also other kinds of analogical figures. There also exist differences which show themselves in moments of similarity between different entities (such as animals, people, furniture, and so forth). Here we can also speak of analogies – entity-analogies. Such analogies between entities

---

4 In Chapter 3 we explained this distinction with reference to the difference between physical space and the original character of space.

are commonly referred to as metaphors. Think of such well-known expressions as "the lion of Western Transvaal" (Genl De La Rey), or of the little child who refers to the joint of his/her finger as the finger's "elbow".

After the *linguistic turn* at the beginning of the 20th century the semantic phenomenon of *metaphoricity* gained in importance. Since metaphors are based upon *entitary anlogies* they ought to be distinguished from *modal analogies*. Whereas it is possible to replace metaphors with ones totally *different* from those used, modal analogies cannot be replaced, except by *synonymous* words.

5.4.2 Concept and idea / analogy and metaphor

The distinction between (modal) analogy and metaphor (entity analogy) – which is of great importance to theology – is deepened when it is connected with the perspective given by the distinction between concept and idea. If we concentrate on the fundamental difference between the dimension of aspects (modalities) and the dimension of entities, it seems that the terms which appeal to the original meaning of a certain aspect[5] can be used in two different ways: *conceptually* and by the use of *ideas* ("idee-matig").

(a) A conceptual use regards those instances where the particular terms (or their analogical contexts) are applied within the limits of a particular modal aspect, e.g. when numerical terms are used to indicate numerical relations (with the help of computations like addition, subtraction, etc.), or when spatial terms are used to describe spatial figures (one or more dimensional), or when kinematic terms are used to describe the relative movement of a body, or when physical terms are used to typify the nature of changes which occur in a physical system.

(b) An idea-use ("*idee-matige gebruik*") of modal terms occurs when the particular term is used to refer to data which transcend the limits of that particular aspect. In this sense an idea is a genuine limit-

---

5   As we have seen in Chapter 3 – e.g. unity and multiplicity – numerical aspect; coherence/extension/whole-parts – spatial aspect; invariance/constancy/continuity – kinematic aspect; dynamic/change/causality – physical aspect; and so forth.

ing-transcending concept which, on the one hand foundationally refers to the original modal meaning of the aspect from which the term comes, but on the other hand also approximatingly refers to that which transcends the limits of the particular aspect but nonetheless can only be indicated with the help of a term coming from this aspect.

By returning again to the school example of a chair, we can explain the distinction between concept and idea better.

We saw that a normal lounge chair functions in reality in a concrete way. If we should now state that such a chair had four legs, we notice only the way in which this chair functions within the limits of the numerical aspect. Even if we ignore the chair's concrete entity nature, and abstracted the numerical aspect theoretically by concentrating on the modal nature of numerical relations (like the question about the nature of natural numbers and calculations like addition, multiplication, etc., which can be defined therefore), our attention remains focused on data found within the limits of the numerical aspect thus giving us conceptual access). In other words: the numerical term which we use is not applied to refer to the complete reality of the chair – it refers only to the way in which the chair functions in one aspect of reality (distinguished from other aspects).

Is it possible to say something about the chair which applies to *all* its facets (aspects) from the gateway of the numerical aspect? It is: "this chair is *unique* – it has *individuality*". Sometimes we refer to the uniqueness of something by saying that it is something quite "apart"/"distinct". These terms undoubtedly make use of our numerical awareness of *distinctness*, of *being distinct*, although it refers to the total existence of the chair and not just to its numerical aspect. The chair is really entirely unique in *all* its aspects! The terms *uniqueness* and *individuality* reveal an idea-use of numerical terms/terms making an appeal to our intuition of numerical multiplicity.

It is not even always necessary to implement different terms if we want to come to an idea-use of numerical notions. Think only of the church confession of the divine Tri-unity – where we use the numerical term unit in an idea context. It is notable that our normal language often makes use of distinguishing terms when it comes to an idea usage. Compare the following examples: in a conceptual context we usually speak of *unity* and *multiplicity* – in an idea-context we prefer the expression: *unity* and *diversity* (e.g. as applicable to creational diversity); conceptually we speak of formation (a term which comes from the historical aspect) – within an idea-context we (and the Bible) speak of *creation*; conceptually we speak of *endlessness* – within an idea-context of *actual infinity* (i.e., the *at once infinite*); etc.

When we speak conceptually about the spatial aspect of the lounge chair we can refer, for e.g., to its *size* (length, breadth and height). The whole-parts relation, which originally appears in the spatial aspect, can also be used in a limit-transcending way, for example when it is used to refer to more than just the spatial aspect of the chair – e.g. when we speak of the chair as a totality (whole).[6] In distinction of the conceptual use of the kinematic term *constancy* (the relative-constant speed at which every physical entity moves), an idea-use of the kinematic gateway makes it possible for us to take account of the relative *identity* (durability/persistence) of the chair as chair – in the midst of changes and even aging we still experience the chair as the *same* chair. This *identity-idea* uses the kinematic point of entry to reality, but it does not only refer to the kinematic aspect of the chair – the chair remains identical with itself in the fullness of its existence (we therefore understand all changes as changes to the same chair!).

In following Van Riessen we can discuss the way in which the first four aspects enable us to form ideas about all of creation:

(i) Everything is unique;

(ii) Everything coheres;

(iii) Everything is constant; and

(iv) Everything changes.

Idea-statements like these do not cancel or oppose each other – rather they presuppose and deepen each other.

There are countless examples of entitary analogies which can be

---

6   The notion of *enkapsis* discussed earlier also instantiates an idea-use of the spatial whole-parts relation, because enakptically bound structures are still referred to as *part*-structures!

used either conceptually or as limit-transcending concepts (ideas/limiting concepts). Many special sciences develop some or other theory in which a particular metaphor plays a key role (conceptual usage).[7] Naturally it also happens that a particular metaphor is over-extended and is actually elevated in a discipline to a fundamental explanatory idea for *all* of reality as it is studied by that particular discipline.[8]

Fortunately, legitimate idea-uses of metaphors exist – without that we would have to go without the manner of speech of the Bible! Think of the key meaning of the idea-use of the following two metaphors about God in biblical revelation: God as *Father* and God as *King*. The concrete faith language of the Bible uses modal terms ideally in an implicit way without any problems when God is spoken of: cf. expressions like the Lord our God is an only Lord (idea-use of a numerical term); God is omnipresent (idea-use of the spatial term); I am who I am (idea-use of the kinematic meaning of constancy); God deals with human beings in a dynamic way (cf. Christ's remark: My Father works until now and so do I and transports all of creation to the Sabbath rest which remains for the people of God [idea-use of physical terms]); God is *life* (a biotic term); God is *almighty* (a historical term); and so on.

The central problem of dialectic theology and negative theology is that it often attempts to use terms in an idea-context and simultaneously to depreciate or negate the sphere (aspect) from which those terms originally come. In negative theology, where it is stressed that we can say nothing positive about God, but can only say what God is *not*, we find many examples of the dialectical negation of the original meaning of terms which are eventually used to phrase a minimum of positive remarks about God (even if it is negated directly afterwards).

> **Comment:** In passing we mention that negative theology reaches back to Plato's dialogue Parmenides which was continued in the Middle Ages and thereafter under the influence of Pseudo-Dionysius the Aeropagite. These problems return in their own way in the thought of Derrida and so-called deconstructionism. Cf. Visagie, 1985:59ff.

---

7   Think, for example, of the strong influence of the mentioned drama-metaphor in sociology where it is a fairly general practice to speak of roles.

8   Think, for example, of the so-called organicism in H. Spencer's sociology – elevated to the level of an all;-pervasie root metaphor.)

The opposite of this approach is presented by the medieval *analogia entis* doctrine which in turn attempts to apply the structure of a (modal or entitary) analogy, conceptually used, to the relation between God and creation.

We focus our attention on the relation of these distinctions for a more meaningful understanding of the fundamental inclination in modern philosophy – and typify at the same time, in coherence with it, the nature of two well-known -isms in the house of theoretical reflection: *rationalism* and *irrationalism*.

5.4.3 Nominalism

Owing to the irreducibility of the numerical and spatial aspects it is also impossible to reduce *universality* (a term with a spatial origin) and *individuality* (a term with a numerical origin) to each other. The *universal* only gives access to *conceptual* knowledge, while the *unique-individual* can only be approached with the aid of limiting concepts (ideas).

> *Rationalism always absolutizes conceptual knowledge at the cost of idea-knowledge, while irrationalism inversely absolutizes ideaknowledge at the expense of conceptual knowledge.*

We have already met Plato's speculative-metaphysical justification of the universal constancy of God's law (order) for creation (Plato's ideas). Aristotle deviated from Plato's view by moving the emphasis from the order *for* to the orderliness *of*. In Aristotle it is known as the so-called *secondary substance*. This view survived into the Middle Ages – *realism* retained a *threefold* existence of universalia: *universalia ante rem* (before the creation as creational ideas in God's Spirit – influence of Plato); *universalia in re* (as the immanent substantial forms of things – influence of Aristotle) and *universalia post rem* (afterwards as universal concepts in the human mind – influence of both).

Nominalism drew a line through the first two – outside the human spirit no universality exists – only the concepts in the human spirit possess universality. Outside the human mind exclusively concrete-individual things exist. This pure individuality is devoid of all universality – it is divorced from the universal *orderliness* of creatures, and from the universal order which God established as determining and limiting law *for* creaturely subjects. The universal concepts or names in the human mind is a substitute which refers to the unencompassable multiplicity of purely individual things outside the human mind – they are only *nomina* for the things existing in their pure *individuality*. Thence the indication *nominalism*.

Is nominalism *rationalistic* or *irrationalistic*? The answer sounds almost paradoxical: it is both! With regard to the universal concepts/names in the human mind, nominalism is rationalistic and with regard to purely individual things outside the human mind, nominalism is *irrationalistic*.

5.4.4 The development of Humanistic thought

By the 15th century after Christ, modern nominalism had rid itself from the faith in a God-given creational order.[9] If creatures have no universal side (no *orderliness*), then it is obvious that it would be difficult to cling to a universally determining and limited (creational) *law for* such creatures. Stripped of all *order for* and all *orderliness* we are left with a *chaotic* and *structureless* multiplicity of things in their concrete individuality.

The lack of order-determination which thus created was "fruitfully" grasped by the *rationalistic* tendencies of modern humanistic philosophy. Immanuel Kant would finally draw the extreme rationalistic consequence of nominalism: if no (God-given) *order for* or creational *orderliness* of things exist outside the human mind, then the human mind must take this vacant position! Subsequently it is not at all surprising that Kant teaches that the human mind actually is the *a priori formal law-giver of nature*: "the mind does not create its laws (a priori) from nature, but prescribes them to nature" (Kant, 1783-ll, par.36; Cf. Kant, 1787-B:163 – we shall return to this point below in our assessment of the problematic status of postmodernism).

The irrationalistic side of nominalism offers an equally "fruitful" breeding ground. Linked to it, we often see the rise of all the irrational-

---

9   Even in theological circles the tendency still exists to delimit God's creation to the creation of individual creatures – without acknowledging in any way the universal creational law instituted by God, or the universal orderliness by means of which creatures express their subjection to the law.

istic tendencies of modern philosophy; the later development of the post-Kantian freedom idealism (in which the ideology of the unique ethnic mind of every trans-individual organic nation appears – followed by Nazism), the emergence of existential philosophy, pragmatism, personalism, neo-Marxism (except Habermas), historicism, the existential-phenomenological movement – in which all honour is given to the unique-individual ("the contingent") and finally the most recent variants of postmodernism.

5.5 The problematic status of postmodernism

In 1992 Zigmunt Bauman published a book with the title: *Intimations of Postmodernity*. The basic thrust of this book is similar to a vast number of publications, coming from diverse areas. It sets out to inform the reader about the impasse of "modernity" / "modernism" in order to highlight the vantage point of "postmodernity" / "postmodernism".[10] In spite of the growing popularity, in certain academic circles, of the conviction that we are living in a "postmodern world," there are also other academics who are not so thoroughly impressed with the claims of *originality* put forward by "postmodernists." When a competent sociological analyst, such as John O'Neill (1995), speaks about *The Poverty of Postmodernism* one may suspect that there is something wrong in the attempt to portray the culture in which we live as being "postmodern." Jurgen Habermas, the well-known philosopher-sociologist from the Frankfurt school, is quite explicit in his rejection of the idea that we have transcended "modernity" as a "form of life":

> The concept of modernity no longer comes with a promise of happiness. But despite all the talk of postmodernity, there are no visible rational alternatives of this form of life. What else is left for us, then, but at least to search out practical improvements within this form of life (1994:107)?

Already in 1981 Harbermas explains that he wants to learn from the mistakes of modernity without giving up its project: "I think that instead of giving up modernity and its project as a lost cause, we should learn from the mistakes of those extravagant programs which have tried to negate modernity"

---

10   Some authors avoid the identification of these two pairs of terms.

(1981:351).

In order to characterize the *postmodern condition*, Richard Middleton and Brian Walsh, for example, commence by using a number of characteristics to identify *modernity*. The general picture of modernity which they portray comprises features such as its "myth of progress," its "realism" that seeks to "grasp the infinite, irreducible complexities of the world as a unified homogeneous totality" and the intellectual rhetoric of "scientific objectivity, nonbiased observation and universal maxims." (1995:14ff., 31-33, 34).

> It may be that what we call "modernity" was an inherently unstable hybrid of realism and autonomy, a transitional station between classical and medieval culture, with its submission to the given, and postmodernity, with its frank admission of human construction (1995:41).[11]

Unfortunately, Middleton and Walsh totally neglects the *historicism* and *irrationalism* of the 19th century.[12] According to their exposition these features exclusively belong to the more recent emergence of "postmodernism." Their (mentioned) statement that modernity is characterized by its "realism", however, is incorrect (Middleton & B.J. Walsh, 1995:31-33). The *nominalistic* position of Renés Descartes is clearly expressed where he says: "number and all universals are only modes of thought."[13] This orientation also explains why Descartes does not acknowledge a contradiction between our "ideas" and "universal essences" outside the human mind: "contradiction [exists] ... in

---

11 Whereas *construction* is assessed to be exclusively postmodern, later on (cf. page 48) it is said that *construction / reconstruction* lies at the root of both the modernist and the postmodernist notion of the "self-constructed self." Nonetheless, on page 56 it is once again claimed that the view that we live in a world of our "own construction" is implicitly postmodern!

12 In a different context, and with the positive aim to argue for the development of a distinctly Christian economics, Hoksbergen unfortunately also shows no historical awareness of the nature of the *historicism* and *irrationalism* of the 19th century. His discussion of the main traditions and themes of postmodernism therefore does not realize that the features highlighted by him in principle were present already at the beginning of the 19th century (cf. Hoksbergen (1994:126-142, 134).

13 Realism is said to be "central to the Cartesian ideal", 1994:41.

our ideas alone"[14]

The whole motive of *logical creation*, dominant in nominalistic humanism since Thomas Hobbes and Immanuel Kant, is also ignored by Middleton and Walsh. The idea of the "social *construction* of reality" directly relates – via Berger, Luckmann, Schutz and Husserl – to Kant, who elevated human understanding, as we have mentioned, to the *formal law-giver* of nature. In Husserl this idea of *construction* was still conceived of in a *rationalistic* way. Existential phenomenology, on the other hand, transformed Husserl's rationalism into an *irrationalistic* perspective. Consequently, the contemporary "postmodern" idea that we create the world we live in (either through thought or through language) simply continues core elements of *modern* humanism!

The image of "modernity" portrayed by someone like Bauman in his project of "postmodernity" suggests that the ideal of (contingent) autonomy, the acknowledgement of perpetual change and the self-constitution of the symbolical constructs of agents are all recent "postmodern" phenomena (cf. Bauman, 1992). However, we want to argue that there are sound historical reasons to question this whole image. In addition to that certain immanent-critical considerations as well as a reference to contemporary reflections on the issue of change may help us to gain a better understanding of certain inescapable elements of theory formation which are not only still present in Bauman's account but which are referring to unavoidable *structural conditions* for scholarship as such.

Looking at the rise of the modern mind since the Renaissance, Kant's *Critique of Pure Reason* stands out as a sign-post of the attempt to *reconquer* the lost territory of the inital motive to be free in the modern (secularized) humanistic sense of *autonomy* (i.e., being obedient to a law prescribed by humankind to itself). This *freedom-ideal*, which was jeopardized by the dominance of the *natural science-ideal* since Descartes, advocates a consistent emphasis on *universality* – something that, in turn, was to be challenged seriously by the 19th and the 20th centuries.

Since the contemporary emphasis on *language* and on the lingual

---

14 Renés Descartes, The Principles of Philosophy, Part I, LVIII, (Translated by John Veitch, London, 1965), 187.

(-symbolic) construction of social reality creates the impression that this is a unique feature characteristic of the recent emergence of the "postmodern" age,[15] we have to highlight one facet of modern *nominalism* dating back to the transition of the medieval to the modern era.

The controversy of nominalism versus realism surfacing during the transitional period between medieval philosophy and modern philosophy provides decisive starting points for the subsequent developments in philosophy. The nominalistic stance considered science to be concerned with *universals* (as the subjective universal image of the real individual entities). Over against the realistic conception of truth as the agreement between thought and essence (*adequatio intellectus et rei*), nominalism shifted the criterion to the inner activity of the human mind – truth concerns the *compatibility of concepts*.

Early modern humanistic philosophy explored this nominalistic attitude in many different ways. We only have to focus upon some crucial statements made by Thomas Hobbes, the British philosopher of early humanism, to realize how misplaced some of the claims of "postmodernity" are. The motive of *logical creation* indeed characterizes the autonomy-ideal and the first manifestations of the modern humanistic natural science-ideal. Nominalism stripped factual reality both from God's *conditioning law-order* and from its universal side – evinced in the *orderliness* of concretely existing entities.[16]

Since *rationalism* claims that universality is the only source of *knowledge*, it is clear that the motive of *logical creation* implicitly transforms subjective human understanding to become the *law-giver* of nature.

Hobbes affirms the nominalistic conception of truth when he states that truth does not inhere in things, but is a feature of names and their comparison in statements.[17] Add to this Hobbes's conviction

---

15 Perhaps covering the last 40 to 50 years, although some may go as far back as Nietzsche.

16 Experimental natural science can only approximates the God-given *conditions for* physical entities by investigating their *orderliness* – the universal side of entities at the factual side of reality.

17 Ernst Cassirer formulates this as follows (*Das Erkenntnisproblem in der Philosophie und Wissenschaft der neueren Zeit*, Volume Two, (3rd edition, Darmstadt 1971), 56): "Die Wahrheit haftet nicht an den Sachen, sondern an den Namen und

that demonstrative science is only possible with regard to those things which, in their generation, are dependent upon human discretion (*arbitrio*),[18] then it becomes clear that already here we are confronted with a conception of the *creative power* of human *thought* and *language* anticipating both Kant's extreme position and Richard Rorty's more recent point of view. Since, according to Kant, the material of experience (sense impressions) is chaotic, the natural order is (formally) made possible through the categories as *forms of thought*. Thus seen, the concepts of understanding in Kant's conception function as *formal law-giver* of nature. They are not derived from experience (a posteriori) but (as mentioned earlier) are (a priori) lying at the basis of experience: *"Categories are concepts, which prescribe laws a priori to phenomena, and thus to nature as the totality of all phenomena."*[19] Although Kant restricted the humanistic science-ideal to the domain of sensorially perceptible "phenomena", these words clearly highlight to what an extent he still adheres to the deification of human understanding as the a priori formal law-giver of nature.

As already mentioned, we may even advance beyond Kant in our assessment of the importance of Hobbes's nominalism by looking at a key-figure within the scene of "postmodernity," Richard Rorty. Richard Bernstein defines the rationalistic tradition (designated by him as "objectivism") as "the basic conviction that there is or must be some permanent, ahistorical matrix or framework to which we can ultimately appeal in determining the nature of rationality, knowledge, truth, reality, goodness, or rightness." (1983:8). In following Mary Hesse,[20] Rorty views "intellectual history" as "history viewed as the history of

---

an der Vergleichung der Namen, die wir im Satze vollziehen: veritas in dicto, non in re consistit" (cf. De Corpore, Part I, Chapter 3, Par.7 & 8). "Truth does not inhere in the things, but belongs to the names and their comparison, as it occurs in statements."

18 "Earum tantum rerum scientia per demonstrationem illam a priore hominibus est, quaram generatio dependet ab ipsorum huminum arbitrio" (De Homine, Chapter X, par.4 – quoted by Cassirer, *Ibid.*, 57).

19 I. Kant, *Kritik der reinen Vernunft* (1781, 17872), (edition Felix Meiner Verlag, Hamburg, 1787), 163.

20 She sees scientific revolutions as "metaphoric rediscriptions" – cf. Rorty, 1989:50.

metaphor." "Old metaphors are constantly dying off into literalness, and then serving as a platform and foil for new metaphors" (1989:16).²¹

5.5.1 The transition from universality to change and individuality

The point he wants to make is that "every specific theoretic view comes to be seen as one more *vocabulary*, one more description, one more *way of speaking*." (1989:57). The germs of this view are fully present in the quoted conceptions of Hobbes!²²

Whereas, roughly speaking, one can say that the 18th century is the period of extreme (conceptual) *rationalism*, the transition to the 19th century can be designated as an acute awareness of the *historical dimension* of reality. By the end of the 18th century this, first of all, was an effect of the pioneering work done by Johann Herder, a contemporary of Immanuel Kant. Korff calls Herder the *German* Rousseau, and Cassirer praises Herder as the Copernicus of the (science of) history (Cassirer, 1957:226). Proß sees in Herder the key figure who, in rejecting the "Aufklärung" (*Enlightenment*), prepared the rise of *romantic historicism*.

Although early romanticism transposes the *universal* to the *unique*, it did not distance itself from the inherent *atomism* (indvidualism) of the 18th century. The step to *holistic irrationalism* was eventually given by Schelling, Fichte and Hegel – three prominent post-Kantian philosophers in Germany during and after the rise of *romanticism*. We should observe that although Herder believes that society is subject to thorough *historical change*, he does not want to advocate an *anchorless relativism*. To curb this unwanted consequence, Herder upholds the *ideal of humanity* which guarantees, as universally binding rule, the *unity* and the *meaning* of history (cf. Cassirer, 1957:228).

Niebuhr, the tutor of Leopold von Ranke (perhaps best known for

---

21 To this Rorty adds: "This account of intellectual history chimes with Nietzsche's definition of 'truth' as 'a mobile army of metaphors'" 1989:17).

22 Rorty "metaphorizes" diverse givens – such as language, conscience, morality, and hopes: "To see one's language, one's conscience, one's morality, and one's highest hopes as contingent products, as literalizations of what once were accidentally produced metaphors, is to adopt a self-identity which suits one for citizenship in such an ideally liberal state" (*Ibid.* 61).

his statement that the science of history studies the past as it actually happened to be), demonstrates the transition from the 18th to the 19th century in a remarkable way. From the romantic movement – including Goethe and Schiller (Germany), Bilderdijk and Da Costa (The Netherlands), and Shelley and Keats (Britain) – Niebuhr received his appreciation of mythical thought. Without relinquishing the imaginative exuberance present in myths and sages, Niebuhr wants to treasure the historical way of thought in its own right.

With an obvious hint to Plato's classical allegory of people living in a cave (*The Republic*), Niebuhr compares the historian with a person who's eyes adapted so effectively to the dark that he can observe things that would be invisible to the newcomer. Where Plato appraises these "shadow-images" *negatively*, Niebuhr assesses them positively – for on occasion he characterizes the work of the historian as "work done under the earth."

In opposition to Plato, who acknowledges only knowledge directed at the true (static) *being* of things as worthwhile, Niebuhr is convinced that only *historical change* provides genuine knowledge. This kind of knowledge is the most appropriate type of knowledge for humanity comprising the vital self-developing of human beings.[23]

5.5.2 Unresolved problems: the emergence of language as new horizon

As opposed to the deification of universal (conceptual) knowledge during the 18th century, we here discern an emphasis on the importance of *historical change*. However, this *irrationalist* and *historicist* reaction against Enlightenment *rationalism* contains hidden problems that would become explicit only during and at the end of the 19th century. It is noteworthy that this process was anticipated by the first critical reactions to Kant's *Critique of Pure Reason*. It was in particular Jacobi, Hammann and Herder who pointed out that Kant neglected the na-

---

23   I have analyzed the successive epistemic ideals of the past three centuries in a different context: Rationalism, historicism and pan-'interpretationism', in: *Facets of Faith and Science*, edited by Jitse van der Meer, University of America Press, Co-published with The Pascal Centre for Advanced Studies in Faith and Science, Volume 2, 1996, pp.99-122.

ture of *language*.²⁴ Herder even calls "man" a "creation of language".²⁵

During the 19th century Wilhelm Dilthey embodied the flourishment of *historicism* and at the same time set into motion a reflection conducive of the socalled "linguistic turn." He reacts intensely to the positivistic mode of thought with its emphasis on *explanation*. He wants to find a new criterion to distinguish between the natural sciences and the humanities. This follows from the fact that the mental world is stamped by the presence of values and aims requiring a new method to capture this teleological domain. In contrast with Kant's critique of pure reason Dilthey develops a critique of *historical reason*. This critique entails the human capacity to understand itself as well as society and its history, constituted by humankind.²⁶ Karl Mannheim, one of the prominent sociologists of the first half of the 20th century and the founder of the sociological subdiscipline known as *sociology of knowledge*, had a solid understanding of the romantic roots of Dilthey's irrationalistic historicism:

> Dilthey is borne by, and may be the most important exponent of, that irrationalistic undercurrent which first became self-aware in Romanticism, and which, in the neo-Romanticism of the present, is on the way, in altered form, to effecting its attack on bourgeous rationalism.²⁷

Only what can be experienced in the context of a historical, world-encompassing coherence, could serve as the *immediately certain*

---

24 That Kant indeed distorted the meaning of history emerged also more clearly during the 19th century – beyond the rise of historicism as such. The discovery of non-Euclidean geometries (by Gauss and Lobatsjevski) relativized Kant's *table of categories* by making it clear to what extent his analysis of *understanding* was *historically* dependent upon Newton's *Principia* (1686).

25 "Der Mensch ist ein freidenkendes, thätiges Wesen, dessen Kräfte in Progression fortwürken; darum sei er ein Geschöpf der Sprache!" (Proß, 1978:73). Also Fichte emphasizes that language mediates the spirituality of reason and consciousness (Reiß, 1966:24).qxq

26 Already during the 18th century Vico claimed that humankind knows *history* better than *nature* since it was *made* by humankind.

27 Karl Mannheim, *Structures of Thinking*, edited by David Kettler, Volker Meja and Nico Stehr and translated by Jeremy J. Shapiro and Shierry Weber Nicholson (London: Routledge & Kegan Paul 1982), 162 – this manuscript was last reviewed by Mannheim in 1946 or 1947.

basis of knowledge acquisition – and only by means of empathy one can attain a genuine understanding (Verstehen) of spiritual reality. The natural sciences *know*, the humanities *understand* (Dilthey, 1927:86). Dilthey no longer supports the positivistic science ideal seeking the typically human in some facet of nature. The historical aspect now occupies this vacancy: to be human means to be *historically conditioned* (1927:275, cf. Diwald, 1963:38 note 11). Harbermas futhermore mentions the implied *linguistic framework* present in Dilthey's hermeneutics:

> We don't understand a symbolic expression without an intuitive prior-understanding (Vorverständnis) of its context, because we are not capable of freely transforming the presence of an unquestioned background knowledge of our culture into an explicit awareness.[28]

The inability of conceptual knowledge to grasp what is unique and individual caused philosophers to look at *language* to bridge the gap. It seems as if *language* can indeed mediate between *universality* and *individuality* in a way which transcends the limitations of *concept formation*.[29] Already Mannheim had a clear understanding of these issues. In connection with the *conceptual basis* of *asserting* he writes:

> Everything subject to assertion is to be identical for everyone in every assertion of it: and the concept thus is universally valid in two ways: referable to all objects of the same kind (the concept "table" is thus applicable to all tables that have ever existed or ever will exist), and valid for all subjects who ever will utter it, and who accordingly always understand the same thing by "table." That this tendency inheres in every concept-formation cannot be doubted; and the creation of such a conceptual plane upon which one concept can be defined by others, with all concepts thereby forming an objective self-contained system, should not be denied. ... In contrast to this, there is also an altogether different tendency in concept-formation, long in existence and rooted in a different movement, and this alternative must not be neglected. It rests on the

---

28 "Einen symbolischen Ausdruck verstehen wir nicht ohne das intuitive Vorverständnis seines Kontextes, weil wir das fraglos präsente Hintergrundwissen unserer Kultur nicht freihändig in explizites Wissen verwandeln können" (Habermas, 1983:17).

29 Strangely enough Derrida still seems to over-emphasize the logical foundation of language with his view that language inevitably enforces the general.

possibility of using every concept, including the most general, as a *name*; and what is to be understood by name in this case is the specific property of word whereby they designate a specific thing in a specific function in its unique relationship to us in our specific conjunctive community. ... That is precisely the miracle of living speech: that it always places each word in a unique context and that it can bestow an *individual meaning* (I am emphasizing – DFMS) to each word from the specific totality of the sentence, and even more, from the undercurrent of the communication flowing from its rhythm and the stream of association.[30]

As a consequence, we can speak about a general (and currently widely acknowledged) shift from *concept* to *meaning*, from *thought* to *language*.

Against this back-ground we may now answer the question whether we really have to see *postmodernity* as a **recent** phenomenon?

5.5.3 The "old face" of "postmodernity": Conclusion

It should now be clear that "postmodernity" and its supposed "new" features are actually "old" humanistic ones. Its key historicistic claims can be traced to their roots in post-Kantian Romanticism and its lingual emphasis was anticipated by nominalism since its very inception (cf. Ockham and Hobbes), and was also suggested by Jacobi, Hamman and Herder even before the end of the 18th century! The key-figure in the genesis of the linguistic turn, in so far as we may see it as an attempt to overcome the limitations of concept-formation with respect to what is unique, contingent and individual, Wilhelm Dilthey, actually lived the greater part of his life in the 19th century. To be sure, what is called *postmodernity* merely constitutes a new *power concentration* of the irrationalistic side of nominalism – under the spell of the disintegration and fragmentation caused by it. This basic orientation even pre-dates *modernity* – in the sense of the 18th century Enlightenment!

---

30 Karl Mannheim (1982:196-197) also clearly grasped something of the *twofold* nature of nominalism: "Nominalism proceeds from the unjustifiable assumption that only the individual subject exists and that meaningful contextures and formations have being only to the extent that individual subjects think them or are somehow oriented toward them in a conscious manner" (cf. 1982:224).

QUESTIONS FOR CHAPTER 5

1. Sketch the historical background to the emergence of the modern university.
2. Analyze the unique nature of scientific thought with reference to the inevitability of a theoretical worldview
3. Analyze philosophically the uniqueness of the university.
4. Typify education in terms of philosophical anthropology.
5. Discuss the cosmically multi-faceted nature of emotional openness.
6. Discuss the difference between education as disclosure and the Greek view of education as forming.
7. Distinguish between analogy and metaphor, and discuss the distinction between concept and idea.
8. Discuss the fundamental influence of nominalism in the development of Western philosphy in view of its inherently paradoxical simultaneous rationalistic and irrationalistic nature.

Literature

Aguirre, E. & Rosas, A. (1985): Fossil man from Cueva Mayor, Ibeas, Spain: New findings and Taxanomic Discussion, in: Tobias, 1985.

Alexander, J.C. (1985): *Neofunctionalism* (London: Sage Publications), 1985;

Alexander, J.C. (1987): *Sociological Theory since World War II, Twenty Lectures* (New York: Columbia University Press), 1987;

Alexander, J.C. (1988): *Action and its Environments* (New York: Columbia University Press), 1988;

Alexander, J.C. (1990a): *Analytic debates: Understanding the relative autonomy of culture*, in: *Culture and Society, Contemporary Debates*, edited by Alexander, J.C. & Seidman, S., (New York: Cambridge University Press), 1990;

Alexander, J.C. (1990b): *Differentiation Theory and Social Change*, co-editor Paul Colomy, New York: Columbia University Press), 1990;

Alexander, J.C. (1990c): *Differentiation Theory: Problems and Prospects*, in: *Differentiation Theory and Social Change*, 1990.

Allesch, G.H. (1931): *Zur nichteuklidischen Struktur des phänomenalen Raumes*, Jena 1931.

Altner, G. & Hofer, H. (1972): *Die Sonderstellung des Menschen*, Stuttgart 1972.

Altner, G. (uitgewer) (1973): *Kreatur Mensch, Moderne Wissenschaft auf der Suche nach dem Humanen*, München 1973.

Apolin, A. (1964): *Die geschichte des Ersten und Zweiten Hauptzatzes der Wärmetheorie und ihre Bedeutung für die Biologie*, in: *Philosophia Naturalis*, 1964.

Ayer, A.J.: *Language, Truth and Logic* (1936), 17de druk London 1967.

Azar, L. (1986): *Book Review* of: Darwinism Defended: A Guide to the Evolution Controversies (geskryf deur Michael Ruse, 1982), in: The New Scholasticism, Volume LX, No.2, Spring 1986 (pp.232-235).Bernays, P.: Über den Platonismus in der Mathematik, in: Abhandlungen zur Philosphie der Mathematik, Darmstadt 1976.

Bauman, Z. (1992): *Intimations of Postmodernity*, Routledge, London 1992.

Bavink, B. (1954): *Ergebnisse und Probleme der Naturwissenschaften*, 10e druk, Zürich 1954.

Bendall, D.S. (uitgewer) (1983): *Evolution from Molecules to Men*, New York 1983.

Bernstein, R. (1983): *Beyond Objectivism and Relativism. Science, Hermeneutics and Praxis*, (Philadelphia: University of Pennsylvania Press 1983.

Bohr, N.: *Atoomtheorie en natuurbeschrijving*, Aula-uitgawe, Antwerpen 1966.

Bohr, N.: Naturwissenschaften, 21, 245, 1933.

Bolk, L. (1926): *Das Problem der Menschwerdung*, Jena 1926.

Born, M., Pymont, B en Biem, W: *Dualismus in der Quantentheorie*, in: Philosophia Naturalis, 1968.

Bromage, T.G. (1985): *Taung facial remodelling: A growth and development study*, in: Tobias, 1985.

Buytendijk, F.J.J. (1970): *Mensch und Tier*, Hamburg 1970.

Cassirer, E. (1910): *Substanzbegriff und Funktionsbegriff*, Untersuchungen über die Grundfragen der Erkenntniskritiek, 3e ongewysigde uitgawe, Darmstadt 1969.

Cassirer, E. (1928): *Zur Theorie des Begriffs*, in: Kant-Studien, Vol.33, 1928.

Cassirer, E. (1929): *Philosophie der symbolischen Formen*, Vol.III, Berlyn 1929.

Cassirer, E. (1957): *Das Erkenntnisproblem in der Philosophie und Wissenschaft der neueren Zeit – Von Hegels Tod bis zur Gegenwart* (1832-1932), Stuttgart, 1957.

Cassirer, E. (1944): *An Essay on Man*, New York 1944.

Chiarelli, B. (1985): Chromosomes and the origin of Man, in: Tobias, 1985.

Clark, D. (1985): *Leaving no Stone Unturned: Archeological Advances and Behavioral Adaptation*, in: Tobias, 1985.

Clarke, R.J. (1985): *Early Acheulean with Homo habilis at Sterkfontein*, in: Tobias 1985.

Dacque, E. (1935): *Organische Morphologie und Paläontologie*, Berlyn 1935.

Dacque, E. (1935a): *Organische Morphologie and Phylogenie*, Berlyn 1935.

Dacque, E. (1940): *Die Urgestalt*, Leipzig 1940.

Dacque, E. (1948): *Vermächtnis der Urzeit*, München 1948.

Darwin, C. (1968): *The Origin of Species*, Penguin-uitgawe, 1968.

De Klerk, W.J. (1978): *Inleiding tot die semantiek*, Durban 1978.

Dilthey, W. (1927): *Der Aufbau der geschichtliche Welt in den Geisteswissenschaften*, reprint of the Berlin-edition, 1927, VandenHoeck & Ruprecht, Göttingen, 1965.

Diwald, H. (1963): *Wilhelm Dilthey, Erkenntnistheorie und Philosophie der Geschichte*, Berlin 1963.

Dobzhansky, Th. (1967): *The Biology of Ultimate Concern*, New York 1967.

Dooyeweerd, H. (1959): *Schepping en Evolutie*, in: Philosophia Reformata, 1959.

Dooyeweerd, H. (1969): *A New Critique of Theoretical Thought*, Collected Works of Dooyeweerd, A-Series, The Edwin Mellen Press, Lewiston, NY, Volumes A1–A4, 1997.

Dooyeweerd, H.: *De Wijsbegeerte der Wetsidee*, 3 Volumes, Amsterdam 1935-1936.

Dooyeweerd, H.: *Het Substantiebegreip in die moderne natuurphilosphie en de theorie van het enkaptisch structuurgeheel*, in: Philosophia Reformata, 2de en 3de kw. 1950,

Driesch, H. (1920): *Philosophie des Organischen*, Leipzig 1920.

Driesch, H. (1931): *Wirklichkeitslehre*, 1931.

Duley, W.W. & Williams, D.A. (1984): *Interstellar Chemistry*, London

1984.

Eibl-Eibesfeldt, I. (1972): *Stammesgeschichtliche Anpassungen im Verhalten des Menschen*, in Gadamer, 1972.

Eigen, M. (1983): *Self-replication and molecular evolution*, in: Bendall, D.S. 1983.

Eisberg, R.M.: *Fundamentals of Modern Physics*, New York 1961.

Eisenstein, I. (1975): *Ist die Evolutionstheorie wissenschaftlich begründet?* in: Philosophia Naturalis, Archiv für Naturphilosophie und die philosophischen Grenzgebiete der exakten Wissenschaften und Wissenschaftsgeschichte, Vol.15, No.3 & 4, 1975.

Faul, M & Boekkooi, J. (1986): *Ancient 'black skull' discovery shakes theory of man's evolution*, report in: The Star, Monday, September 15 1986 (p.10).

Friedrich, H. (uitgewer) (1973): *Mensch und Tier*, Ausdruckformen des Lebendigen, München 1973.

Gadamer, H-G, & Vogler, P. (1972): *Neue Anthropologie*, Vol.II, Stuttgart 1972.

Gehlen, A. (1965): *Theorie der Willensfreiheit und frühe Philosophische Schriften*, Berlyn 1965.

Gehlen, A. (1971): *Der Mensch, Seine Natur und seine Stellung in der Welt*, 9e druk, Frankfurt am Main 1971.

Gieseler, W. (1974): *Die Fossilgeschichte des Menschen*, in: Heberer (pp.171-517), 1974.

Greenberg, J.M. (1981): *The Largest molecules in space* (II), in: Nederlands Tijdschrift voor Natuurkunde A47 (1), 1981.

Goerttler, K. (1972): *Morphologische Sonderstellung des Menschen im Reich der Lebensformen auf der Erde*, in: Gadamer, 1972.

Goulian, M., Kornberg, A. & Sinsheimer, R.L. (1967): *Synthesis of infectious Phage* ^{a} X 174 DNA, in: *Biochemistry*: Goulian et al, Vol.58, 1967.

Greene, J.C. (1981)): *Science, Ideology, and World View*, London 1981.

Greenfield, L.O. (1985): *The Study of Human Evolution and the Description of Human Nature*, in: Tobias 1985.

Grene, M. (1974): *The Understanding of Nature, Essays in the Philosophy of Biology*, (Boston Studies in die Philosophy of Science, Vol.III), Boston 1974.

Hübner, J. (1966): *Theologie und biologische Entwicklungslehre*, München 1966.

Haas, J. (1959): *Naturphilosophische Betrachtungen zur Finalität und Abstammungslehre*, in: Die stammesgeschichtliche Werden der Organismen und des Menschen, Vol.I, Vienna 1959.

Haas, J. (1968): *Sein und Leben, Ontologie des organischen Lebens*, Karlsruhe 1968.

Haas, J. (1974): *Das organische Leben*, in: Gott, Mensch, Universum, Köln 1974.

Habermas, J. (1983): *Moralbewußtsein und kommunikatives Handeln*, Frankfurt am Main: Surhkamp Verlag 1983.

Habermas, J. (1981): *Modernity versus Postmodernity*, New German Critique 22, reprintied in J.C. Alexander & S. Seidman, *Culture and Society, Contemporary Debates*, New York: Cambridge University Press, 1990.

Habermas, J. (1994): *The past as future*, interviewed by Michael Heller, translated by Peter Hohendahl, Londen: University of Nebraska Press, 1994.

Haeffner, G. (1982): *Philosophische Antropologie*, Stuttgart 1982.

Hallonquist, E. (1971): *The Age of The Earth*, reprint from the Bible-Science Newsletter (Bible-Science Association of Canada), August 1971.

Harrison, G.A. & Weiner, J.S. & Tanner, J.M. & Barnicot, N.A. (1970): *Biologie van de Mens* 1, Utrecht/Antwerpen 1970.

Hart, H. (1984): *Understanding our World*, An Integral Ontology, New York 1984.

Hebeda, E.H. and others (1973): *Excess Radiogenic argon in the precambrian avanavero dolerite in western Suriname* (South America), Earth and Planetary Science Letter 20 (189-200), North Holland Publishing Company, 1973.

Heberer, G. (uitgewer) (1974): *Die Evolution der Organismen, Ergebnisse und Probleme der Abstammungslehre*, Band III: Phylogenie der

Homoniden, Stuttgart 1974.

Hoksbergen, R. (1994): *Is There a Christian Economics?: Some Thoughts in Light of the Rise of Postmodernism*, Christian Scholars Review, Vol. XXIV:2, December 1994.

Heisenberg, W. (1956): *Das Naturbild der heutigen Physik*, Rowohlt, Hamburg 1956.

Heitler, W. (1970): *Der Mensch und die naturwissenschaftliche Erkenntnis*, Braunschwieg 1970.

Heitler, W. (1976): *Ueber die Komplementarität von Lebloser und lebender Materie*, Abhandlungen der mathematisch-naturwissenschaftlichen Klasse, Jahrgang 1976, Nr.1, Mainz 1976.

Heitler, W. (1977): *Die Natur und das Göttliche*, Verlag Klett & Blamer Zug 1977.

Heitler, W. (1981): *Naturwissenschaft ist Geisteswissenschaft*, Zurich 1981.

Henke, W. & Rothe, H. (1980): *Der Ursprung des Menschen*, Stuttgart 1980.

Holz, Fr. (1975): *Die Bedeutung der Methode Galileis für die Entwicklung der Transzendentalphilosophie Kants*, in: Philosophia Naturalis, 1975.

Howells, W. (1967): *Mankind in the Making*, A Pelican Book, 1967.

Husserl, E. (1954): *Die Krisis der europäischen Wissenschaften und die transzendentale Phänomenologie* (1936), Husserliana Vol.VI, The Hague 1954.

Huxley, A.F. (1983): *How far will Darwin take us?*, in: Bendall, D.S. 1983.

Huxley, J. (1968): *Evolution in Action*, A Pelican Book, 1968.

Jansen, P. (1975): Arnold Gehlen, Die antropologische Kategorienlehre, Bonn 1975. Jaspers, K. (1948): *Philosophie*, 2e druk, Berlyn 1948.

Jelínek, J.J. (1985): *The European, near east and north african finds after Australopithecus and the principal consequences for the picture of human evolution*, in Tobias, 1985.

Jevons, F.R. (1964): *The Biochemical Approach to Life*, New York 1964.

Jonas, H. (1973): *Organismus und Freiheit, Ansätze zu einer philosophischen Biologie*, München 1973.

Kant, I.: *Kritik der reinen Vernunft* (1781-A/17872-B), Felix Meiner-uitgawe, Hamburg 1967.

Kant, I. (1968): *Kritik der Urteilskraft* (1790, 1793, 1799), Darmstadt 1968.

Kant, I.: *Prolegomena zu einer jeden künftigen metaphysik die als Wissenschaft wird auftreten können* (1783), Felix Meiner-uitgawe, Hamburg 1969.

Kerkut, G.A. (1960): *Implications of Evolution*, New York 1960.

Kitts, D.B. (1974): *Paleontology and Evolutionary Theory*, in: Evolution, 28. September 1974.

Koehler, O. (1973): *Vom unbenannten Denken*, in: Friedrich 1973.

Kugel, J. (1982): *Filosofie van het Lichaam*, Wijsgerige beschouwing over het menselijk gedrag, Utrecht 1982.

Kugler, R. (1967): *Philosophische Aspekte der Biologie Adolf Portmanns*, Zürich 1967.

Laitman, J.T. (1985): *Evolution of the upper respiratory tract: The fossil evidence*, in: Tobias, 1985.

Landmann, M. (1969): *Philosophische Anthropologie*, Berlyn 1969.

Laszlo, E. (1971): *Introduction to Systems Philosophy*, New York 1971.

Le Gros Clark, W.E. (1964): *The fossil evidence for Human Evolution*, 2e revised and extended edition, London 1964.

Leakey, L.S.B. & Goodall, V.M. (1970): *Unveiling man's Origins*, London 1970.

Leakey, R.E. (1973): *Skull 1470, Discovery in Kenya of the earliest suggestion of the genus Homo – nearly three million years old*, in: National Geographic, Vo.143, No.6, June 1973.

Leakey, R.E. & Lewin, R. (1978): *People of the Lake*, Mankind and its Beginnings, New York 1978.

Leinfeller, W. (1966): *Ueber die Karpelle verschiedener Magnoliales I*, Oesterreischische Botanische Zeitschrift, 113, 1966.

Lorenz, K. (1973): *Ueber tierisches und menschliches Verhalten, Aus dem Werdegang der Verhaltenslehre*, Gesammelte Abhandlungen, Band II, 10e druk, München 1973.

Lorenz, K. (1980): *Die Rückseite des Spiegels*, Versuch einer Naturgeschichte des menschlichen Erkennens, München 1980.

Malthus, Th.R. (1970): *An Essay on the Principle of Population*, A Pelican Book, 1970.

Mannheim, K. (1982): *Structures of Thinking*, edited by David Kettler, Volker Meja and Nico Stehr and translated by Jeremy J. Shapiro and Shierry Weber Nicholson, London: Routledge & Kegan Paul 1982.

McHenry, M.M. & Skelton, R.R. (1985): *Is Australopithecus africanus ancestral to Homo?* in: Tobias, 1985.

McMullin, E. (1983): *Values in Science*, Proceedings of the Philosophy of Science Association (PSA), Volume 2, 1983.

Merleau-Ponty, M. (1970): *Phenomenology of Perception*, London 1970.

Meyer, A. (1964): *The Historico-Philosophic Background of modern Evolution-Biology*, Leiden 1964.

Middleton, J.R. & Walsh, B.J. (1995): *Truth is Stranger than it used to be*, Downers Grove: InterVarsity Press, 1995.

Miller, S.L. & Orgel, L.E. (1974): The Origins of Life on Earth, New Yersey 1974.

Monod, J. (1972): *Zufall und Notwendigkeit*, München 1972.

Munson, R. (uitgewer) (1971): *Man and Nature*, Philosophical Issues in Biology, New York 1971.

Narr, K.J. (1959): *Die Abstammungslehre im Licht der Kulturgeschichte*, in: Das stammesgeschichtliche Werden der Organismen und des Menschen, Vol.I, Vienna 1959.

Narr, K.J. (1973): *Kulturleistungen des frühen Menschen*, in: Altner 1973.

Narr, K.J. (1974): *Tendenzen in der Urgeschichtsforschung*, in: Fortschritt im Heutigen Denken? Freiburg/München 1974.

Nida, E.A. (1979): *Componential analysis of meaning*, New York 1979.

Olthuis, J.: The Word of God and Creation, in: *Tydskrif vir Christelike Wetenskap* (Journal for Christian Scholarship), 1st & 2nd quarter, 1989 (pp.25-37).

O'Neill, J. (1995): *The Poverty of Postmodernism*, London: Routledge, 1995.

Oparin, A.I.: *The Origin of Life*, New York 1953.

Orgel, L.E.: *The Origins of life on Earth*, New Yersey 1974.

Orgel, L.E. & Sulston, J.E. (1971): *Polynucleotide replication and the Origin of Life*, in: *Prebiotic and Biochemical evolution*, ed. A.P. Kimball & J. Oró, London 1971.

Overhage, P. (1959): *Das Problem der Abstammung des Menschen*, in: *Das Stammesgeschichtliche Werden der Organismen und des Menschen*, Vol.I, Vienna 1959.

Overhage, P. (1959a): *Um die Ursachliche Erklärung der Hominisation*, Leiden 1959.

Overhage, P. (1959c): *Keimesgeshichte und Stamme*, in: Die stammesgeschichtliche Werden der Organismen und des Menschen, Vol.I, Vienna 1959.

Overhage, P. (1967): *Zur Frage einer Evolution der Menschheit während des Eiszeitalters*, Part III, in: Acta Biotheoretica, Vol.XVII, 1967.

Overhage, P. (1972): *Der Affe in dir*, Frankfurt am Main 1972.

Overhage, P. (1973): *Die Evolution zum Menschen hin*, in: Gott, Mensch, Universum, Köln 1973.

Overhage, P. (1977): *Die biologische Zukunft der Menschheit*, Frankfurt am Main 1977.

Overhage, P. & Rahner, K. (1965): *Das Problem der Hominisation*, 3e revised uitgawe, Basel 1965.

Pannenberg, W. (1968): *Was ist der Mensch? Die Anthropologie der Gegenwart im lichte der Theologie*, Göttingen 1968.

Passmore, J. (1966): *A Hundred Years of Philosophy*, A Pelican Book, 1966.

Planck, M. (1910): *Die Stellung der neueren Physik zur mechanischen Naturanschauung* (1910), in: Max Planck, Vorträge und Erinnerungen, 9e herdruk of the 5e druk, Darmstadt 1973.

Plessner, H. (1965'): *Die Stufen des Organischen und der Mensch*, Berlyn 1928.

Plessner, H. (1975): *Autobiographical article: Helmut Plessner*, in: Pongratz 1975.

Plessner, H. (1975a): *Zur Anthropologie der Sprache*, in: Philosophia Naturalis, Vol.15, Section 4, 1975.

Polanyi, M. (1967): *Life Transcending Physics and Chemistry*, in: Chemical

Engineering News, August 21, 1967.

Polanyi, M. (1968): *Life's Irreducible Structure*, Science, Vol.160, June 21, 1968.

Polanyi, M. (1969): *Personal Knowledge*, 3e druk, London 1969.

Pongratz, L.J. (1975): Philosophie in Selbstdarstellungen, Hamburg 1975.

Popper, K. (1972): *Objective Knowledge*, Oxford University Press 1972.

Portmann, A. (1965): *Vom Ursprung des Menschen*, Basel 1965.

Portmann, A. (1967): *Probleme des Lebens,* Eine Einführung in die Biologie, Basel 1967.

Portmann, A. (1969): *Biologische Fragmente zu einer Lehre vom Menschen*, 3rd extended and revised edition, Basel 1969.

Portmann, A. (1969a): *Einführung in die vergleichende Morphologie der Wirbeltiere*, 4th extended edition, Stuttgart 1969.

Portmann, A. (1970): *Der Mensch ein Mängelwese?*, chapter in: Entlässt die Natur den Menschen?, München 1970.

Portmann, A. (1973): *Biologie und Geist*, Frankfurt am Main 1973.

Portmann, A. (1973a): *Der Weg zum Wort*, in: ERANOS Vol 39, Leiden 1973.

Portmann, A. (1974): *An den Grenzen des Wissens*, Düsseldorf 1974.

Portmann, A. (1975): *Homologie und Analogie*, Ein Grundproblem der Lebensdeutung, in: ERANOS Vol.42, Leiden 1975.

Portmann, A. (1977): *Die biologischen Grundfragen der Typenlehre*, in: ERANOS Volume 43, Leiden 1977.

Pretorius, A. von L. (1986): *Wetenskap, Mens en Toekoms – Evaluering van die Sistemefilosofie van Ervin Laszlo*, Ph.D-thesis (unpublished), RAU, Johannesburg 1986.

Wolfgang Proß (ed.) (1978):, *Johann Gottfried Herder, Abhandlung über den Ursprung der Sprache, Text, Materialen, Kommentar*, Carl Hanser Verlag 1978.

Rauche, G.A. (1966): *The Problem of Truth and Reality* in Grisebach's Thought, Pretoria 1966.

Rauche, G.A. (1971): *Truth and Reality in Actuality*, Durban 1971.

Rauche, G.A. (1985): *Theory and Practice in Philosophical Argument, A Metaphilosophical View of the Dynamics of Philosophical Thought*, Published by The Institute for Social and Economic Research, University of Durban Westviille, Durban 1985.

Reed, C.A. (1985): *Energy-Traps and Tools*, in: Tobias, 1985.

Reiß, H. (1966): *Politisches Denken in der deutschen Romantik* (Bern: Francke Verlag 1966.

Rensch, B. (1959): *Evolution above the species level*, London 1959.

Rensch, B. (1968): *Discussion Remarks*, attached to Von Bertalanffy 1968a: Symbolismus und Anthropogenese, in: Handgebrauch und Verständigung bei Affen und Frühmenschen, Stuttgart 1968.

Rensch, B. (1969): *Die fünffache Wurzel des panpsychistischen Identismus*, in: Philosophia Naturalis, Vol.11, 1969.

Rensch, B. (1971): *Biophilosophy*, London 1971.

Rensch, B. (1973): *Gedächtnis, Begriffsbildung und Planhandlungen bei Tieren*, Hamburg 1973.

Roodyn, D.B. en Wilkie, D.: *The Biogenesis of Mitochondria*, London 1968.

Rorty, R. (1989): *Contingency, Irony and Solidarity* (New York: Cambridge University Press 1989.

Scheler, M. (1962): *Die Stellung des Menschen im Kosmos* (1928), 6e druk, Bern-München 1962.

Schelling, F.W.J. (1968): *Schriften von 1806-1813*, Ausgewählte Werke, Vol.4, Darmstadt 1968.

Scherer, G. (1980): *Strukturen des Menschen*, Grundfragen philosophischer Antropologie, Essen 1980.

Schindewolf, O.H. (1956): *Zeugnisse der Urzeit*, Reden bei der feierlichen Uebergabe des Rektorates zu Beginn des Sommersemesters am 8. Mai 1956, Rede des neuen Rektors, Professor Dr. Otto H. Schindewolf, Tübingen 1956.

Schindewolf, O.H. (1969): *Ueber den 'Typus' in morphologischer und phylogenetischer Biologie*, Wiesbaden 1969.

Schopf, W. & Barghoorn, E.S. (1967): *Alga-like fossils from the early precambrian of South Africa*, in: Science 156, 1967.

Schrödinger, E. (1955): What is Life? The Physical Aspect of the Living Cell, Cambridge 1955.

Schubert-Soldern, R. (1962): *Mechanism and Vitalism*, London 1962.

Schubert-Soldern, R. (1959): *Materie und Leben als Raum und Zeitgestalt*, München 1959.

Schuurman, E. (1972): *Techniek en Toekomst*, Assen 1972.

Schrotenboer, P. (1971): The marks of the institutional church, in: *Journal for Christian Scholarship*, 3rd quarter 1971.

Schwartz, J.H. (1985): *Toward a synthetic analysis of Hominid Phylogeny*, in: Tobias, 1985.

Simpson, G.G. (1969): *Biology and Man*, New York 1969.

Simpson, G.G. (1971): *Man's Place in Nature*, Section from "The Meaning of Evolution" (revised uitgawe Yale University 1967), Herdruked in Munson, 1971.

Sinnott, E.W. (1963): *The Problem of Organic Form*, London 1963.

Sinnott, E.W. (1972): *Matter, Mind and Man*, The Biology of Human Nature, New York 1972.

Spann, O. (1963): *Naturphilosophie*, Gesamtausgabe, Band 15, 1963.

Strauss, D.F.M. (1977): *Evolusionisme en die vraag na Grondnoemer*, In: Woord en Wetenskap, Feesbundel opgedra aan prof F.J.M. Potgieter, edited by 'VCHO', Bloemfontein 1977.

Strauss, D.F.M. (1980): *Inleiding tot die Komologie*, Bloemfontein 1980.

Strauss, D.F.M. (1981): *Woord, Saak en Betekenis*, in: Acta Academica, UOFS, Bloemfontein 1981.

Strauss, D.F.M. (1983): *Evolusie, Kernpunte van die moderne Afstammingsleer onder die soeklig* (42 pp.), Bloemfontein 1983.

Strauss, D.F.M. (1983a): Individuality and Universality in Reformational Philosophy, in: Reformational Forum, Vol. I, No.1, 1983.

Strauss, D.F.M. (1984): *An analysis of the structure of analysis*, (The Gegenstand-relation in discussion), in: Philosophia Reformata, 1984.

Strauss, D.F.M. (1985): *Taal en Historiciteit als Bemiddelaars tussen Geloven en Denken*, in: Philosophia Reformata, 1985.

Thorpe, W.H. (1978): Purpose in a World of Chance, Oxford 1978.

Tobias, P.V. (uitgewer) (1985): *Hominid Evolution*, New York 1985.

Tobias, P.V. (1985a): *The former Taung Cave System in the light of contemporary reports and its bearing on the skull's provenance: Early deterrents to the acceptance of Australopithecus*, in: Tobias, 1985.

Trincher, K. (1985): *Die Dualität der Materie*, in: Philosophia Naturalis, Vol.22, part 3, 1985.

Troll, W. (1949): *Die Urbildlichkeit der organische Gestaltung*, Experientia 1, 491, 1949.

Troll, W. (1951): *Biomorphologie und Biosystematik als typologische Wissenschaften*, Studium Generale 4 (376-389), 1951.

Troll, W. (1973): *Allgemeine Botanik*, revised and uitgebreide uitgawe, Stuttgart 1973.

Van Peursen, C.A. (1966): *Lichaam-Ziel-Geest*, Utrecht 1966. Van Riessen, H. (1948): *Filosofie en Techniek*, Kampen 1948.

Van Riesen, H. (1970): *Wijsbegeerte*, Kampen 1970.

Visagie, P.J. (1988): *Methods and Levels of Archeological Discourse Analysis – with Special Reference to J Derrida*, Winter Interim, Spring 1988 (pp.49-71).

Von Bertalanffy, L. (1968): *Organismic Psychology and Systems Theory*, Clarke University Press, Massachusetts 1968.

Von Bertalanffy, L. (1968a): *Symbolismus und Anthropogenese*, in: Handgebrauch und Verständigung bei Affen und Frühmenschen, edited by H. Hubner, Stuttgart 1968.

Von Bertalanffy, L. (1973): *General System Theory*, Penguin University Books, 1973.

Von Eickstedt, E. (1934): *Rassenkunde und Rassengeschichte*, Stuttgart 1934.

Von Königswald, G.H.R. (1968): *Problem der ältesten menschlichen Kulturen*, in: Handgebrauch und Verständigung bei Affen und Frühmenschen, ed. B Rensch, Stuttgart 1968.

Von Uexküll, J. & Kriszat, G.(1970): *Streifzüge durch die Imwelten von Tieren und Menschen*, uitgawe Conditio Humana, Stuttgart 1970.

Von Uexküll, J. (1973): *Theoretische Biologie* (1928), Frankfurt am Main

1973.

Weiner, J.S. (1955): *The Piltdown Forgery*, London 1955.

Weiszäcker, C.F. (1971): *Voraussetzungen der Naturwissenschaftlichen Denkens*, München 1971.

Wolf, K.L. (1951): *Urbildliche Betrachtung*, Studium Generale 4 (365-375), 1951.

Woltereck, R. (1940): *Ontologie des Lebendigen*, Stuttgart 1940.

Zimmerman, W. (1962): *Die Ursachen der Evolution*, in: Acta Biotheoretica, Vol.XIV, 1962.

Zimmerman, W. (1967): *Methoden der Evolutionswissenschaft*, in: Die Evolution der Organismen, Vol. I, 3e uitgebreide uitgawe (uitgewer G. Heberer), Stuttgart 1967.

Zimmerman, W. (1968): *Evolution und Naturphilosophie*, Berlyn 1968

Index

A

abstraction	14, 73, 78, 101, 171, 172, 173
activities	19, 22, 26, 27, 55, 58, 67, 70, 88, 90, 92, 107, 117, 135, 136, 147, 148, 154, 166, 171, 172, 174, 176, 177
adaptation	85
Adam	160
Africa	32, 37, 62, 150, 152, 177
Altner	58
America	64, 198
analogies	100, 111, 113, 120, 122, 139, 143, 144, 164, 185, 186, 188
Analysis	5, 48, 56, 70, 74, 78, 81, 91, 101, 107, 118, 123, 140, 144, 147, 149, 165, 172, 199
animals	43, 44, 47, 48, 49, 50, 51, 52, 53, 54, 55, 56, 58, 59, 68, 77, 85, 92, 94, 95, 97, 136, 141, 142, 143, 159, 185
anticipatory	109, 113, 121, 122, 175
antithesis	25, 26, 34, 35, 139, 162, 163
Apolin	102
Aristotle	13, 80, 98, 151, 171, 190
arithmetization	97, 98
art work	85
atom	16, 18, 43, 44,

	45, 50, 51, 52, 53, 55, 67, 85, 96, 106, 123, 130, 131, 132, 133, 134, 135, 137, 152, 197		127, 135, 136, 137, 138, 139, 140, 145, 156, 163, 164, 165, 189
Augustine	27, 162	bodily structures	69, 72
awareness	51, 70, 77, 80, 89, 92, 98, 121, 122, 131, 179, 181, 185, 187, 193, 197, 200	Bohr	131
		Bolk	58
		Bolzano	97
		Boyer	97
		Buber	63, 64
		building	47, 48, 100, 123, 137, 141, 183
B		business	20, 21, 24, 26, 33, 35, 37, 95, 123, 128, 144, 146, 147, 150, 153, 178
bacteria	46, 141		
Bauman	192, 194		
beauty	70, 85, 106, 166		
Bell	98		
Bernays	98		
Bernstein	196	**C**	
Bible	16, 17, 18, 19, 20, 25, 26, 27, 28, 29, 30, 31, 39, 65, 109, 110, 115, 118, 188, 189	calling	14, 21, 23, 33, 36, 39, 57, 61, 113, 158, 161, 162, 167, 174
		Calvin	19, 21, 22, 23, 24, 66, 109, 162
biology	13, 44, 45, 46, 75, 85, 127, 134, 137, 138, 139	Cantor	97, 98, 120, 121
		capacity	31, 53, 86, 147, 171, 199
biotic	44, 45, 46, 48, 54, 59, 60, 68, 69, 70, 71, 72, 73, 84, 85, 86, 88, 89, 90, 91, 93, 96, 97, 107, 108, 109, 111,	capitalism	23, 24
		career	21, 23, 175
		Carnot	102
		Cassirer	80, 195, 196, 197

certainty   54, 80, 91, 175
Christ   20, 25, 26, 29, 30,
                 31, 32, 33, 34, 35,
                 36, 38, 39, 44,
                 66, 67, 109, 110,
                 111, 115, 116,
                 117, 118, 151,
                 159, 160, 161,
                 162, 163, 191
Christian   14, 16, 20, 22, 24,
                 25, 26, 28, 29, 30,
                 31, 33, 36, 37, 38,
                 39, 60, 61, 83,
                 110, 111, 112,
                 113, 118, 158,
                 161, 162, 166,
                 167, 193
church institute 20, 22, 29, 31,
                 32, 33, 34, 36,
                 39, 160, 161
Clausius   102
coherence   46, 87, 91, 94, 96,
                 97, 98, 99, 100,
                 104, 105, 106,
                 107, 108, 109,
                 111, 124, 136,
                 163, 164, 165,
                 173, 174, 175,
                 176, 181, 185,
                 186, 190, 199
competence   86, 89, 128, 143,
                 144, 150, 154,
                 176, 177, 179,
                 183
concepts   19, 53, 54, 85, 92,
                 97, 108, 119, 123,
                 144, 163, 172,
                 189, 190, 191,
                 195, 196, 200
conservatism   114
constancy   82, 83, 101, 103,
                 104, 105, 106,
                 111, 131, 186,
                 188, 189, 190
cosmology   15
culture   27, 37, 54, 55, 56,
                 63, 81, 151, 177,
                 180, 183, 192,
                 193, 200

D

Darwin(ism)   16, 43, 44, 45, 46,
                 47, 48, 50, 51, 61,
                 106, 134
De Klerk   92
death sentence   112
Dedekind   97, 98
Descartes   27, 131, 193, 194
development   5, 19, 23, 24, 27,
                 44, 46, 47, 48, 60,
                 61, 73, 86, 98,
                 102, 114, 117,
                 123, 127, 148,
                 149, 169, 173,
                 179, 184, 191,
                 192, 193
Dilthey   199, 200, 201
distinction   26, 30, 34, 37, 39,
                 40, 44, 47, 55, 56,

	65, 66, 70, 71, 74, 83, 91, 92, 93, 95, 99, 103, 104, 105, 114, 119, 120, 121, 123, 125, 128, 135, 139, 141, 142, 150, 153, 159, 161, 162, 163, 164, 165, 169, 174, 175, 176, 181, 184, 185, 186, 187, 188, 202		132, 145, 146, 147
dualism			26, 34, 35, 36, 37, 40, 70, 163
E			
Einstein			82, 103, 104
effect			14, 21, 36, 46, 82, 100, 102, 113, 117, 152, 157, 165, 173, 197
electrons			131, 132, 133, 134
elements			24, 67, 71, 84, 102, 121, 137, 194
direction	5, 14, 15, 26, 27, 28, 35, 37, 40, 48, 52, 54, 83, 102, 110, 151, 160, 174, 176, 177, 178		
F			
facets			14, 15, 25, 57, 65, 74, 85, 88, 95, 109, 110, 136, 173, 175, 184, 187, 198
diversity	5, 15, 16, 20, 27, 29, 74, 77, 78, 79, 80, 81, 83, 85, 87, 89, 91, 93, 94, 95, 96, 97, 99, 101, 103, 105, 107, 108, 109, 111, 113, 115, 117, 119, 121, 122, 123, 136, 174, 179, 182, 188	faith	5, 16, 17, 21, 22, 26, 34, 37, 45, 60, 64, 66, 85, 87, 93, 108, 109, 110, 111, 114, 115, 118, 128, 147, 153, 157, 161, 162, 166, 167, 175, 189, 191, 198
Diwald	200		
Dobzhansky	46, 47, 51		
Dooyeweerd	64, 65, 67, 68, 72, 81, 103, 107, 112,	family	22, 29, 48, 65, 92, 144, 145, 146,

Index | 221

	148, 149, 151, 153, 158, 161, 184
fossils	47, 48, 49, 50, 55, 142
freedom	14, 27, 28, 52, 54, 57, 64, 70, 86, 112, 150, 151, 152, 176, 180, 192, 194

G

Galileo	82, 101, 103, 104
gateway	119, 127, 128, 173, 187, 188
Gehlen	54, 58
Goerttler	53
grace	20, 21, 22, 25, 32, 34, 37, 107, 159, 161, 163, 166, 169
guidance	16, 68, 70, 87, 164, 175, 179
guilt	112, 113

H

Haas	138
Habermas	70, 192, 200
Hart	57, 84, 114
heart	18, 21, 22, 25, 27, 29, 35, 36, 38, 40, 61, 65, 66, 67, 68, 69, 110, 113, 116, 118, 160, 162, 174
historicism	105, 107, 108, 111, 192, 193, 197, 198, 199
Hoksbergen	193
holism	45, 134
holy	16, 20, 21, 29, 30, 117, 118, 119, 158, 159, 160
humankind	5, 14, 16, 18, 19, 20, 21, 22, 23, 25, 27, 29, 38, 41, 43, 44, 46, 50, 51, 52, 55, 57, 58, 59, 60, 61, 62, 63, 64, 66, 67, 69, 107, 113, 139, 158, 175, 179, 183, 194, 199
Husserl	194

I

illogical	19, 26, 54, 57, 93
illustration	14, 38, 44, 173
individual	14, 15, 18, 28, 29, 46, 51, 53, 57, 61, 63, 64, 77, 86, 132, 142, 144, 146, 150, 151, 152, 153, 161, 172, 190, 191, 192, 195, 200, 201
institute	20, 21, 22, 29, 30, 31, 32, 33, 34, 36, 37, 38, 39, 155,

J

Jesus	115, 116
Jonas	138, 139
jural	91, 93, 107, 108, 111, 113, 117, 123, 154, 176, 180
juridical	87, 128, 129, 147, 154, 156
justification	27, 119, 169, 172, 174, 175, 190

K

Kant	54, 131, 191, 194, 196, 197, 198, 199
kinematic	93, 101, 102, 103, 104, 105, 111, 131, 136, 143, 165, 172, 173, 186, 188, 189
kingdom	23, 25, 26, 27, 28, 29, 30, 31, 32, 33, 35, 36, 40, 55, 59, 67, 68, 71, 86, 117, 123, 127, 129, 131, 133, 135, 137, 139, 141, 142, 143, 145, 147, 149, 158, 160, 161, 160, 161, 169, 191
Kitts	50
Kuyper	161

L

Laitman	52
Landmann	42
language	31, 32, 51, 52, 53, 54, 92, 94, 123, 135, 144, 187, 189, 194, 196, 197, 198, 199, 200, 201
law	15, 16, 17, 18, 19, 20, 25, 31, 57, 58, 59, 63, 64, 71, 83, 86, 87, 89, 91, 96, 100, 101, 102, 104, 105, 108, 111, 112, 113, 114, 117, 118, 119, 120, 122, 132, 137, 138, 142, 150, 151, 153, 154, 156, 157, 169, 170, 171, 176, 177, 190, 191, 194, 195, 196
Leakey	49, 54
legal	37, 85, 86, 87, 88, 89, 91, 105, 107, 108, 112, 113, 114, 117, 128, 162, 163, 166, 167

Index | 223

	129, 149, 150, 152, 153, 154, 156, 157, 176, 177, 179	metaphor	184, 185, 186, 189, 197
		methodology	39, 171
		Middleton	193, 194
logical	19, 22, 53, 54, 57, 62, 78, 85, 90, 93, 100, 123, 165, 172, 173, 175, 177, 194, 195, 200	modalities	91, 93, 94, 95, 99, 100, 101, 102, 111, 120, 122, 123, 124, 139, 140, 142, 143, 144, 163, 172, 173, 180, 185, 186, 187, 189, 190
Lorenz	54, 58		
love	22, 25, 26, 36, 63, 64, 65, 66, 67, 82, 106, 107, 108, 110, 113, 115, 117, 118, 123, 128, 154, 155, 156, 157, 158, 161, 167		
		moment of death	88, 89, 90, 91
		morphology	142
		movement	17, 24, 52, 59, 81, 82, 85, 86, 96, 100, 101, 102, 103, 104, 105, 127, 130, 131, 172, 173, 181, 186, 192, 198, 200

M

Mannheim	199, 200, 201		
marriage	29, 33, 37, 64, 65, 116, 119, 123, 145, 146, 154, 155, 156, 157, 158, 161, 163	mutation	45, 46, 47, 61

N

		Narr	55, 56
		nation	15, 26, 28, 29, 30, 38, 39, 119, 145, 159, 160, 192
material	28, 42, 43, 44, 45, 51, 56, 57, 61, 67, 70, 71, 72, 92, 94, 106, 130, 133, 135, 137, 138, 139, 140, 141, 165, 183, 196	natural	18, 20, 23, 25, 26, 28, 32, 46, 55, 56, 57, 58, 59, 61, 62, 64, 71, 79, 80,
Melchizedek	117		

neighbour	86, 100, 102, 106, 114, 129, 130, 132, 136, 139, 141, 145, 147, 148, 187, 194, 195, 196, 199, 200 25, 36, 65, 67, 110, 113	**P** Parmenides philosophy	81, 82, 83, 130, 189 5, 13, 14, 15, 16, 21, 27, 28, 44, 64, 67, 78, 79, 80, 81, 82, 84, 100, 122, 123, 130, 131, 138, 174, 184, 185, 190, 191, 192, 194, 195
Newton	102, 131		
Niebuhr	134, 197, 198		
nominalism	142, 184, 190, 191, 195, 196, 201		
normative	18, 32, 54, 55, 57, 68, 69, 70, 71, 72, 85, 96, 110, 118, 119, 120, 123, 129, 155, 157, 161, 167, 174, 178, 179, 180, 181	Planck Plato	102 13, 27, 36, 42, 43, 83, 142, 151, 183, 189, 190, 198
		Polanyi	173
		Popper	5, 173
		Portmann	47, 53, 54, 55, 56, 59, 60, 143
		postmodernism	6, 184, 191, 192, 193
nucleus	131, 132, 133, 134	private law	119, 153, 176, 177
numerical	92, 98, 103, 104, 107, 120, 121, 122, 127, 130, 172, 180, 186, 187, 189, 190	protestantism protista	23 46, 141, 142
		R	
		radical	14, 26, 28, 30, 31, 33, 35, 36, 40, 65, 110, 118, 133, 147, 161, 164
O			
Oakley	55		
obedience	20, 23, 26, 110, 115, 117, 124, 151, 154, 158, 159, 161, 184	rationalism	64, 107, 190, 194, 195, 197, 198, 199
Overhage	53, 55		

realism	142, 190, 193, 195	Spencer	189
rebirth	29	sphere(s)	20, 21, 25, 32, 34, 39, 67, 72, 89, 96, 133, 134, 150, 153, 154, 156, 162, 177, 183, 189
Reed	14, 23, 24, 27, 28, 33, 47, 52, 54, 57, 64, 70, 81, 86, 112, 150, 151, 152, 176, 180, 191, 192, 194		
		stewardship	108, 124, 161
reformation	16, 17, 22, 23, 24, 31, 35, 36, 38, 40, 94, 109, 171	Strauss	31, 120, 133, 158, 171
		suspended	88, 155
relativism	103, 105, 111, 197	Synagogue	161
Renaissance	16, 151, 194	**T**	
Rensch	41, 53	technique	55, 69, 73
Repko	88	theology	18, 21, 43, 105, 115, 128, 186, 189
republic	43, 150, 198		
Ridderbos	162	theory	16, 27, 42, 43, 44, 45, 46, 48, 50, 58, 60, 61, 72, 83, 97, 102, 103, 104, 105, 111, 120, 121, 131, 133, 140, 141, 142, 152, 171, 172, 173, 178, 179, 189, 194
Rorty	196, 197		
Rothe	48, 49		
Russell	19, 54, 62		
S			
Schelling	100, 152, 197		
Schuurman	73		
Simmel	28		
Simpson	16, 44, 46, 55, 57, 61, 106	thyroid	71, 72
		traditionalism	114
slavery	69, 86	Trincher	93, 135
Smit	69	Troll	142
Socrates	13, 41	typicality	130, 175, 178
sovereignty	32, 96, 150, 183		

U

ultraviolet	59
Umwelt	57, 136
universal	18, 57, 61, 92, 94, 101, 103, 113, 114, 116, 118, 128, 139, 140, 142, 143, 172, 177, 190, 191, 193, 195, 197, 198
university	19, 20, 21, 26, 29, 35, 37, 38, 41, 93, 144, 146, 150, 162, 169, 170, 171, 173, 174, 175, 176, 177, 178, 179, 198

V

Van Riessen	80, 130, 188
Venter	171, 172, 175
Vertebrates	51
Visagie	27, 189
vitalism	45, 134, 138, 139, 140
Von Bertalanffy	71, 137

W

Water molecule	133, 134
Weber	23, 24, 199
Weierstrass	97, 99
Wolters	27, 28

Z

Zeno	81, 82, 121, 130
Zwingli	23

CREATURES SUBJECTED TO CREATIONAL LAWS

Aspects, Entities and Societal Institutions

	Law-Spheres (Aspects)		**Meaning-nuclei**
HUMAN BEINGS (SOCIAL LIFEFORMS & CULTURAL THINGS)	Certitudinal ▲	Church	certainty (to be sure)
	Ethical ▲	Family	love/troth
	Juridical ▲	State	retribution
	Aesthetical		beautiful harmony
	Economical ▲	Business	frugality/avoid excesses
	Social		social intercourse
	Sign-mode		symbolical signification
	Cultural-historical ▽		formative power/control
	Logical		analysis
ANIMALS	Sensitive-psychical		sensitivity/feeling
PLANTS	Biotical		organic life
THINGS	Physical		energy-operation
	Kinematic		unif. motion/constancy
	Spatial		continuous extension
	Numerical		discrete quantity

▽ Foundational function of church, state and business ▲ Qualifying function

www.ingramcontent.com/pod-product-compliance
Lightning Source LLC
Chambersburg PA
CBHW050632300426
44112CB00012B/1768